Comparative-Historical Methods

SAGE has been part of the global academic community since 1965, supporting high quality research and learning that transforms society and our understanding of individuals, groups and cultures. SAGE is the independent, innovative, natural home for authors, editors and societies who share our commitment and passion for the social sciences.

Find out more at: **www.sagepublications.com**

Comparative-Historical Methods

Matthew Lange

Los Angeles | London | New Delhi
Singapore | Washington DC

Los Angeles | London | New Delhi
Singapore | Washington DC

SAGE Publications Ltd
1 Oliver's Yard
55 City Road
London EC1Y 1SP

SAGE Publications Inc.
2455 Teller Road
Thousand Oaks, California 91320

SAGE Publications India Pvt Ltd
B 1/I 1 Mohan Cooperative Industrial Area
Mathura Road
New Delhi 110 044

SAGE Publications Asia-Pacific Pte Ltd
3 Church Street
#10-04 Samsung Hub
Singapore 049483

Editor: Chris Rojek
Editorial assistant: Martine Jonsrud
Production editor: Katherine Haw
Copyeditor: Jane Elliott
Marketing manager: Ben Griffin-Sherwood
Cover design: Wendy Scott
Typeset by: C&M Digitals (P) Ltd, Chennai, India
Printed by: CPI Group (UK) Ltd, Croydon, CR0 4YY

© Matthew Lange 2013

First published 2013

Library of Congress Control Number: 2012934289

British Library Cataloguing in Publication data

A catalogue record for this book is available from the British Library

MIX
Paper from
responsible sources
FSC
www.fsc.org   FSC® C013604

ISBN 978-1-84920-627-3
ISBN 978-1-84920-628-0 (pbk)

Table of Contents

List of Figures and Tables

About the Author

 Matthew Lange has a Ph.D. from Brown University and is Associate Professor of Sociology at McGill University. His work focuses on states, development, colonialism, ansd ethnic violence. Lange's books include *Educations in Ethnic Violence* (Cambridge, 2012), which explores how education affects ethnic violence, and *Lineages of Despotism and Development* (Chicago, 2009), which analyzes how different forms of British colonialism initiated different developmental trajectories. He is co-editor of *States and Development* (Palgrave Macmillan, 2005) and *The Oxford Handbook of the Transformations of States* (Oxford, Forthcoming) and has published articles in the *American Journal of Sociology*, *World Development*, *Social Forces*, *Studies in Comparative International Development*, *Commonwealth & Comparative Politics*, *Social Science History*, the *International Journal of Comparative Sociology*, and *Nationalism & Ethnic Politics*. His work uses comparative-historical methods, and he specializes in mixing methods.

1

Comparative-Historical Methods: An Introduction

Since the rise of the social sciences, researchers have used **comparative-historical methods** to expand insight into diverse social phenomena and, in so doing, have made great contributions to our understanding of the social world. Indeed, any list of the most influential social scientists of all time inevitably includes a large number of scholars who used comparative-historical methods: Adam Smith, Alexis de Tocqueville, Karl Marx, Max Weber, Barrington Moore, Charles Tilly, and Theda Skocpol, are a few examples. Demonstrating the continued contributions of the methodological tradition, books using comparative-historical methods won one-quarter of the American Sociological Association's award for best book of the year between 1986 and 2010, despite a much smaller fraction of sociologists using comparative-historical methods.

Given the contributions made by comparative-historical researchers, it is apparent that comparative-historical methods allow social scientists to analyze and offer important insight into perplexing and pertinent social issues. Most notably, social change has been *the* pivotal social issue over the past half millennium, and social scientists have used comparative-historical methods to offer insight into this enormous and important topic. State building, nationalism, capitalist development and industrialization, technological development, warfare and revolutions, social movements, democratization, imperialism, secularization, and globalization are central processes that need to be analyzed in order to understand both the dynamics of the contemporary world and the processes that created it; and many—if not most—of the best books on these topics have used comparative-historical methods.

Despite the great contributions made by comparative-historical analyses of social change, there is very little work on exactly what comparative-historical methods are. Unlike all other major methodological traditions within the social sciences, there are no textbooks on comparative-historical methods; moreover, present books reviewing comparative-historical analysis touch on methods only briefly, focusing most attention on the types of issues analyzed by comparative-historical scholars and important figures within the research tradition. Thus, comparative-historical methods have produced some of the best works in the social sciences; many of the best social scientists use them to analyze vitally important social issues, but there is little discussion of what such methods actually are.

This omission is unfortunate for comparative-historical analysis; it is also unfortunate for the social sciences in general. Indeed, the works and issues analyzed by scholars using comparative-historical methods have dominated the social sciences since their emergence, so an understanding of comparative-historical methods helps improve our understanding of the entire social scientific enterprise. Moreover, comparative-historical methods—as their name implies—are mixed and offer an important example of how to combine diverse methods. Given inherent problems with social scientific analysis, combining methods is vital to optimize insight, but competition and conflict between different methodological camps limit methodological pluralism. Comparative-historical methods, therefore, offer all social scientists an important template for how to gain insight by combining multiple methods. Finally, yet related to this last point, comparative-historical methods also offer an example of how to deal with another dilemma facing the social sciences: balancing the particular with the general. The complexity of the social world commonly prevents law-like generalizations, but science—given the dominance of the natural sciences—privileges general causal explanations. The social sciences are therefore divided between researchers who offer general nomothetic explanations and researchers who offer particular ideographic explanations. Comparative-historical analysis, however, combines both comparative and within-case methods and thereby helps to overcome this tension, and to balance ideographic and nomothetic explanations.

In the pages that follow, I help to fill the methodological lacuna surrounding comparative-historical methods. This book is not meant to be an overview of everything comparative and historical; rather, using broad strokes, it paints a picture of the dominant methodological techniques used by comparative-historical researchers. For this, I summarize past methodological works, review the methods used in past comparative-historical analyses, and integrate all into a single statement about the methodological underpinnings of comparative-historical analysis. In so doing, I also offer new interpretations of what comparative-historical methods are, their analytic strengths, and the best ways to use them.

Defining Comparative-Historical Analysis

Comparative-historical methods are linked to a long-standing research tradition. This tradition was previously referred to as comparative-historical sociology, but Mahoney and Rueschemeyer (2003) refer to it as **comparative-historical analysis** in recognition of the tradition's growing multidisciplinary character. In addition to sociology, comparative-historical analysis is quite prominent in political science and is present—albeit much more marginally—in history, economics, and anthropology.

As the Venn diagram in Figure 1.1 depicts, comparative-historical analysis has four main defining elements. Two are methodological, as works within the research tradition employ both within-case methods and comparative methods. Comparative-historical analysis is also defined by epistemology. Specifically, comparative-historical works pursue social scientific insight and therefore accept the possibility of gaining insight through comparative-historical and other methods. Finally, the unit of analysis is a defining element, with comparative-historical analysis focusing on more aggregate social units.

A **methodology** is a body of practices, procedures, and rules used by researchers to offer insight into the workings of the world. They are central to the scientific enterprise, as they allow researchers to gather empirical and measurable evidence and to analyze the evidence in an effort to expand knowledge. According to Mann (1981), there is only one methodology

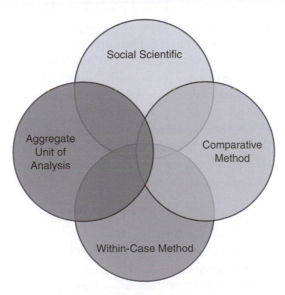

Figure 1.1 Venn diagram of comparative-historical analysis

within the social sciences. It involves eight steps: (1) formulate a problem, (2) conceptualize variables, (3) make hypotheses, (4) establish a sample, (5) operationalize concepts, (6) gather data, (7) analyze data to test hypotheses, and (8) make a conclusion. He suggests that the only methodological differences in the social sciences are the techniques used to analyze data— something commonly referred to as a **method**. Because particular techniques commonly require particular types of data, methods are also linked to different strategies of data collection.

All works within comparative-historical analysis use at least one **comparative method** to gain insight into the research question. By **insight**, I mean evidence contributing to an understanding of a case or set of cases. As described in considerable detail in Chapter 5, common comparative methods used within comparative-historical analysis include narrative, Millian, Boolean, and statistical comparisons. All of these comparative methods compare cases to explore similarities and differences in an effort to highlight causal determinants, and comparative-historical analysis must therefore analyze multiple cases. Although some comparative methods offer independent insight into the research question, others must be combined with the second methodological component of comparative-historical analysis: within-case methods.

Within-case methods pursue insight into the determinants of a particular phenomenon. The most common within-case method is causal narrative, which describes processes and explores causal determinants. Narrative analysis usually takes the form of a detective-style analysis which seeks to highlight the causal impact of particular factors within particular cases. Within-case analysis can also take the form of process tracing, a more focused type of causal narrative that investigates mechanisms linking two related phenomena. Finally, comparative-historical researchers sometimes use pattern matching as a technique for within-case analysis. Different from both causal narrative and process tracing, pattern matching does not necessarily explore causal processes; rather, it uses within-case analysis to test theories.

Within-case methods constitute the "historical" in comparative-historical analysis—that is, they are temporal and analyze processes over time. Moreover, they commonly analyze historical cases. This historical element has been a commonality unifying works within the comparative-historical research tradition to such an extent that works using within-case methods that do not analyze historical/temporal processes should not be considered part of the research tradition.

In addition to methods, comparative-historical analysis is also defined epistemologically. **Epistemology** is a branch of philosophy that considers the scope and possibility of knowledge. Over the past few decades, there has been growing interest in postmodern epistemological views that deny the possibility of social scientific knowledge. They take issue with **positivism**, which suggests that social scientists can gain knowledge about social relations by using social scientific methods. Instead, the postmodern view suggests it is impossible to decipher any social laws because of the sheer complexity of social relations. These works go beyond Max Weber's claims that social scientists should pursue *verstehen*—or understanding—instead of social laws, suggesting that even a limited understanding is impossible. *Verstehen* is impossible, according to this view, because discourses impede the scientific study of human relations. Most basically, our social environments shape human values and cognitions in ways that severely bias our analysis of social relations and—in combination with extreme social complexity—prevent any insight into the determinants of social relations.

It is not my intention to discuss the merits and demerits of postmodern epistemological views, but such a position necessarily prevents a work from being an example of comparative-historical analysis. In particular, when a researcher denies the ability of social scientific methods to provide causal insight, they are inherently anti-methodological. Further, because methodology is the primary defining element of comparative-historical analysis and because comparative-historical analysis is focused on causal analysis, postmodern works are epistemologically distinct from comparative-historical analysis and should be considered separate from the research tradition.

The final definitional element of comparative-historical analysis concerns the unit of analysis. Traditionally, all works that are considered examples of comparative-historical analysis have taken a structural view and explore meso- and macro-level processes—that is, processes involving multiple individuals and producing patterns of social relations. Along these lines, Tilly (1984) described comparative-historical analysis as analyzing big structures and large processes, and making huge comparisons. As such, states, social movements, classes, economies, religions, and other macro-sociological concepts have been the focus of comparative-historical analysis. This focus does not prevent comparative-historical researchers from recognizing the causal importance of individuals. For example, Max Weber was a founding figure of comparative-historical analysis and paid considerable attention to individuals. More contemporary social scientists using comparative-historical methods also employ individual-level frameworks that consider individual-level action. Both Kalyvas (2006) and Petersen (2002), for example, analyze the causes of violence and focus on individual-level mechanisms. However, in doing so, Weber, Kalyvas, and Petersen all analyze how the structural and institutional environments shape individual actions and, thereby, the actions of large numbers of people. Even when analyzing individual-level processes, therefore, comparative-historical researchers retain a structural focus and consider the interrelations between individual and structure.

While one might justify this final definitional element based on historical precedent, there are practical reasons to limit the category of comparative-historical analysis to works at the meso- and macro-level. Individual-level analyses that do not link individuals to structure are inherently different from the analysis of collective units, as scholars of the latter analyze collective processes and dynamics rather than individual thought processes and actions. Most notably, micro-analysis draws on individual-level data to understand the perceptions, interests, motivations, and actions of a single person and is, therefore, very biographical. Biography can also be an important component of more macro-level analyses, but such analyses also include structural analysis. That is, because meso- and macro-level analysis explores causal processes involving a number of people, it analyzes common structural and institutional factors shaping how large numbers of people act. As a consequence, familial, religious, economic, and political institutions as well as warfare, population growth, and other events that affect the lives of large numbers of people hold prominent positions in comparative-historical analysis.

Using all four defining elements, the size of the body of work that constitutes comparative-historical analysis is greatly reduced, leaving a large body of work that is similar to comparative-historical analysis in several ways but is not an example of it because the work lacks at least one of the four defining elements. Thus, Said's *Orientalism* (1978) and other postmodern works that compare cases and use narrative analysis to explore meso/macro-level processes are not examples of comparative-historical analysis because they are not social scientific: they deny the ability to gain insight into our social world through comparative and within-case methods. Similarly, Acemoglu, Johnson, and Robinson's (2001, 2002) statistical analyses of colonial legacies are social scientific, analyze macro-processes, and use comparative methods; but they are not examples of comparative-historical analysis because they omit within-case analysis. Next, Tilly's *The Contentious French* (1986) offers a social scientific analysis of the French political system through the use of within-case methods, but the book is not a clear example of comparative-historical analysis because it does not gain insight through the explicit use of inter-case comparison. Notably, all three of these are influential works of exceptional quality. By excluding them, I am not suggesting that they are inferior to comparative-historical analysis in any way; they simply do not conform to the main defining elements of the methodological tradition.

Despite my use of a specific definition, the boundaries of comparative-historical analysis are very blurred. Some works clearly use within-case methods to answer their research questions but do not make explicit comparisons that explore similarities and differences. Others use comparative methods to gain insight into their research questions but include brief case studies that offer little insight. Similarly, some researchers question—but do not deny—the possibility of social scientific insight, and some analyses focus primarily on micro-level processes while briefly considering how the structural environments shape the micro-level. Ultimately, I am not concerned with delineating precise cut-off lines because the quality of an analysis is not determined by whether or not it is an example of comparative-historical analysis. Instead, I have defined comparative-historical analysis in an effort to clarify the major elements of the research tradition. A comparison of comparative-historical methods with other major methodological traditions in the social sciences is also helpful in this regard.

Social Scientific Methods: A Review

Comparative-historical methods are one of several methodological traditions used by social scientists in their efforts to understand our social world. In this section, I briefly review the major social scientific methods—statistical, experimental, ethnographic, and historical—and compare them to comparative-historical methods. I conclude that comparative-historical analysis employs a hodge-podge of methods and therefore has affinities with almost all other methodological traditions. Indeed, the main distinguishing characteristic of comparative-historical analysis is that it combines diverse methods into one empirical analysis that spans the ideographic-nomothetic divide.

Nomothetic/Comparative Methods

Different methodological traditions take a positivistic approach and attempt to provide **nomothetic explanations** of social phenomena. That is, they pursue insight that is generalizable and can be applied to multiple cases. At an extreme, nomothetic explanations pursue law-like generalizations that apply to the universe of cases, something implied by its name ("nomos" is Greek for law). Given the dominance of the natural sciences and their ability to offer insight that applies to the universe of cases, nomothetic explanations are commonly—but incorrectly—viewed as more scientific, so researchers who attempt to make the social sciences as scientific as possible commonly pursue this type of explanation. Rarely, however, do they go to the extreme of pursuing social laws that apply to the universe of cases, believing that extreme social complexity makes social laws impossible. So, instead of exploring the causes of ethnic violence in the former Yugoslavia in the early 1990s, these works explore common determinants of several episodes of ethnic violence, but they rarely try to discover a cause of all episodes of ethnic violence.

Methods pursuing nomothetic explanations necessarily analyze multiple cases because it is impossible to generalize based on one or a few cases. Although a researcher might simply complete numerous case studies, nearly all researchers pursuing nomothetic explanations gain insight from inter-case comparison. The two most common comparative methods used to provide nomothetic insight are statistics and controlled laboratory experiments.

Statistical Methods

The most popular and formalized methodological tradition in the social sciences is **statistical methods**, a massive methodological category that includes a number of subcategories. Statistics attempts to approximate controlled experiments by analyzing natural variation among a set of cases. The insight gained from statistical methods is derived primarily from inter-case comparison, although an increasing number of works use time-series data and also analyze variation within cases over time. For statistical comparison, variables are operationalized for a number of cases to explore whether one variable is commonly related to another among the set of cases. If there is a strong relationship between variables among the set of cases, the statistical analysis provides evidence that the two might be causally related. Thus, if a cross-sectional study finds that per capita GDP is strongly and negatively related to the incidence of civil war, it provides evidence that national wealth deters civil war in some way, as the natural variation among cases shows that non-wealthy countries are at a heightened risk of civil war.

Statistical methods are advantaged in several ways. By including multiple variables in the same model, statistics allows researchers to test different theories simultaneously. Statistics also allows researchers to estimate causal effects and risks. Third, cross-sectional statistics analyzes several cases and offers insight that is generalizable across the set. It therefore allows researchers to pursue nomothetic insight. Finally, statistics is very formalized, which makes possible the replication of findings, and has numerous techniques that can be matched to best suit the analysis at hand.

Like all methodological traditions, statistics also has shortcomings. First, statistical results are commonly open to question for two reasons: statistical analysis is based on numerous assumptions that are commonly broken, and there is no way of determining which model is most appropriate for any statistical analysis (and results vary according to the model). Even if one accepts the validity of the statistical findings, correlation is not the same as causation, and frequently statistical methods are unable to provide insight into whether a relationship is causal or spurious. Indeed, statistical findings have difficulty highlighting causal mechanisms that underlie relationships, as they provide little ideographic—or case-specific—insight into causal processes. Finally, statistical methods commonly cannot be used because some social phenomena either lack appropriate data sets or have an insufficient number of cases.

Experimental Methods

Experimental methods are most prominent in psychology and attempt to use controlled laboratory experiments on humans. Notably, statistical methods are a central element of this methodological tradition. What separates experimental methods from standard statistics is data collection, as researchers using experimental methods manipulate subjects and then use statistical methods to analyze the impact of this treatment. Standard statistical methods, on the other hand, explore natural variation instead of variation caused by a treatment.

Researchers using controlled laboratory experiments usually assign subjects to different treatment groups to see whether the various groups react differently based on their different treatments. For example, to analyze whether gender stereotypes shape our perceptions of others, a researcher might tell one-third of the subjects that a toddler is a boy, tell one-third of the subjects that a toddler is a girl, and deliberately conceal the child's sex to the remaining subjects. After the subjects have played with the toddler, the researcher can then interview the subjects and ask them to describe the personality traits of the toddler, noting whether the treatment—what they have been told regarding gender— affects how the subjects perceive the toddler (see Seavey, Katz, and Zalk 1975).

Although the use of different treatment groups is common, researchers using experimental methods sometimes give the same treatment to all subjects but analyze whether they react differently to the treatment based on some measurable characteristic of the individual subjects. For example, a researcher exploring how self-esteem affects violent action might ask subjects to complete questionnaires that allow the researcher to assess the self-confidence of the subjects. The researcher could then ask the subjects to write an essay, have an employee critique the essays harshly, and then give each of the subjects an opportunity to retaliate against the employee who critiqued their paper by blowing a loud horn at them. Finally, the researcher could measure each subject's retaliatory act by timing how long the subject honked the horn, to see whether there is a relationship between an individual's self-confidence and the length of the retaliation (see Bushman and Baumeister 1998).

Experimental methods provide very powerful insight into general determinants of causal processes. Relative to statistics, they offer researchers a superior ability to manipulate a particular factor while controlling for others, an advantage allowing researchers to gain more precise insight into causal determinants. Most notably, controlled laboratory experiments are much less likely to produce spurious findings, have a greatly superior capacity to offer insight into causal mechanisms, and measure causal effects with much greater accuracy. The main disadvantage of experimental methods—and the factor that prevents them from being used more broadly—is their impracticality. Notably, experimental methods are most appropriate for simple micro-level processes and become difficult—if not impossible—for processes involving large numbers of people. For example, it is virtually impossible to use experimental methods to explore directly the causes of social revolutions or the rise of capitalism. Similarly, experimental methods cannot easily be used to analyze either processes lasting extended periods of time or complex social phenomena requiring multiple treatments and interactions. Finally, for moral reasons, experimental methods cannot be used to analyze phenomena when the treatment is potentially harmful to the well-being of the subject. Thus, a researcher cannot explore the impact of severe verbal abuse by a stranger on feelings of self-worth among adolescents because the subjects could be harmed by the treatment.

When researchers are unable to use experimental methods, they can try to approximate them through natural experiments, which use natural variation in an effort to isolate the impact of certain factors (see Diamond and Robinson 2010). Unlike laboratory experiments, researchers attempting natural experiments cannot control for all factors and manipulate only one. Instead, they select cases that were very similar in many ways but subsequently differed in one key way. The researcher is thereby able to compare the cases and estimate the impact of the difference. Unfortunately, even the most similar of cases cannot control for all influential factors, so one cannot be as confident in their findings. This is especially the case given that a natural experiment commonly compares only two cases, not the hundreds or thousands of cases compared through more controlled experiments. Moreover, it can be very difficult to find appropriate natural experiments to answer all types of research questions.

Ideographic/Within-Case Methods

Whereas statistical methods and experimental methods compare multiple cases in pursuit of nomothetic explanations, several social scientific methods specialize in providing case-specific—or ideographic—insight. Such analyses explore either what happened in a particular case or what the characteristics of a particular case were through in-depth analysis of the case. Authors pursuing this type of analysis commonly believe that extreme social complexity caused by free will and multicausality prevents researchers from making discoveries that can be extended across a large set of cases. They therefore strive either to pursue findings that can be applied to only one case or to show how social processes unraveled very differently in multiple cases.

It is possible to pursue **ideographic explanations** through comparative methods, as comparisons might not highlight commonalities or strong relationships. Most commonly, however, researchers employ within-case methods when making ideographic explanations. Two prominent examples of within-case methodologies are ethnographic and historical methods.

Ethnographic Methods

Ethnographic methods are the dominant method within anthropology, and a substantial minority of researchers in sociology and political science use them. They are commonly used for the study of culture within a particular group of people, ranging from elites, to ethnic groups, to criminals, to students.

Ethnographic methods have two distinct components. The first is concerned with how to gather data through participant observation and interviews. Much of this literature discusses appropriate ways to find subjects, observe and interact with subjects, and gather data from subjects. For example, a researcher using ethnographic methods to analyze elite culture has to figure out sites to observe elite culture, how to find elites for interviews, how to conduct the interviews, and what questions to ask. The second component deals with how to analyze and present the findings. These ethnographic analyses lay out and interpret the data, thereby giving an account of the phenomenon under analysis. The analyses usually take the form of a narrative description and commonly present photographs, texts, and tables. Unlike statistics and controlled experiments, ethnographic analyses commonly are not formalized, and the ultimate insight gained from them depends on both the quality of the data and the analytical skills of the researcher. Such skills primarily involve making sense of the data, recognizing patterns, and being able to present the findings clearly. Interpersonal skills are also very important as they are vital to the data collection process.

Two notable strengths of ethnographic methods are its ability to offer descriptive insight into the characteristics of a phenomenon and its ability to analyze complex phenomena. Most notably, ethnographic methods are usually the best means of gaining insight into motivations, perspectives, values, rituals, and other factors commonly considered as subcomponents of culture. These advantages help to explain their dominance in anthropology and why researchers using ethnographic methods commonly take a more interpretivist approach. Along with these advantages, however, ethnographic methods also have three notable disadvantages. First, ethnographic methods cannot be used for many historical phenomena, as the past cannot be observed directly and relevant individuals might not be available for interview. So, while ethnographic methods would be an excellent source of insight into the causes and characteristics of the French Revolution, they cannot now be used for this research question. Second, ethnography pursues case-specific insight for a particular time and place and is therefore poorly suited for nomothetic explanation. This is not to say that ethnography cannot provide generalizable insight. Lipset, Trow, and Coleman's (1956) *Union Democracy*, for example, offers a superb ethnographic analysis of the International Typographical Union and offers generalizable insight into the mechanism underlying Michels's (1911/1968) iron law of oligarchy. Still, gaining nomothetic insight from ethnography requires that one either perform multiple ethnographic analyses or link the ethnographic analysis of one case to a larger theory or literature. Third, ethnographic methods require willing participants, and it can be very difficult to find willing participants when researchers want to analyze delicate topics which reveal the private lives of individuals. Moreover, even if a researcher finds participants willing to allow her or him to analyze sensitive issues, it is possible that the participants will modify their behavior when being observed or respond inaccurately to interview questions in order to portray themselves to the researcher in the most positive light. Researchers must therefore critically assess the validity of the data they collect through ethnographic methods.

Historical Methods

Historical methods, also known as historiography, are the most common analytic techniques used in the discipline of history. They are generally used to explore either what happened at a particular time and place or what the characteristics of a phenomenon were like at a particular time and place. Similar to ethnographic methods, methodological discussions of historiography focus on both data collection and data analysis. The first includes guidelines for finding historical data, as this is a major concern of historians. The second component consists of guidelines for interpreting and presenting data. These guidelines generally describe how to judge the validity of historical data but rarely discuss how the data is analyzed once its validity has been assessed. This overlooked element is central to the historical method and involves piecing together the evidence to make a conclusion about the research question.

Researchers can use historical methods to analyze diverse phenomena. For instance, a researcher might investigate the processes leading to Truman's decision to drop nuclear bombs on Japan. For this, the researcher might analyze biographies, diaries, and correspondence between Truman and other officials involved in deciding to use nuclear weapons. They might also interview officials or close confidants of deceased officials. In gathering this data, the researcher must consider the source of the data and its apparent validity and accuracy. Then, the researcher must analyze the collection of data to assess the influences on Truman, his state of mind, and the sequence of events leading up to his decision to use nuclear weapons. Alternatively, researchers interested in the structure of families in the English countryside during the mid-nineteenth century would rely on different types of sources. They might use census data to get information on the members of households; legal documents about marriage, divorce, inheritance, and household responsibilities; and newspapers, magazines, diaries, and other relevant literature that provides information on household relations. After gathering the data, the researcher must then assess the validity of the data, analyze the collection of data to gain insight into the structure of families, and write a narrative that presents the evidence.

Not surprisingly, historical methods are able to provide insight into the characteristics and determinants of historical phenomena. Similar to ethnographic methods, they offer considerable insight into complex phenomena and processes. Indeed, historical and ethnographic methods are commonly used to analyze the same types of phenomena, the main difference being that ethnographic methods analyze contemporary examples whereas historical methods analyze examples from the past. In this way, data collection and type of data are commonly the only factors separating ethnographic methods from historical methods. Historical methods are also similar to ethnographic methods because their insight is limited to particular cases, as historical methods analyze particular phenomena in particular places at particular times. As a consequence, they are ill-suited for nomothetic explanations. Historical methods are also disadvantaged because they cannot generate their own data and therefore depend on the presence of historical sources. As a consequence, such methods cannot be used to analyze phenomena that lack appropriate data.

Comparative-Historical Methods in Comparative Perspective

Comparative-historical methods combine comparative and within-case methods, and therefore have affinities with both comparative/nomothetic methods and within-case/ideographic methods. Similar to statistical and experimental methods, comparative-historical methods employ comparison as a means of gaining insight into causal determinants. Similar to ethnographic and historical methods, comparative-historical methods explore the characteristics and causes of particular phenomena.

Comparative-historical analysis, however, does not simply combine the methods from other major methodological traditions—none of the major comparative methods is very common in comparative-historical analysis. Indeed, only a small—albeit growing—portion of comparative-historical analyses uses statistical comparison, and laboratory-style experimental methods are not used by comparative-historical researchers. There are several reasons for the marginal position of statistics within comparative-historical analysis. Most notably, within-case methods have been the dominant method used in the research tradition, and the basic logics of statistics and within-case methods differ considerably, with the former focusing on relationships between variables and the latter focusing on causal processes (see Mahoney and Goertz 2006). As a consequence, comparative-historical researchers commonly avoid statistics and simply focus on causal processes. Additional reasons for the limited use of statistical comparison within the comparative-historical research tradition include the limited availability of historical data needed for appropriate statistical analyses and the small number of cases analyzed by comparative-historical researchers. Experimental methods are excluded from comparative-historical analysis for two main reasons. First, comparative-historical scholars ask research questions about concrete real-world phenomena, such as, "What caused the American civil rights movement?" Controlled experiments, on the other hand, can only provide insight into general issues, for example, "Are people with higher or lower self-confidence more likely to retaliate aggressively?" Second, comparative-historical analysis focuses on social processes like revolutions, economic development, and state building that involve many people within a complex social environment over an extended period. For practical and moral reasons, such phenomena cannot be replicated in controlled environments.

Instead of statistics and controlled experiments, the most common comparative methods employed in comparative-historical analysis are small-N comparisons. These comparisons usually explore how causal processes are similar and different and, in so doing, pay attention to the impact of context and causal mechanisms. Different from statistical comparison, such comparisons are usually not an independent source of insight, pursue insight that can be applied to a fewer number of cases, and focus on more specific details.

Besides comparative methods, comparative-historical scholars employ several different types of within-case methods. Ethnography can and is used for within-case analysis and is therefore part of the comparative-historical methodological toolkit. Comparative-historical researchers only rarely use it with great rigor, however, because ethnographic methods are usually used for very descriptive works that attempt to increase understanding about a particular group of people, their livelihoods, and their culture. Comparative-historical analysis, on the other hand, usually has a broader research agenda than understanding culture. As a consequence, ethnography can only provide partial insight into most of the questions asked by comparative-historical researchers. In addition, comparative-historical methods are used to analyze multiple cases, and ethnographic work is so intensive that it is very difficult to analyze more than one case in a single work. As a result, it is rare for ethnographic work to be comparative, although there are exceptions, such as Geertz's *Islam Observed* (1968). Finally, in general ethnographic methods cannot be used to analyze historical phenomena, so they are usually not appropriate for comparative-historical analysis. For all of these reasons, comparative-historical scholars rarely employ ethnographic methods themselves, although they commonly gather data from ethnographic analyses to use for their comparative-historical analyses.

Historical methods are much more commonly employed within comparative-historical analysis. In particular, comparative-historical researchers frequently use historical methods to gather, assess, and present data. Yet, because of the breadth of the questions analyzed by comparative-historical researchers and the multiple cases under analysis, comparative-historical researchers rely primarily on data from secondary sources, and many do not use historical methods to collect and assess data. Instead, they gather data from historical secondary sources and use this data for their comparative-historical analyses.

While using ethnographic methods and historical methods as sources of data, comparative-historical methods differ fundamentally from each in their analysis of the data. Whereas ethnographic and historical methods are primarily descriptive and document the characteristics of social phenomena, comparative-historical methods analyze data to offer insight into causal determinants. For this, comparative-historical researchers commonly employ three different within-case methods. These methods are all similar to those used by detectives and involve sorting through the available evidence and attempting to reconstruct causal scenarios in an effort to gain insight into the determinants of social phenomena. The three methods differ based on the type of inference they pursue: causal narrative offers insight into causal processes, process tracing explores causal mechanisms, and pattern matching tests theories.

Comparative-historical methods are also distinct from all other major methodological traditions in the social sciences because they have a much more extensive and diverse methodological toolkit. Indeed, comparative-historical methods include multiple types of comparative methods and multiple types of within-case methods. Researchers combine them in different ways and for different purposes. Considering the latter, they sometimes combine methods for triangulation, sometimes combine methods to exploit the strengths of different methods, and sometimes combine methods to improve the insight that can be gained by the individual methods.

Relatedly, comparative-historical methods are also unique because they pursue both ideographic and nomothetic explanations. The within-case methods offer ideographic insight, whereas the comparative methods offer more nomothetic insight. Their combination, in turn, weakens both the ideographic bent of the within-case methods and the nomothetic bent of the comparative methods, and pushes the researcher to consider both ideographic and nomothetic explanations.

Most comparative-historical researchers value ideographic explanations deeply, and both Skocpol and Somers (1980) and Tilly (1984) recognize ideographic explanation as a common goal of comparative-historical researchers. However, the methods of comparative-historical analysis are actually biased against this type of explanation. Most notably, comparative methods require multiple cases and usually seek insight that can be extended beyond a single case, and scholars pursuing purely ideographic explanations usually restrict their analysis to a single case. As a consequence, ideographic explanations are relatively rare in comparative-historical analysis but very common in history and historical sociology.

At the same time, comparisons highlight differences as well as similarities, and some comparative-historical researchers focus on the differences highlighted through comparison. These works show how each case is unique and does not follow any common logic. Notably, the failure of such comparisons to discover commonalities does not imply that ideographic explanations are in any way inferior to more nomothetic explanations. As Tilly notes, an ideographic explanation is not a "bungled attempt at generalization" (1984, 88). Instead, it seeks to find variation, not explain it. Such difference-oriented comparisons are valuable because they highlight the great diversity and complexity of the social world and show how social phenomena are commonly unique. They therefore serve as a corrective to comparative works that seek to stretch generalizations to the extreme. It is thus not by coincidence that most ideographic analyses in comparative-historical analysis seek to correct the universalism of different theories.

One master of this difference-oriented strategy was Reinhard Bendix. Several of his books combined detailed within-case analysis with small-N comparison, and both methods ultimately highlighted the uniqueness of each case. His 700-page *Kings or People* (1978) offers a notable example. This book analyzes a subject that was the focus of much of Bendix's work—authority—and explores how popular sovereignty came to succeed hereditary monarchy in diverse countries throughout the world. It analyzes and compares England, France, Germany, Japan, Russia, and China and is divided into two analytic sections. The first analyzes how monarchs founded, legitimized, and protected their rule; the second explores the emergence of popular sovereignty and traces the development of popular sovereignty in his cases up to the mid-twentieth century. His three main points are that (1) demonstration effects contributed to the emergence of popular sovereignty but that popular sovereignty still emerged relatively independently; (2) preexisting institutions, history, and beliefs shaped the emergence of popular sovereignty; and (3) the major causes of the emergence of popular sovereignty were changes in ideas, beliefs, and justifications. Notably, all three could be generalized and thereby offer some nomothetic insight. Still, as Tilly remarks, "Through their stress on the causal influence of conditions that are unique to each state, the three assumptions push the whole analysis back toward individualization" (1984, 93). In this way, Bendix's ultimate conclusion is that the processes leading to popular sovereignty were distinctive in all of his cases and did not follow a single pathway to modernity.

Different from an ideographic strategy, a nomothetic strategy privileges methods that offer insight into multiple cases, and this is a notable strength of comparative methods. A number of social scientists view nomothetic explanations as more scientific than ideographic explanations. This is because the natural sciences produce more law–like findings that apply to the universe of cases, and they therefore commonly privilege methods that offer general insight. Because of this methodological bias, nomothetic analyses frequently do not employ within–case methods, an omission that removes them from the realm of comparative-historical analysis. When researchers do employ within-case methods, a nomothetic analysis commonly privileges the comparative analysis and simply uses the within-case analysis to supplement the comparisons by either scoring variables or highlighting common mechanisms. The danger of this epistemological and methodological bias, however, is that social relations are much more unpredictable than atoms, molecules, and stars, and generalizations in the social sciences usually come at a price: they abstract reality and overlook actual causal processes.

Some comparative-historical analyses undoubtedly suffer from these problems associated with a focus on nomothetic insight, but there is a general bias within the research tradition against these types of work. Indeed, just as comparative methods prevent works from being overly ideographic, within-case methods impede overly nomothetic explanations. Within-case methods, for example, force researchers to consider particular historical and social contexts and to—first and foremost—try to get the within-case analyses right. As a result, most comparative-historical researchers who pursue nomothetic insight take a more moderate position and avoid claims of universal laws. Instead, as Mahoney and Rueschemeyer claim, they almost always "suggest that an explanation is contingent on complex and variable conditions" (2003, 10).

Skocpol's *States and Social Revolutions* (1979) offers a well-known example of a work that attempts to balance ideographic and nomo-thetic explanation. Skocpol sets out to increase general insight into the causes of social revolutions and, through a comparative-historical analy-sis of several cases, shows how both state breakdown and peasant mobi-lization capacity are vital to social revolution. Still, she offers detailed analyses of individual cases that provide considerable ideographic insight. Moreover, she limits her analysis to a subset and notes that her cases have particular characteristics that make them different from other more recent revolutions: they were non-colonies with limited interna-tional dependence, their revolutions occurred during a certain time period, and the cases were agrarian bureaucracies at the time of the revolutions. These factors differentiate them from more recent revolu-tions, and have led Skocpol to claim that her findings are not likely to apply to cases outside of her subset.

This middling position of comparative-historical analysis within the ideographic-nomothetic continuum has made the research tradition a target of criticism from both sides. Historians, for example, commonly criticize comparative-historical analysis for sacrificing "good history" for the sake of generalization. Alternatively, several more positivistic social scientists believe covering laws are the purpose of the social sciences and criticize comparative-historical analysis for privileging internal validity over external validity. The position of most comparative-historical researchers, however, is that ideographic and nomothetic explanations are both important and that one should not be sacrificed for the other. Indeed, both the particular and the general are vital to any understand-ing of social relations, and comparative-historical methods force researchers constantly to consider both.

Book Outline

Having described what comparative-historical analysis is and compared comparative-historical methods to other major methodological traditions in the social sciences, the remainder of this book reviews the origins and basic elements of comparative–historical methods. Chapter 2 offers a historical overview of the methodological tradition and reviews major scholars and works within it. It also describes the topics researchers commonly analyze through comparative–historical methods and the disciplines that use comparative–historical methods. Chapter 3 begins to review the actual methods employed in comparative–historical analysis by describing the main within–case techniques used by comparative–historical scholars to produce and analyze evidence. Chapter 4 continues to analyze within–case methods and reviews how researchers employ within–case methods to explore two influential aspects of causal processes: temporality and inter–case relationships. Chapter 5 turns to comparative methods and explores the ways comparative–historical researchers use them to gain insight. It describes large–N and small–N comparisons as well as sub–types of each. Chapter 6 discusses different ways that comparative–historical researchers combine within–case and comparative methods and the benefits derived from different combinatorial strategies. Although Chapters 3 through 6 consider the actual methodological techniques that are used to analyze data, Chapter 7 discusses three non-analytic aspects of comparative–historical methods: data, case selection, and theory. Finally, Chapter 8 concludes by reviewing major points highlighted in the chapters and discussing the important analytical strengths of comparative–historical methods.

Glossary

Comparative methods: Diverse methods used in the social sciences that offer insight through cross-case comparison. For this, they compare the characteristics of different cases and highlight similarities and differences between them. Comparative methods are usually used to explore causes that are common among a set of cases. They are commonly used in all social scientific disciplines.

Comparative-historical analysis: A prominent research tradition in the social sciences, especially in political science and sociology. Works within this research tradition use comparative-historical methods, pursue causal explanations, and analyze units of analysis at the meso- or macro-level.

Comparative-historical methods: The collection of methods commonly employed for comparative-historical analysis. These include a variety of comparative and within-case methods. Comparative-historical methods necessarily combine at least one comparative method and one within-case method.

Epistemology: A branch of philosophy that considers the possibility of knowledge and understanding. Within the social sciences, epistemological debates commonly focus on the possibility of gaining insight into the causes of social phenomena.

Ethnographic methods: A type of social scientific method that gains insight into social relations through participant observation, interviews, and the analysis of art, texts, and oral histories. It is commonly used to analyze culture and is the most common method of anthropology.

Experimental methods: The most powerful method used in the social sciences, albeit the most difficult to use. It manipulates individuals in a particular way (the treatment) and explores the impact of this treatment. It offers powerful insight by controlling the environment, thereby allowing researchers to isolate the impact of the treatment.

Historical methods: Also known as historiography, it is the dominant method in the discipline of history. Such methods focus largely on finding data, judging the validity of the data, and accurately presenting the data through narrative analysis. Historical methods can be used to analyze causal processes but are most commonly used in history to describe social phenomena.

Ideographic explanation: Causal explanations that explore the causes of a particular case. Such explanations are not meant to apply to a larger set of cases and commonly focus on the particularities of the case under analysis.

Insight: Evidence contributing to an understanding of a case or set of cases. Comparative-historical researchers are generally most concerned with causal insight, or insight into causal processes.

Method: A technique used to analyze data. Commonly, a method is aligned with a particular strategy for gathering data, as particular methods commonly require particular types of data. "Method" is therefore commonly used to refer to strategies for both analyzing and gathering data.

Methodology: A body of practices, procedures, and rules used by researchers to offer insight into the workings of the world.

Nomothetic explanation: Causal explanations that apply to the universe of cases. They are commonly associated with positivism. Because the physical sciences pursue nomothetic explanations, they are frequently—albeit incorrectly—perceived by some as being more scientific than ideographic explanations.

Positivism: An epistemological approach that was popular among most of the founding figures of the social sciences. It claims that the scientific method is the best way to gain insight into our world. Within the social sciences, positivism suggests that scientific methods can be used to analyze social relations in order to gain knowledge. At its extreme, positivism suggests that the analysis of social relations through scientific methods allows researchers to discover laws that govern all social relations. Positivism is therefore linked to nomothetic explanations. Other positivists believe social complexity prevents the discovery of social laws, but they still believe that the scientific method allows researchers to gain insight into the determinants of social phenomena.

Statistical methods: The most common subtype of comparative methods. It operationalizes variables for several cases, compares the cases to explore relationships between the variables, and uses probability theory to estimate causal effects or risks. Within the social sciences, statistics uses natural variation to approximate experimental methods. There are diverse subtypes of statistical methods.

Verstehen: Meaning "understand" in German, the term was used by Max Weber to designate a particular epistemological position in the social sciences at odds with extreme varieties of positivism. It suggests that social scientists cannot discover social laws and should simply strive to understand social phenomena. The term is commonly associated with interpretivism, which claims that it is impossible to gain concrete knowledge about the determinants of social action and that social scientists should simply attempt to interpret the meaning of action to gain insight into its determinants.

Within-case methods: A category of methods used in the social sciences that offer insight into the determinants of a particular phenomenon for a particular case. For this, they analyze the processes and characteristics of the case.

2

An Intellectual History and Overview of Comparative-Historical Analysis

The Comparative-Historical Pedigree: Two Generations of Work

Comparative-historical methods have been around for a long time. For example, Ibn Khaldun used them in his fourteenth-century history of the world. During the Enlightenment, key figures such as Montesquieu and Adam Smith also employed comparative-historical methods for their major works, including Montesquieu's *The Spirit of the Laws* (1748/1952) and Smith's *The Wealth of Nations* (1776/1976). Although Montesquieu and Smith greatly influenced subsequent comparative-historical researchers, it was not until the mid-nineteenth century—with the scientific revolution, rampant social change, and the emergence of democratic movements—that comparative-historical analysis truly emerged as a research tradition. The scientific revolution promoted a proliferation of research in diverse areas to expand knowledge about the world, and many began the pursuit of a science of social relations. This social scientific push was further magnified by the enormous social changes that occurred in Europe. These changes involved capitalism, industrialization, state building, and imperialism and provoked interest in and concern about the causes of such social change. Democratization, in turn, strengthened the belief that humans could take control of their social environment and transform it to suit their needs. Together, these factors fueled widespread interest in gaining insight into—and possibly controlling—the major social changes that were at hand.

Among the earliest and most influential social scientists were Alexis de Tocqueville, Karl Marx, and Max Weber—all of whom used comparative-historical methods. After Weber's death in 1920, there was a lull in comparative-historical analysis. By the late-1950s and 1960s, however, a new generation of comparative-historical scholars had emerged and began to produce modern classics using comparative-historical methods—scholars such as Karl Polanyi, Reinhard Bendix, Shmuel Eisenstadt, and Barrington Moore. Although initially small in size and with limited influence in the social sciences, this second generation flourished and became more mainstream by the 1970s and 1980s. At this time, its most influential practitioners included Charles Tilly, Immanuel Wallerstein, Theda Skocpol, Perry Anderson, Michael Mann, and many others. This second generation never faded and continues to thrive to this day, with many of the best works and most respected social scientists using comparative-historical methods.[1]

The First Generation of Comparative-Historical Analysis

Figure 2.1 gives a time-line showing the founding figures of comparative-historical analysis. Because the founding figures of the social sciences used comparative-historical methods, a review of the founding figures of comparative-historical analysis overlaps considerably—but not completely—with a review of the founding figures of the social sciences. One reason for this overlap is that the social sciences began with a strong historical bent. This is most evident in four influential founding figures of the social sciences: Alexis de Tocqueville, Karl Marx, Friedrich Engels, and Max Weber.

Alexis de Tocqueville (1805–59) was from a wealthy aristocratic family that was briefly exiled by the French Revolution, and he supported himself

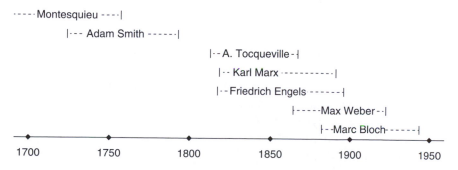

Figure 2.1 Time-line of the first generation of comparative-historical analysis

as a politician for most of his life. Tocqueville was also a respected pundit and wrote several works that have left a powerful and lasting influence on the social sciences. His *The Old Regime and the Revolution* (1856/1998) analyzes the causes and consequences of the French Revolution. His explanation focuses on the high tax burden suffered by the peasants, unequal land distribution, and—especially—state centralization during the period of absolutism. Tocqueville's two-volume *Democracy in America* (1835, 1840/2000) is also a classic in both political science and sociology, and helped cement his position as a founding figure of comparative-historical analysis. The book is a thorough empirical analysis of the workings and causes of American democracy up until the 1830s. Although a case study, the analysis also has a strong comparative component, as Tocqueville constantly compares the United States and Europe in an effort better to understand the causes of their differences. Most notably, Tocqueville is famous for pointing to rampant associationalism as an important determinant of successful democratization in the United States and the remnants of aristocracy as a powerful deterrent to democratization in Europe.

Karl Marx (1818–83) and Friedrich Engels (1820–95) were also founding figures of the social sciences and, like Tocqueville, had an enormous impact on comparative-historical analysis. Both were born in present-day Germany, Marx the son of a lawyer and Engels the son of an industrialist. They began collaborating in 1845 and wrote many of the most influential Marxist works together over the next four decades. Although Marx received most of the credit (and criticism) for this body of work, many scholars now recognize that Engels was an influential partner, potentially even more important than Marx in the development of Marxism (Collins 1994, 56).

Marx and Engels believed that societies evolved through progressive stages and that the stages were based on different modes of economic production. They believed, in turn, that class conflict caused one mode of production to transform into another. Much of their empirical work offers a comparative-historical analysis showing how class conflict contributed to the transformation from one mode of production to another. In comparison with the work of Alexis de Tocqueville, their empirical analyses were less thorough and had a much greater theoretical component. Whereas Tocqueville started with a question and tried to answer it through empirical analysis, Marx and Engels generally started with their theory and tried to show its validity through comparative-historical analysis (although their theory was undoubtedly based on their prior observations). In this way, Marx and Engels's legacy in comparative-historical analysis is primarily theoretical.

Of the two, Engels's independent work conforms to comparative-historical analysis most closely. His *Origins of the Family, Private Property, and the State* (1884/2010) actively exploits both comparative and historical methods to investigate the impact of capitalist development on the family structure and female subordination. It is recognized as the first work linking the family structure and patriarchy to the economic system, is backed up by comparative-historical analyses of several societies, and continues to be a very influential work.

Like Marx and Engels, Max Weber (1864–1920) was from Germany and is recognized as one of the most influential founding figures of both sociology and comparative-historical analysis. The son of a prominent civil servant and politician, Weber was a trained lawyer and legal historian, worked as a university professor, and was very active in German politics. He was a prolific researcher who wrote extensively on a variety of topics. While wide ranging, almost all of his writings focus on the determinants of broad-based social change, with a special interest in how Western Europe emerged as the global economic and political power. Unlike Marx and Engels, Weber did not propose a grandiose theory of social development, believing rather that social change is too complex to reduce to a couple of covering laws.

Weber influenced sociology and comparative-historical analysis in many ways. He developed several concepts that remain central to comparative-historical analysis, including bureaucracy, rationalization, legitimate authority, domination, and social action. His conceptualizations are most notable in *Economy and Society* (1922/1968), his posthumous opus, which lays out hundreds of concepts that he used to gain insight into how the social world works. It is commonly recognized as one of the most important books ever written in sociology. A poll by the International Sociological Association, for example, placed it as the single most influential sociological book of the twentieth century, with nearly twice as many votes as C. Wright Mills's *The Sociological Imagination* (1959) which took second place.

Much more than Tocqueville, Marx, and Engels, Weber clearly used comparative-historical methods. Weber was a prolific reader of history, and some claim that he knew more about world history than any of his contemporaries. He used history, in turn, as a means of analyzing and attempting to gain a better understanding of the changing social world. His were not simply historical analyses, however; Weber actively sought to compare phenomena in an effort to understand the determinants of their similarities and differences.

Weber's most famous comparative-historical analysis is *The Protestant Ethic and the Spirit of Capitalism* (1905/2001). The book was actually written as a series of essays that were eventually combined into a single volume. The resulting book is only part of a much larger body of Weber's work that collectively explores the impact of religion on economic transformation. *The Protestant Ethic and the Spirit of Capitalism* concludes that Protestantism—and, in particular, Calvinism—contributed to a strong work ethic and promoted the reinvestment of profits, thereby contributing to capitalist development. Alternatively, his analyses of other religions conclude that no other major religion affected economic action in similar ways. Importantly, Weber's analysis is considerably more complex than this brief synopsis, as he notes that many factors contributed to the rise of capitalism and that non-religious factors also interacted with and shaped the Protestant ethic.

Weber's influence also comes from his work on comparative-historical methods. Indeed, Weber was the first researcher to consider closely the methodological underpinnings of comparative-historical analysis. He believed that social scientific analysis must offer insight into social action and, therefore, must focus on individual actions and the ways in which social relations shape such actions. To explore social action, Weber devised **ideal types**, or concepts that are crafted to emphasize one characteristic of a phenomenon. These concepts are then used as a **heuristic device** to compare phenomena and explore the extent to which cases conform to the ideal type. *Economy and Society* laid out hundreds of Weber's most famous ideal types, and *The Protestant Ethic and Spirit of Capitalism* is his most famous comparative-historical analysis that uses ideal types. Most notably, *The Protestant Ethic and Spirit of Capitalism* used Weber's ideal type of value-rational action and showed how Calvinism contributed to capitalist development by instilling values that pushed individuals to act in particular ways that contributed to capitalist development.

Despite comparative-historical researchers commonly proclaiming Weber the most important and influential comparative-historical researcher of all time, Kalberg (1994) notes that comparative-historical researchers largely overlook Weber's methodological work. Specifically, few researchers use ideal types for social scientific analysis, and Weber's ideal types are generally taught in theory classes, not methods classes. Moreover, most comparative-historical researchers take a more macro-level approach that pays less attention to individual action. That is, they do not ignore the individual but fail to explore rigorously the mutual influence of individual and structure, which was a central concern of Weberian methods.

Marc Bloch (1886–1944) was a French historian and must also be considered a founding figure of comparative-historical analysis. He studied in Germany, where he was influenced by Max Weber. After returning to France, he helped found the *Annales* School of history (so called for their journal, *Annales d'histoire économique et sociale*), which championed social scientific analysis through history. He also wrote methodological pieces on historiography and historical comparison, and completed historical analyses with a clear social scientific component. If not for his untimely death at the hands of the Nazis (he was Jewish and a member of the French Resistance), his lifetime would probably have spanned the divide between the first and second generations of comparative-historical analysis and his influence on comparative-historical analysis would likely have been greater.

Bloch wrote about diverse topics. In *The Royal Touch* (1924/1990), he analyzed the common belief that the king could cure scrofula (a type of tuberculosis) by touching the infected individual. The analysis offers a comparative analysis of both France and England that examines why people believed in the curing power of the royal touch and how it affected relations between the monarchs and their subjects. Bloch also wrote extensively about feudalism (1939/1965) and rural class relations (1931/1970), the latter of which explores the impact of agricultural relations on revolution. All of these works are social histories exploring the causes of long-term social change and offer extremely broad analyses that consider the interplay between politics, economics, and culture. As such, they exemplify some of the hallmarks of comparative-historical analysis.

Along with the Tocquevillian, Marxist, and Weberian traditions, a few founding figures of the social sciences were structural functionalists. Similar to Marxist theory, structural functionalism proposed a grand theory of social transformation from one stage to another. Auguste Comte (1798–1857), the founder of modern sociology and a co-national and contemporary of Tocqueville, was one of the earliest structural functionalists. He proposed a theory of sociocultural evolution suggesting the need to analyze societies using an historical perspective. Famed philosopher Herbert Spencer (1820–1903) popularized the social evolutionary views of structural functionalism even further. Most notably, he proposed that all societies evolved from military society, which was simple and undifferentiated, to industrial society, which was complex and differentiated. Similarly, Emile Durkheim (1858–1917), who founded sociology as an academic discipline, accepted an evolutionary perspective claiming that societies transform from simple to complex.

Although structural-functionalist theory focuses on historical change and therefore seems to have an affinity with comparative-historical methods, the leading figures of this theoretical perspective focused primarily on contemporary societies and contributed little to the comparative-historical tradition. Comte and Spencer, for example, were very theoretical, and their empirical analyses were quite ahistorical. Similarly, most of Durkheim's work does not take a historical perspective. Indeed, Ragin and Zaret (1983) claim Durkheim's work is overwhelmingly antihistorical, viewing Durkheim rather as a founding figure of the quantitative research tradition, because his major works operationalize variables and test relationships as a means of social scientific insight. Because of his very limited historical analysis, Durkheim is the founding figure of sociology with the least influence on comparative-historical analysis.

By the 1930s, structural functionalism had established itself as the leading theoretical tradition in sociology, especially in the United States. This dominance and, in turn, the growing popularity of surveys and statistical analysis contributed to a twenty-five-year lull in the comparative-historical research tradition.

The Second Generation of Comparative-Historical Analysis

After World War II, comparative-historical analysis began a comeback, albeit a slow one that did not reestablish itself as a distinct research tradition until the 1970s and 1980s. Figure 2.2 gives a time-line of key figures in this second generation of comparative-historical analysis. Although social scientists from diverse countries contributed to this comparative-historical renaissance, the United States was the methodological movement's epicenter. To a large extent, this comeback was promoted by growing disillusionment in structural functionalism and a return by many sociologists to the theories and methods of the other founding figures, most notably Marx and Weber. Moreover, researchers returned to comparative-historical methods because they offered considerable insight into some of the major social issues of the 1960s and

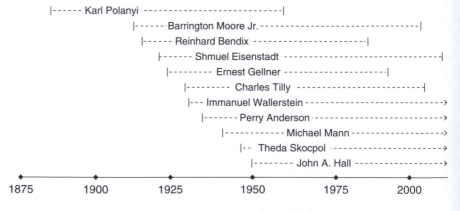

Figure 2.2   Time-line of the second generation of comparative-historical analysis

1970s, such as the civil rights movement, the Vietnam War, and the cold war. As Mahoney and Rueschemeyer (2003) note in their edited review of the research tradition, comparative-historical analysis flourished during this second generation, thereby establishing itself as a major research tradition in the social sciences. The explosion is so great that it is impossible to review all the exceptional researchers and works that emerged during this period. Below, I present a handful of the most influential comparative-historical researchers during the second generation.

Although not a comparative-historical researcher, per se, C. Wright Mills (1916–62) helped promote the reemergence of the research tradition. He was an American sociologist who was influenced greatly by Marx and Weber. Mills strongly opposed structural functionalism and demanded the historical analysis of social phenomena. Most notably, his *The Sociological Imagination* (1959) proclaimed that any social scientific analysis must consider the origins of a society, how it has changed, and how history is being made. Despite his premature death, Mills's work was enormously influential in American sociology, and several subsequent comparative-historical scholars recognize Mills as a major source of inspiration and influence.

Another apparent cause of the American-centered second generation of comparative-historical analysis was the immigration of several Europeans to North America prior to and during World War II. Karl Polanyi (1886–1964) was among the earliest and most influential of the second generation of comparative-historical researchers. He was born in the Austro-Hungarian Empire but spent his most productive years in Great Britain, the United States, and Canada. Polanyi's most influential work was his critically acclaimed *The Great Transformation* (1944). This work offers a comparative-historical analysis of the rise of market society in an effort to understand the forces that contributed to the rise of fascism. In it, he describes how market society subordinates all social relations to the market mechanism, thereby hindering the ability of individuals to provide for themselves when the market mechanism fails. Although not a Marxist, Polanyi therefore shared Marx's concern with the harmful effects of capitalist development, but he did not accept the Marxist doctrine.

Like Polanyi, Reinhard Bendix (1916–91) was a central European who emigrated to North America in reaction to Hitler's rise to power, although Bendix was younger and received his higher education in the United States. Bendix's most renowned comparative-historical works are *Work and Authority in Industry* (1956), which explores the conditions that allow entrepreneurs to gain autonomy; *Nation-Building and Citizenship* (1964), which explores the development of different authority systems; and *Kings or People* (1978), which explores how parliamentary democracy came to succeed hereditary rule. He was also interested in theory and wrote a book on Max Weber (1977). Indeed, Weber influenced Bendix, and Weber's concepts and views are evident throughout Bendix's work—most notably, his concern with the long-term development of authority. Like much of Weber's work, Bendix also used comparative-historical methods to highlight differences between cases and thereby the uniqueness of each case.

Shmuel Eisenstadt (1923–2010) was also from central Europe, although—unlike Polanyi and Bendix—he emigrated to Palestine in the 1930s instead of North America. Along with his work in Israel, he was also a professor at Harvard, Stanford, and the University of Chicago, so he did influence (and was, in turn, influenced by) the reemergence of comparative-historical analysis in the United States. His earliest and most famous book was *The Political Systems of Empires* (1963). In it, Eisenstadt offers a comparative-historical analysis of diverse bureaucratic empires and explores factors causing their rise and transformation. Although influenced by Weber, he is more closely aligned with a structural functionalist approach. As noted previously, this approach has always been more marginal in comparative-historical analysis, a factor that limited Eisenstadt's subsequent influence in the research tradition.

Barrington Moore Jr. (1913–2005) was a contemporary of both Bendix and Eisenstadt and, like them, a trained sociologist. He was not a recent immigrant, however, and hailed from a wealthy New England family. Although author of several books, he is most renowned for *Social Origins of Dictatorship and Democracy* (1966). This book offers a comparative-historical analysis of several countries and explores the processes leading to political and economic modernization. Ultimately, it draws heavily on Marxist theory and suggests that the strength of classes and class conflict play an important role in the modernization process. More than any of the books written by early figures of the second generation of comparative-historical analysis, *Social Origins of Dictatorship and Democracy* remains a classic and is still taught by political scientists and sociologists. Indeed, it is commonly considered the piece that did the most to rejuvenate comparative-historical analysis and revive it from its post-Weber lull.

Moore was the doctoral advisor of Charles Tilly (1929–2008), Theda Skocpol (1947–), and several other subsequent comparative-historical researchers who helped establish comparative-historical analysis as a major research tradition. Moore's influence, therefore, extends well beyond his empirical work.

Tilly was a prolific writer, with over fifty books and monographs and some six hundred articles to his name. He wrote on diverse topics but is best known for his work on social movements, democracy, and state formation. At their core, most of his analyses explore collective mobilization and focus on historical examples, usually Western Europe. Like Weber, he is difficult to categorize because his keen historical awareness caused him to note the uniqueness of individual cases, but his sociological training pushed him to make broad general claims. Although a prolific researcher whose quality and quantity of works is potentially unmatched, Tilly's greatest legacy might very well be his teaching, as he advised hundreds of doctoral students throughout his career and thereby trained numerous comparative-historical researchers. Tilly also made valuable methodological contributions to comparative-historical analysis. Toward the end of his life, he wrote about mechanisms and how to use them for social scientific analysis. Earlier, his highly influential *Big Structures, Large Processes, Huge Comparisons* (1984) helped lay out some potential problems with comparative-historical analysis as well as ways of avoiding them.

Skocpol was also a student of Moore and has greatly influenced comparative-historical analysis. Her *States and Social Revolutions* (1979) is commonly placed alongside Moore's *Social Origins of Dictatorship and Democracy* (1966) as one of the two most central modern classics of the research tradition. In it she offers an analysis of social revolutions in France, Russia, and China. Skocpol also helped formalize comparative-historical analysis as a distinct discipline in two ways. First, she edited *Vision and Method in Historical Sociology* (1984), which reviewed the works of prominent comparative-historical researchers from the second generation and helped lay out what comparative-historical analysis actually is. Second, she was the first from the second generation to write about comparative-historical methods and thereby sparked subsequent methodological work and debate (Skocpol 1979; Skocpol and Somers 1980).

Immanuel Wallerstein (1930–) is another very influential comparative-historical sociologist from the second generation. His early work offers comparative-historical analyses of sub-Saharan Africa, but his most famous books analyze the entire world. *The Modern World-System* (1974) and the subsequent volumes with the same title (1980, 1989, 2011) offer the basis of world-systems theory. In them, Wallerstein uses comparative-historical methods to explore how the positioning of a region within the hierarchy of the world system has enormous implications for regional development. In so doing, Wallerstein offers strong evidence against modernization theories of development and suggests that the position of regions like Africa in the world-system helps to explain their limited development. Wallerstein is greatly influenced by Marx and Engels, although he applies their theory on a global level. Besides his empirical work, Wallerstein founded and directed the

Fernand Braudel Center for the Study of Economies, Historical Systems and Civilization, an influential research center that has produced many new comparative-historical researchers.

Although immigrants from central Europe helped reinvigorate comparative-historical analysis's second generation, the second generation was also influenced—albeit more belatedly—by several British sociologists, most of whom also immigrated to North America. Perry Anderson (1938–) was an influential editor of the *New Left Review* and has written a number of comparative-historical analyses. He is a rare comparative-historical researcher because he is a Marxist and his research actively engages Marxist theory. Underneath his Marxist veneer, however, one can also see a strong Weberian influence. His empirical works explore a number of topics with particular relevance to Marxism, but his main impact on the comparative-historical research tradition came through two acclaimed books: *Passages from Antiquity to Feudalism* (1974b) and *Lineages of the Absolutist State* (1974a). Both books were published in the same year and speak to one another. Besides offering insightful analyses of social change, the books also pursue ideological objectives: they stress the uniqueness of Western Europe and suggest that it is the sole region with a history suitable for socialism, thereby explaining the gruesome failures of socialist experiments elsewhere.

Michael Mann (1942–) is another influential British comparative-historical researcher. He is best known for his four-volume work, *The Sources of Social Power* (1986, 1993, 2013). The first volume explores the sources of social power up to 1760, the second analyzes the rise of classes and national states between 1760 and 1914, and the final volume considers globalization and empire. Together, the volumes offer an enormous comparative-historical analysis of the origins of the modern world—the subject that impassioned the first comparative-historical researchers and continues to dominate the research tradition.

Ernest Gellner (1925–95) is another influential British comparative-historical researcher. Gellner was born in France, raised in Prague, but spent most of his life in Great Britain. In this way, he was similar to Polanyi, Bendix, and Eisenstadt, as all four were central European Jews who had emigrated to avoid Nazi atrocities. His academic training was in philosophy, but he was also a social anthropologist who wrote extensively on social change, work that has had a lasting influence on the comparative-historical research tradition. His most famous work is *Nations and Nationalism* (1983), which described how industrialization promoted nationalism by creating a need for cohesion and standardization. All of his comparative-historical work has an extremely strong theoretical component. That is, although all comparative-historical works are inherently guided by theory, Gellner's writings actively combine theory and analysis, with theory arguably taking precedence.

During the 1980s, both Gellner and Mann taught at the London School of Economics (LSE). Indeed, Gellner, Mann, and a third comparative-historical researcher at LSE—John A. Hall (1949–)—collaborated and pushed one another to produce some of their most influential works during the mid-1980s. Like Gellner, Hall actively combines theory with comparative-historical analysis and gives theory a very important position, referring to his own work as "philosophic history" (1985, 3). Hall's *Powers and Liberties* (1985), for example, asks the classic comparative-historical question: Why did the West rise instead of other regions of the world? In it, he reviews, critiques, and combines the theories of Marx, Adam Smith, and Weber, offering a broad historical review that helps to elucidate his own theoretical position. Hall's argument and findings focus on the autonomous power of religion, the state, and the economy in Western Europe and how all three strengthened one another in a synergistic fashion, whereas one usually constrained the other two in other major civilizations. Much of his subsequent work has focused on the state as an influential historical actor, and he therefore played an important role in "bringing the state back in" to comparative-historical analysis (see Evans, Rueschemeyer, and Skocpol 1985).

The Subjects and Disciplines of Comparative-Historical Analysis

As a broad research tradition, the comparative-historical literature analyzes a variety of phenomena. Still, the tradition has largely retained the focus of the earliest comparative-historical researchers, mainly broad-based social change and development. Within this general area, comparative-historical analysis continues to explore issues of state building, democratization and regime change, capitalist development, revolutions, imperialism, and nationalism.[2] There are notable differences between the first and second generations of comparative-historical analysis, however. Most importantly, early works focused primarily on Europe and—to a lesser extent—major non-European civilizations, whereas more recent works pay considerable attention to all regions of the world.

More recent comparative-historical analyses also diverge from earlier examples because they have begun to analyze new subjects. Earlier comparative-historical researchers did not analyze some phenomena that are now commonly analyzed by comparative-historical researchers because the phenomena are rather new and were only beginning to take shape during the first generation of comparative-historical analysis. The analysis of welfare states is one notable example.[3] Other phenomena belatedly became subjects of comparative-historical analysis, not because they are new but because of a growing recognition of their importance. For example, most early comparative-historical researchers paid scant attention to gender, ethnicity, race, and globalization; but comparative-historical researchers now pay considerable attention to all four.[4]

Regardless of the subject, contemporary comparative-historical researchers continue to share the macro- and meso-level bias of their predecessors. Indeed, comparative-historical researchers still focus overwhelmingly on major social institutions and structures and their transformations over time. Precedent may well be a cause of this continuity. In addition, comparative-historical methods have a comparative advantage for the analysis of such phenomena. Most notably, an historical analysis is necessary to analyze long-term transformations in institutions, and both within-case and comparative methods offer important yet different insight into large and long social processes. At the same time, statistical, experimental, and ethnographic methods are less suited to historical and macro-level analyses.

Although recognizing this bias, there are an increasing number of works in the research tradition that attempt to shift comparative-historical analysis toward the micro-level and place greater emphasis on agency. Some explore how individuals are able to have considerable influence on social processes when they possess considerable power and resources. Along these lines, Lachmann (2000) analyzes the important influence of organizationally powerful elites on capitalism and state building in early modern Europe. Similarly, path dependence has become an important analytical concept of comparative-historical analysis and helps elucidate how agency can affect broad social change (see Chapter 3 below). Others have turned to the micro-level out of theoretical preference, as several comparative-historical researchers use a rational-choice perspective and accept its methodological individualism.[5]

Given the diverse topics that can be analyzed through comparative-historical methods, it is hardly surprising that researchers from diverse disciplines use comparative-historical methods. Most notably, comparative-historical analysis first emerged in sociology, and it continues to be one of many important research traditions within this discipline. Sociology traces its origins to the founding figures of comparative-historical analysis, and nearly all of the early comparative-historical researchers from the second generation were sociologists. Despite their sociological backgrounds, the works of these early researchers almost always analyzed politics and, therefore, bridged the gap between sociology and political science. This still continues, with political sociologists comprising the majority of contemporary comparative-historical researchers in sociology.

Although initially concentrated almost exclusively in sociology, the research tradition spread to political science by the 1980s and 1990s. This is clearly seen in the movement of several second-generation researchers into political science departments (such as Bendix, Skocpol, and Tilly). As Hall (2003) notes, the research tradition that dominated comparative politics up until the 1980s contributed to the belated presence of comparative-historical analysis in political science. Specifically, a type of ideographic institutionalism was dominant until the 1950s, and this tradition simply described political institutions; structural functionalism was dominant during the 1950s and 1960s and was quite ahistorical; and statistical analysis dominated in the 1970s and 1980s. Statistics remains an influential research tradition in comparative politics, but comparative-historical analysis began to make inroads during the 1980s and, especially, the 1990s; it is presently a major research tradition in comparative politics. Political scientists are presently producing as many comparative-historical analyses as sociologists—if not more. A few prominent contemporary political scientists using comparative-historical methods include David Collier, Ruth Berins Collier, Peter Hall, Evelyne Huber, Atul Kohli, James Mahoney, Joel Migdal, Paul Pierson, Dan Slater, Kathleen Thelen, Deborah Yashar, and Daniel Ziblatt.

The sociologists and political scientists who use comparative-historical methods commonly explore the same issues, since most comparative-historical sociologists are also political sociologists. Thus some prominent comparative-historical researchers, like James Mahoney and Edgar Kiser, are affiliated with both sociology and political science departments. Others, like John Stephens, have a degree in one discipline but teach in another. So there continues to be considerable overlap between sociology and political science within the comparative-historical research tradition. Some general disciplinary differences do exist, however. Not surprisingly, sociologists and political scientists do not always analyze the same topics. For example, comparative-historical researchers in political science are more likely to analyze parties and federalism, whereas comparative-historical researchers in sociology are more likely to explore family and culture. Another general disciplinary difference concerns methods, as political scientists are more likely to pay greater attention to methods and to use statistics as part of their comparative-historical analyses. The dominance of statistical analysis in comparative politics at the time comparative-historical analysis emerged within the subdiscipline has contributed to the greater prevalence of statistics. Specifically, the dominance of statistical analysis forced comparative-historical researchers in comparative politics to consider and justify their methods and caused many to employ statistics within their comparative-historical analysis. Finally, comparative-historical analysis in political science and sociology differs according to ideographic/nomothetic orientation. Although ideographic explanations were the norm in political science prior to the 1950s, they have been marginalized ever since—as is evident in the renaming of the discipline from simply politics or government to political science. Alternatively, ideographic explanations are more acceptable in sociology (as evinced by historical sociology, a sister tradition that focuses on ideographic explanations), although there is a strong tendency to pursue nomothetic explanations as well.

Sciologists and political scientists dominate comparative-historical analysis, but researchers from other disciplines also use the methods. History is one example as a few historians produce work that squarely falls within the realm of comparative-historical analysis. More importantly, several historians have had a large impact on comparative-historical analysis. Marc Bloch is the most notable example. His colleague, Fernand Braudel (1902–85), was another prominent historian in the *Annales* School, and both Bloch and Braudel influenced Moore, Tilly, Wallerstein, and other prominent comparative-historical researchers. Recognizing this influence, Wallerstein named his research center after Braudel.

Although part of the research tradition, very few historians are squarely within it. This marginality is primarily the result of self-selection, as historians commonly shy away from comparative-historical analysis. One reason for their avoidance is that historians tend to be much more concerned with descriptive ideographic explanations, causing them to avoid the enormously broad and comparative questions asked by comparative-historical researchers. Similarly, Kocka claims that comparison has become increasingly rare in history for three reasons: (1) the analysis of multiple cases promotes a greater dependence on secondary sources and increases an inability to read primary sources in their original language, and the use of primary sources in the original language is a major principle of modern historical scholarship; (2) the comparison of cases presupposes that they are separate from one another, but historians refute claims of separateness and actively analyze interdependence; and (3) historians shy away from comparisons over concerns of unit homogeneity (2003, 41).

Increasingly, economists are entering the comparative-historical research tradition. Their presence is not new, however, as Adam Smith (1723–90) must be viewed as being a founding figure of comparative-historical analysis. His major work, *The Wealth of Nations* (1776/1976), is not only an early example of comparative-historical analysis but has had great theoretical influence on the research tradition as well. Douglass North and other contemporary economic historians also employ comparative-historical methods. Similarly, a number of development economists like Daron Acemoglu and Dani Rodrik have used comparative-historical analysis to explore the determinants of economic change. However, contemporary economists have remained peripheral in the research tradition for various reasons. For example, the theoretical orientations of economists are much more constrained than those employed by most political scientists and sociologists. Specifically, nearly all economists employ a rational-choice framework, but rational-choice theory is only one of many theoretical perspectives used in political science and sociology. Second, statistics is the dominant method employed by economists, and most economists do not employ within-case methods. Those few economists who do use within-case methods, in turn, employ them largely to supplement statistics rather than as an independent method. Alternatively, although comparison is an important method in comparative-historical analysis, within-case methods are usually central. Lastly, contemporary economists focus on nomothetic explanations and almost completely disregard ideographic explanations.

Finally, comparative-historical methods are also used in anthropology, although the method is very rare in the discipline. This rarity is the result of the centrality of ethnographic and archeological methods in most anthropological subdisciplines, methods that hinder comparative analysis because of the enormous demands of completing such research. Moreover, ethnographic work usually takes an interpretivist approach and views comparative-historical analysis as overly nomothetic. Those few anthropologists who use comparative-historical methods are usually either social anthropologists or comparative linguists. Among the former, Karl Polanyi and Ernest Gellner have already been mentioned. In addition, Eric Wolf, Clifford Geertz, and Marshall Sahlins are prominent examples of social anthropologists who employ both comparative and historical methods. Comparative-historical analysis by social anthropologists generally differs from the comparative-historical analyses of most other disciplines because of their much greater attention to culture and their strong preference for ideographic explanations. Although comparative linguists also employ comparative-historical methods, their methods and subjects are very distinct from those of other comparative-historical researchers. However, Marc Bloch was influenced by their work and used the comparative methods of historical linguists as a guide for his own historical comparisons.

Summary

This chapter offers an historical overview of the comparative-historical research tradition. It traces the long and storied lineage of comparative-historical analysis, highlighting two distinct generations of scholarship that include many of the most respected and influential social scientists of all time. It also considers the issues analyzed by comparative-historical researchers and describes the different disciplines that use comparative-historical methods.

The first section of this chapter notes that a few founding figures of comparative-historical analysis discussed methodology. Most notably, Weber laid out comparative-historical methods based on ideal types (see Kalberg 1994; Weber 1904/1997). Although most famous for his methodological work dealing with historiography, Bloch also discussed how historical comparisons can be used to gain insight into social processes. He focuses on narrative comparisons that pair countries with similar origins and highlights key similarities and differences that help to explain the causes of their subsequent transformations (see Bloch 1967). Skocpol also discussed the comparative method. Her writings differ greatly from those of Bloch, as she draws on John Stuart Mill's methods of comparison. More recently, David Collier and several of his former students—including James Mahoney, John Gerring, and Jason Seawright—have written on different aspects of comparative-historical methods (see Brady and Collier 2004; Gerring 2007; Mahoney 1999, 2000b). Much of this work compares small-N methods to statistics and attempts to highlight their different logics. These and other works have played a very important role in clarifying the methodological underpinnings of comparative-historical analysis, but to date no single work has brought together the diverse elements of the methodological tradition and offered a general overview of its basic components, leaving some wondering what—precisely—comparative-historical methods are and how researchers use them to gain insight into their research questions. The remainder of this book focuses on these issues.

Notes

1 Comparative-historical researchers have debated whether there have been two or three waves, with Adams, Clemens, and Orloff (2005) claiming that a third generation has emerged that is different from the second in terms of subject matter and epistemology. More exactly, this debate concerned historical sociology, but the arguments hold for comparative-historical analysis. Like Mahoney (2006), I do not recognize a third wave because my historical review focuses on the temporal division between the first and second generations, and there is no temporal division between the so-called second and third waves.

2 For state building, see Centeno 2002; Chibber 2003; Ertman 1997; Gorski 2003; Silberman 1993; Tilly 1975, 1990; Ziblatt 2006. For democratization and regime change, see Collier and Collier 1991; Haggard and Kaufman 1995; Luebbert 1991; Mahoney 2001b; O'Donnell 1979; Rueschemeyer, Stephens, and Stephens 1991; Slater 2010; Yashar 1997. For capitalist development, see Arrighi 1994; Evans 1995; Haggard 1990; Lachmann 2000; Kohli 2004. For revolutions, see Goldstone 1991; Goodwin 2001; Paige 1975; Skocpol 1979; Tilly 1978; Wickham-Crowley 1993. For imperialism, see Barkey 2008; Boone 2003; Kohli 2004; Lange 2009; Mahoney 2010; Mamdani 1996; Steinmetz 2007. For nationalism, see Anderson 1983; Breuilly 1982; Brubaker 1992; Gellner 1983; Marx 1998; Wimmer 2002; Yashar 2005.

3 See Esping-Andersen 1990; Flora and Heidenheimer 1981; Heclo 1974; Huber and Stephens 2001; Orloff 1993; Pierson 1994; Sandbrook et al. 2007; Stephens 1980. See Amenta (2003) for a review.

4 See Castells 1996; Charrad 2001; Gal and Kligman 2000; Htun 2003; Lustick 1993; Mann 2005; Marx 1998; McNeill and McNeill 2003; O'Connor, Orloff, and Shaver 1999; Patterson 1982; Wimmer 2002; Yashar 2005.

5 See Bates 1981; Bates, Grief, Levi, Rosenthal, and Weingast 1998; Hechter 2000; Kalyvas 2006; Kiser and Baer 2005; Levi 1988.

Glossary

Heuristic device: An artificial construct that is used to analyze social phenomena in an effort to gain insight into the phenomena.

Ideal types: Heuristic devices created by Max Weber and used as a comparative tool. Ideal types exaggerate some element of social relations to such an extent that no case conforms to them completely. Weber created multiple ideal types to analyze the same phenomenon and used them as a comparative tool to see the extent to which a case conforms to one or another.

3

The Within-Case Methods of Comparative-Historical Analysis

According to the definition provided in Chapter 1, comparative-historical analysis has two main methodological components that are evident in the name of the research tradition. This chapter provides an overview of the "historical" component, something commonly referred to as within-case methods. It reviews the types of within-case methods commonly used in comparative-historical analysis and describes the different ways researchers employ within-case methods to offer insight into the research question.

Such an overview is important because within-case methods are overlooked in most methodological discussions, and many social scientists fail to understand either their logic or value. In their well-respected guide on how to complete qualitative research, for example, King, Keohane, and Verba (1994) ignore within-case methods and claim that all causal insight is gained from inter-case comparison. As a result, they claim no causal insight can be gained from a single case study. Contrary to such claims, comparative-historical researchers recognize that within-case methods are capable of producing considerable causal insight and do not play second fiddle to comparative methods (Rueschemeyer 2003; Rueschemeyer and Stephens 1997; Steinmetz 2004)—indeed, within-case methods are the primary source of causal inference in most comparative-historical analyses.

Within-case methods analyze data to offer insight into the characteristics and causal processes of particular cases. They are able to take a holistic view, analyze complex phenomena, highlight mechanisms, and consider diverse factors and their interactions. The insight offered by within-case methods is largely descriptive and ideographic. That is, these methods describe what happens in particular instances and explore the causes of one particular social phenomenon in one particular setting, insight that is not meant to apply to the universe of cases but nonetheless has the potential to produce insight that can be applied to additional cases.

Defining a Case

Within-case methods are commonly referred to as case study methods, as they are used to analyze one particular case of a phenomenon. According to Gerring, a case is "a spatially delimited phenomenon (a unit) observed at a single point in time or over some period of time" (2007, 19). Within the social sciences, cases can be individual humans or different types of social aggregates, the latter ranging from couples and households to the entire world system. Within comparative-historical analysis, country is easily the most common unit of analysis, and most works usually analyze country-level phenomena, such as national states and national markets. Several analyses, however, select cases that are either subregions within a country (such as states in the United States) or supra-state entities (such as European Union or world systems) (see Snyder 2001; Wallerstein 1974).

Cases can be very difficult to delimit. Tilly (1984), for example, notes that comparative-historical researchers commonly analyze "societies" but claims that societies are fictitious and, therefore, immensely difficult to delimit. Commonly, researchers equate society with the national state; however, this can be very problematic, as borderland regions might have denser relations and more shared cultural traits with the populations on the other side of the border than within their own national borders. Snyder (2001) notes that an analysis of subnational units can help limit this problem, but even subnational units can be very difficult to delimit. As one geographer concludes in his discussion of region:

> In summary, regions do exist, they do have meaning, and we can deline-
> ate them. However, they are not clear-cut areas in which activities are
> confined. Rather, regions are useful more as a system of classification;
> they are imperfect generalizations of the underlying spatial complex,
> which itself can be better described as the connections of countless
> individuals, farms, plants, and businesses. (Morrill 1970, 186)

In this way, researchers analyzing any aggregate social units must carefully consider what the appropriate unit actually is and any potential problems delimiting it.

Besides spatial boundaries, researchers must also consider the most appropriate temporal boundaries because cases commonly persist over extended periods of time. An analysis of China, for example, could extend back thousands of years. The research question, however, helps delimit the case. For example, an analysis of the Chinese Revolution would be likely to focus on the period between 1911 and 1949, whereas an analysis of capitalist development in China would probably focus on the period after 1976.

Secondary Within-Case Methods

There are two basic types of within-case methods—which I refer to as primary and secondary within-case methods—both of which have several subtypes. All comparative-historical analyses, in turn, simultaneously employ both types of within-case method, making within-case analysis a multi-method affair. As depicted in Figure 3.1, primary within-case methods offer evidence for the overall analysis, and comparative-historical researchers commonly employ multiple primary within-case methods. Secondary within-case methods, on the other hand, combine and synthesize the diverse evidence produced by the primary within-case methods to arrive at a conclusion, and researchers usually use only one type of secondary within-case method in an analysis.

Secondary within-case methods are the focus of most assessments of within-case methods and are commonly considered the core of within-case analysis. Despite their name, therefore, they are not of secondary importance; rather the name highlights that they necessarily follow and depend on primary within-case methods. Most basically, secondary within-case methods analyze a variety of data offering insight into a particular phenomenon and then present the results. The methods resemble detective work, as the researcher is forced to collect and sift through evidence in an effort to make sense of the case. As with a good detective, the researcher must not only gather clues that offer insight into who committed the "crime", but also use impressive analytic skills to assemble the evidence and draw as much insight from it as possible. Thus, within-case analysis is only as good as its data and the analytic skills of the researcher, as the method is very dependent on the researcher's ability both to compile and to assess the data.

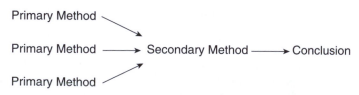

Figure 3.1 Primary and secondary within-case methods in comparative-historical analysis

Similar to detective work, there is no formal methodological procedure for using secondary within-case methods, but researchers usually follow a three-step process: they gather evidence about the phenomenon under analysis, then they analyze the evidence in an effort to gain insight into its characteristics and determinants, and finally they present their results. Despite a clear three-step procedure, researchers almost always go back and forth among the three steps during the research process, as a review of the evidence in step two might reveal the need for additional data and therefore prompt a return to step one, or the writing of the results in step three might spark ideas that cause either additional data gathering or a reanalysis of the preexisting data.

Although detective work is an appropriate analogy, using secondary within-case methods is different from detective work in important ways. Most notably, detectives try to figure out who committed crimes, and all crimes are committed by people. Social scientists using secondary within-case methods, on the other hand, look for a variety of culprits taking diverse forms—ranging from individuals to events to institutions. The "culprits" shaping social processes, in turn, play a variety of roles, with some having direct effects while others contribute to the outcome indirectly. In this way, social scientists using within-case methods analyze and attempt to explain complex phenomena with very complex determinants. Moreover, detective work has only one goal—to figure out "who done it." Social scientists, on the other hand, commonly use secondary within-case methods to pursue three different goals, resulting in three different subtypes of secondary within-case methods: causal narrative explores the determinants of social phenomena, process tracing explores mechanisms, and pattern matching tests theories.

Causal Narrative

Most comparative-historical analyses use **causal narrative** as their secondary within-case method. It is an analytic technique that explores the causes of a particular social phenomenon through a narrative analysis; that is, it is a narrative that explores what caused something. To use this technique, the researcher compiles evidence, assesses it, and presents a sequential causal account.

Notably, this definition is different from that given by Sewell (1996) and Mahoney (2000b), who define causal narrative as a technique for comparing sequences across cases. Although potentially causing confusion, I use the term "causal narrative" to refer to narratives about causation because it is a more evident match between name and method. As discussed in Chapter 5, I refer to the technique of comparing sequences across cases through narrative as narrative comparison.

As the name suggests, causal narratives take a narrative form. A **narrative** is a sequential account—or story—of an event or series of events which organizes material chronologically to provide an overview of either what happened or the characteristics of some social phenomenon. As such, a narrative has two main components. First, narratives describe one or more *events*. According to Griffin, an event is "a distinguishable happening, one with some pattern or theme that sets it off from others, and one that involves changes taking place within a delimited amount of time" (1993, 1096). Because these events spark change, social scientists analyze them as potential causes of a specific outcome. Examples of events with considerable social repercussions include Hurricane Katrina, the 1983 anti-Tamil riots in Sri Lanka, the marriage of Ferdinand and Isabella, the signing of the Oslo Accord in 1993, and the American presidential election in 2000. As these examples indicate, events are unique, as they occur in a particular time and place, and involve and affect particular individuals. Technically speaking, they are commonly aggregates of multiple yet related events. For example, the 1983 Tamil riots occurred in different places over a certain period of time and therefore involved multiple events, but they can be considered to be a single event because the sub-events were related to one another and took similar forms.

The second key element of a narrative is *temporality*. Narratives offer temporal orderings of sequences leading to and following events. Thus, a narrative analysis of the 1983 anti-Tamil riots might describe the conditions and events leading up to the riots, the actual actions that comprised the riots, the outcomes and subsequent events that followed the riots, or a combination of the three. In addition, the narrative will describe the temporal ordering of these events in a way that shows how they unfolded over time.

Most researchers using narratives to analyze the determinants of social processes believe events and processes are "the fundamental building blocks" of social scientific analysis and use narratives to analyze causal processes (Abbott 1992, 428). Narrative descriptions in the form of stories of unfolding and interacting events allow researchers to take a holistic analytic approach that considers context, sequence, and conjuncture. In so doing, they help researchers gain an understanding of how social processes unfold, which is necessary for causal analysis. Causal narratives are, therefore, necessarily descriptive. This description must consider the actual sequences and processes that drive the transformations under analysis. As Collier (2011, 824) writes, "To characterize a process, we must be able to characterize key steps in the process, which in turn permits good analysis of change and sequence." Such an analysis, in turn, must describe the historical and social context in which the processes are unfolding. These two are commonly intertwined, as the context helps explain the process.

The form of a causal narrative depends on the subject under analysis, but comparative-historical researchers commonly employ the secondary within-case method to analyze large processes involving numerous factors that occur over an extended period of time. This is because comparative-historical researchers usually ask large questions, and causal narrative is a highly appropriate technique for analyzing the dynamics and causes of big processes. Indeed, it is able to consider simultaneously the impact of diverse factors and to analyze processes over time.

Similar to the other secondary within-case methods, the actual analytic techniques of causal narrative are informal and depend on the skill of the researcher. A handful of researchers, however, have attempted to formalize a narrative technique that creates a more standardized analysis and forces researchers to consider the relevance of each component of the narrative analysis. Griffin (1993) describes one such technique, which he calls event-structure analysis. This technique asks researchers first to create a diagram of actions and factors that, in the researcher's view, define the event in question. Then, using a computer program, the researcher answers questions probing his or her knowledge of the process to help to clarify the researcher's causal reasoning and argument. After completing the program, the researcher can then write a new causal narrative including only those elements that appear relevant. Few researchers using causal narrative actually employ such a formal technique. Many researchers, however, use a less formalized technique during the second (analytic) step of the research process. This involves creating elaborate causal diagrams to help organize their arguments and consider the causal relevance of each factor in the diagram. This step, in turn, is commonly followed by a return to the first data-gathering step in an effort to gain additional evidence to test the causal diagram.

Causal narrative is an excellent method for analyzing complex processes and concepts, as it allows detail and a more holistic analysis that considers multiple factors as well as their interactions and sequencing. It is particularly suitable for exploratory studies and is capable of providing considerable insight into causal mechanisms. On the negative side, analyses of complex processes involving many factors and interactions have only limited parsimony. Similarly, the findings are usually particular to the case under analysis. If the goal of the analysis is generalizable insight, the method is therefore inappropriate unless several cases are included in the analysis. Finally, there is no standard tool for assessing the validity of a causal narrative, meaning that researchers can construct competing causal narratives and might be unable clearly to assess their validity. The latter is particularly problematic when data are too limited to test competing views or when contradictory data exist.

Despite focusing most of her methodological discussion on comparison, Skocpol's celebrated *States and Social Revolutions* (1979) provides insightful causal narratives that document the factors and processes leading to social revolution in France, Russia, and China. Indeed, Sewell (1996) notes that her comparative analysis would be of little value without the strength of the causal narratives she presents for each case. The book offers an insightful example of how researchers use causal narrative to gain insight.

Skocpol's basic argument focuses on both state breakdown and the capability of peasants to mobilize revolts. Mahoney (1999) carefully diagrams Skocpol's causal narrative of state breakdown in France, which was only a small part of the country's narrative but still includes nearly forty causally relevant factors, and I reproduce his diagram in Figure 3.2.

As depicted in the diagram, Skocpol highlights three causal clusters implicated in state breakdown leading to revolution in France: agrarian backwardness, international pressure, and state autonomy—all of which were promoted by at least six factors. According to Skocpol's causal narrative, for example, agrarian backwardness (point 4 in the diagram) promoted state breakdown by causing a fiscal crisis (point 25). A complex causal sequence, in turn, led to this outcome. First, three factors (points 1 through 3) promoted general agricultural backwardness: property relations inhibited the introduction of new agricultural techniques, thereby limiting agricultural production; the tax system of pre-revolutionary France discouraged improvements in agricultural productivity; and sustained economic growth impeded innovation. Agrarian backwardness, in turn, promoted weak domestic demand for industrial goods (point 5), which obstructed industrialization (point 8) and the ability of France to compete with England (point 10). Commercialization—in combination with a poor domestic transportation system (point 6) and rapid population growth (point 7)—also contributed to very limited economic growth (point 9). In turn, limited economic growth and an inability to compete with England both contributed to the French state's severe financial difficulties, which Skocpol highlights as a key factor leading to the French Revolution.

This example, showing only a fraction of Skocpol's causal narrative of the French case, demonstrates how complex causal narratives can be. Indeed, narratives are able to describe complex causal chains and show how one factor leads to another while, at the same time, supporting the causal argument with evidence. Given the complexity of the narrative, particular causal claims can be somewhat hidden or become lost in an extended narrative analysis. In such a situation, the evidence supporting the causal claims can also be difficult to identify. George and Bennett (2005) therefore recommend that researchers use diagrams to present clearly the argument of causal narratives, to make the causal claims more explicit and, thereby, allow the audience more easily to understand and

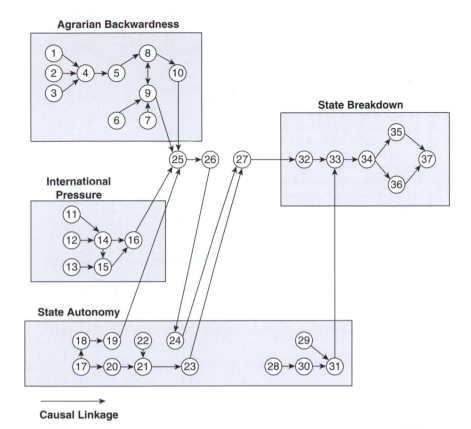

Agrarian Backwardness

International Pressure

State Autonomy

State Breakdown

Causal Linkage

FIG. 1.—Narrative analysis showing conditions for the state breakdown in France (all page numbers are from Skocpol[1979]):

1 Property relations prevent introduction of new agricultural techniques (p. 55)
2 Tax system discourages agricultural innovation (p. 55)
3 Sustained growth discourages agricultural innovation (p. 55)
4 Backwardness of French agriculture (esp. vis-à-vis England) (p. 56)
5 Weak domestic market for industrial goods (pp. 55–56)
6 Internal transportation problems (p. 56)
7 Population growth (p. 56)
8 Failure to achieve industrial breakthrough (p. 56)
9 Failure to sustain economic growth (p. 56)
10 Inability to successfully compete with England (p. 56)
11 Initial military success under Louis XIV (p. 54)
12 Expansionist ambitions of state (p. 54)
13 French geographical location vis-à-vis England (p. 60)
14 Sustained warfare (pp. 54, 60, 60)
15 State needs to devote resources to both army and navy (p. 60)
16 Repeated defeats in war (pp. 54,60,61,63)
17 Creation of absolutist monarchy, decentralized medieval institutions still persist (pp. 52–53)
18 Dominant class often exempted from taxes (pp. 60–61)
19 State faces obstacles generating loans (p. 61)

(Continued)

(Continued)

20   Socially cohesive dominant class based in proprietary wealth (pp. 56–59; 61–61)
21   Dominant class possesses legal right to delay royal legislation (p. 62)
22   Dominant class exercises firm control over offices (pp. 61–62)
23   Dominant class is capable of blocking state reforms (pp. 61–64)
24   Dominant class resist financial reforms (pp. 62)
25   Major financial problems of state (p. 63)
26   State attempts tax/financial reforms (p. 64)
27   Financial reforms fail (pp. 63–64)
28   Recruitment of military officers from privileged classes (p. 65)
29   Military officers hold grievances against the crown
30   Military officers identify with the dominant class resistance (pp. 64–65)
31   Military is unwilling to repress dominant class resistance (pp. 64–65)
32   Financial crisis deepens (p. 64)
33   Pressures for creation of the Estates-General (p. 64)
34   King summons the Estates-General (p. 64)
35   Popular protests spread (p. 66)
36   Conflict among dominant class members in the Estates-General; paralysis of old regime (p. 65)
37   Municipal revolution; the old state collapses (pp. 66–67)

Figure 3.2   Mahoney's diagram of Skocpol's causal narrative

© Mahoney, J., *American Journal of Sociology*, 104: 4 (1999) University of Chicago.

assess the validity of the argument. As described previously, it also forces researchers to consider the relevance of each component of the causal narrative, thus helping to strengthen the analysis itself.

Process Tracing

The methodological work on comparative-historical analysis can be confusing because many terms have not been formalized. In this way, what I call causal narrative, others call narrative appraisal or **process tracing**. The latter term is also used by some to designate a particular, more focused type of causal narrative. George (1979; George and Bennett 2005) coined the term and employed it to refer to a technique used to explore potential causal processes and mechanisms linking two related factors. These factors are either related statistically among a set of cases or linked to one another in an apparent causal sequence for a specific case. Thus, instead of analyzing what causes something, process tracing differs from causal narrative because it starts with a pre-established relationship and explores potential causal processes and mechanisms linking the two. I use "process tracing" throughout this book strictly as defined by George.

Because mechanisms are central to process tracing, it is useful to take an excursus to consider precisely what a **mechanism** is. Although there is considerable disagreement, a mechanism is commonly referred to as a "black box" that explains a causal relation or sequence (Hedstrom 2008; Hedstrom and Swedberg 1998; Mahoney 2001a). As depicted in Figure 3.3, the black

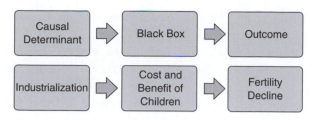

Figure 3.3 Mechanisms as black boxes

box links a cause and an outcome, and suggests that the cause induces transformation in a way that generates the outcome. This transformation usually cannot be observed directly. Thus, a mechanism is the transformative action through which the cause produces the effect.

Figure 3.3 also depicts the relationship between industrialization and fertility decline as a specific example. Many studies find a strong relationship between industrialization and fertility decline, and causal mechanisms are the reasons underlying this relationship. Although several distinct mechanisms appear to underlie the relationship, a number of scholars studying this issue point to a rational-choice mechanism, as children in industrial societies become both less valuable and much more expensive to raise. Specific mechanisms concern the growing importance and cost of schooling with industrialization, the growing cost of providing for children given that an increasing number of products must be purchased by the household instead of produced by the household, the value of child labor on the farm but the restriction of child labor outside of it, and the advent of social security for the elderly in industrialized societies. Thus, there are multiple rational-choice mechanisms that link industrialization to fertility decline and some of them— such as education and social security—are only indirectly related to industrialization. In showing that the same mechanisms can be generated by different factors (limits to child labor, social security, purchasing goods instead of producing them, etc.), the example also shows how mechanisms have the potential to explain causal relations in diverse settings and in multiple ways.

At its most basic, process tracing involves gathering data for a particular case, analyzing the data to explore mechanisms underlying a relationship, and presenting the analysis through a narrative. Because identifying causal mechanisms requires a thorough understanding of the causal process, researchers using process tracing must have a thorough knowledge of the particular case and process under analysis. Moreover, because the researcher is attempting to find mechanisms linking particular factors, the researcher must have a thorough knowledge of the literature on both the independent and dependent variables in order to have an idea of potential reasons they might be causally related. That said, researchers must also be open to mechanisms that have not previously been considered.

Because mechanisms are very difficult to observe, researchers using process tracing are rarely able to find conclusive evidence showing the mechanism in action. Instead, researchers must offer evidence that both the hypothesized cause and the outcome existed and that the outcome followed the hypothesized cause. Once this has occurred, the researcher looks for evidence that offers insight into whether or not the mechanism explains the relationship between the hypothesized cause and the outcome. This commonly involves hypothesis testing, where the researcher suggests that certain factors and conditions should be present if the mechanism explains the relationship (Mahoney, 2012). For example, if the rational-choice mechanism underlies the relationship between industrialization and fertility decline, one would hypothesize that children provide less monetary benefits in industrial societies. Researchers can explore these hypotheses by analyzing and comparing the monetary benefits offered by children in both industrial and non-industrial societies or by comparing the monetary benefits of children over time in a society that has experienced industrial transformation. Similarly, researchers using process tracing can test hypotheses to rule out alternative mechanisms. In this way, process tracing has key similarities with pattern matching, another within-case method that focuses on testing hypotheses (described in the next section).

Process tracing also has important similarities with causal narrative. Indeed, the method of process tracing—data gathering, analysis, and narrative presentation—is identical to that of causal narrative. Moreover, they both analyze causal processes. Important differences separate the two, however. First, process tracing commonly has a more limited focus than causal narrative. It is more focused in two ways: process tracing usually focuses on one determinant, whereas causal narrative usually focuses on several; and process tracing commonly analyzes only a segment of a causal sequence, but causal narrative usually analyzes a much longer causal chain and, therefore, analyzes the causal process over a more extended period of time. Another difference concerns mechanisms. Process tracing is explicitly focused on discovering causal mechanisms that explain a particular causal relationship between a cause and an outcome, whereas causal narrative commonly focuses on presenting larger and longer causal processes. Although mechanisms are inherently part of most causal narratives, they are not usually the focus and can be hidden in the causal narrative. Finally, relative to causal narrative, process tracing is usually closer to the nomothetic end of the ideographic-nomothetic continuum. This is because mechanisms are basic theoretical propositions explaining a causal relationship and can be applied to multiple cases. Indeed, causal narrative is like detective work because it attempts to find the cause of a particular outcome, while process tracing attempts to find more generalizable mechanisms linking two related factors in the hope of highlighting a mechanism that helps to explain additional cases. To stick with the detective work analogy, a causal narrative tries to figure out why someone committed a particular murder, whereas process tracing tries to figure out why someone committed a murder during a recession in an effort to understand more clearly why murder rate and recession are positively related to one another.

Process tracing can be a very powerful method that provides important insight into causal processes yet—like all other methodologies—has its advantages and disadvantages. Most notably, it is very well suited to providing insight into causal mechanisms. Relative to causal narrative, it is also more parsimonious because it is usually much more focused. Relatedly, it is also more generalizable, as a mechanistic analysis focuses on meso-level theory that can potentially be transferred to a larger set of cases. However, the detailed data needed for process tracing limit the number of cases that can be analyzed using it, so process tracing does not usually produce generalizable results by itself. Compared to causal narrative, process tracing is disadvantaged because it provides a less holistic analysis and can only be employed when there is a pre-established relationship—either statistical or sequential. As a consequence of the latter, process tracing cannot be used for exploratory studies that attempt to analyze the causes of a particular causal phenomenon.

Process tracing—and mechanism-oriented analysis in general—began to gain popularity in comparative-historical analysis in the late 1980s and early 1990s, and "process tracing" and "mechanism" have only relatively recently gained entry into the lexicon of comparative-historical scholars. Today, nearly all works within the comparative-historical tradition attempt to highlight mechanisms—and many formally employ process tracing. One relatively early example of process tracing is Rueschemeyer, Stephens, and Stephens's (1991) *Capitalist Development and Democracy*. The authors begin the book by noting contradictions in the quantitative and qualitative literatures on the impact of capitalist development on democracy. The quantitative literature consistently finds a strong and positive relationship between the two, and suggests that capitalist development causes democracy by promoting liberal values and strengthening the middle class. The authors note that the qualitative literature, however, finds that capitalists and the middle class commonly oppose democratic expansion, thereby suggesting that common assumptions about the mechanism linking capitalist development and democracy are incorrect. The book therefore analyzes alternative mechanisms with the potential to explain the strong relationship between capitalist development and democracy. In effect, they are applying a type of critical process tracing where they question common understandings about a potential mechanism linking two variables and search for alternative mechanisms that might better explain the relationship.

As a work that uses process tracing as its secondary within-case method, the structure of *Capitalist Development and Democracy* differs considerably from works that depend primarily on causal narrative. Most notably, the book lacks causal narratives—such as those found in Skocpol's *States and Social Revolutions*—that provide an overview of what happened and then analyze the complex process leading to this outcome. Instead, *Capitalist Development and Democracy* offers a more focused narrative analysis which considers ways in which capitalist development shapes democratization. It is, therefore, less of a historical story and more of a structured and focused analysis.

Rueschemeyer, Stephens, and Stephens's book explores causal mechanisms through case studies of over thirty countries from Europe, Latin America, and the Caribbean. Ultimately, they find that democracy depends on a powerful working class, able to assert itself and pressure the government into allowing working-class participation in politics. Coinciding with the qualitative literature, they find that capitalists and the middle class usually attempt to prevent this group from gaining suffrage and thereby limit democratization. Yet, the authors find that capitalist development still promotes democratization because—contrary to the standard Marxist view—capitalist development actually strengthens the collective power of workers. It does so largely by shaping their mobilizational resources. For example, industrialization promotes urbanization, which allows workers to live among each other in high concentrations; in addition, they interact with one another on the job. Both urban life and work in factories, in turn, promote collective identities and allow communication among one another. Because of these conditions, workers are able to organize labor unions and labor-based parties—powerful mobilizing organizations that commonly pressure governments to promote lower-class incorporation.

Besides strengthening the relative power of the working classes, the authors also find that capitalist development weakens the landed elite. This landed class maintains its position based on wealth and privilege and is, therefore, strongly opposed to any form of democratization. Their weakening at the hands of capitalist expansion provides a boost to democratization and helps explain the statistical relationship between capitalist development and democratization.

Rueschemeyer, Stephens, and Stephens conclude that capitalist development promotes democracy by readjusting the power of classes in ways that strengthen the groups that are most in favor of democracy (the working class) or limited democracy (the bourgeois and middle classes). Conversely, it weakens the group that is most opposed to it (the landed elites). The ultimate causal mechanism linking capitalist development to democracy, therefore, deals with power. Overall, the book is a prime example of process tracing because it uses case studies to explore causal mechanisms linking related variables.

Pattern Matching

Pattern matching is the third secondary method used for within-case analysis. Campbell (1975) coined the term in an article discussing how general causal insight can be gained from a single case study. As its name suggests, pattern matching is a technique used to explore whether or not the pattern of a case matches the pattern predicted by a theory. As such, it involves using a case study to test a pre-established theory by checking to see if the case follows the predictions of the theory. Because most theories have multiple predictions that can be tested by a single case, Campbell claims that pattern matching allows a researcher to use a single case to provide multiple points of insight into the validity of a theory. When competing theories predict different outcomes, pattern matching can be employed to test the theories. Thus, if one theory claims that foreign direct investment (FDI) promotes economic development and another claims that it deters it, a researcher can use pattern matching to analyze how FDI affects economic development in one case. For example, one might explore how FDI affects job growth, economic output, and technological advances in production.

Pattern matching is starkly different from the other two secondary within-case methods. Most notably, the goal of causal narrative and process tracing is to highlight causal processes, but pattern matching often disregards causal processes and focuses on testing theory. Relative to the other secondary within-case methods, pattern matching is therefore advantaged at testing theories (but requires preexisting theories) and disadvantaged at offering insight into particular causal processes. Because of its more theoretical orientation, theory obviously plays a more central role in pattern matching. For example, theory dictates what data are gathered for pattern matching because researchers collect only the data that offer insight into a theory. Moreover, the analysis of the data by pattern matching involves comparing a case to a theory to see if the former conforms to the latter. Finally, the presentation of results derived from pattern matching focuses on whether a case conforms to the theory.

Because pattern matching allows one to test theories through within-case analysis, it is most commonly used by comparative-historical researchers who pursue what Skocpol and Somers (1980) call "parallel demonstration of theory"—showing that a theory holds for multiple cases. Skocpol and Somers list Eisenstadt's (1963) *The Political Systems of*

Empires and Paige's (1975) *Agrarian Revolution* as examples of works that offer a theoretical framework and then use within-case methods to highlight how the cases match the pattern suggested by the theory. A more contemporary example is Wickham-Crowley's *Guerrillas and Revolutions in Latin America* (1993), a book that attempts to explain the strength and success of guerrilla movements in Latin America since 1956. Although the book uses pattern matching, it is not a clear example of parallel demonstration of theory because Wickham-Crowley does not have a privileged theory, tests different theories, and has mixed findings.

Chapter 6 of *Guerrillas and Revolutions in Latin America*, which explores the impact of agrarian structure and its transformations on the strength of guerrilla movements, offers a particular example of Wickham-Crowley's use of pattern matching. In it, he analyzes Cuba, Venezuela, Guatemala, Colombia, Peru, and Bolivia—all of which experienced guerrilla movements with different degrees of success during the first phase of guerrilla movements in Latin America. In turn, he uses pattern matching to test two different theories: modified versions of Jeffrey Paige's (1975) theory on agricultural structure and peasant revolt and James Scott's (1979) theory of moral economy. As such, the chapter includes multiple case studies of Latin American countries and uses each case to test two competing theories.

To assess whether the cases support the theories, Wickham-Crowley reviews the available evidence from past analyses and government statistics, and uses both qualitative and quantitative evidence. Most commonly, he gathers regional-level quantitative data that partially operationalize a characteristic related to a theory and explores whether the characteristic is related to regional variation in guerrilla activity. For example, he uses departmental data from Colombia on the expansion of coffee production to test the moral economy theory, suggesting that this expansion should have disrupted the livelihoods of small producers and created conflict over land. Using data on the number of violent incidents in each department, he then tests the relationship between the two and finds that both are strongly and positively related to one another, thereby supporting the theory. In all other cases, however, he does not use formal statistics to assess his quantitative evidence; tables are generally used listing the variable scores of regions within a country, and Wickham-Crowley places an asterisk after the name of the regions that experienced violence. Using these tables, one can therefore view whether there is a general relationship between the variable scores and violence.

In all cases, Wickham-Crowley also offers brief narrative analyses that help to explain and interpret the data and provide the contextual insight needed to use internal comparisons for pattern matching. In addition, the narratives offer some independent insight that can be used for pattern matching. For his analysis of Peru, for example, he uses narratives to describe the labor structure, conflict, and peasant support for insurgents in different regions in order to test whether they support the different theoretical perspectives.

Table 3.1 lists my scoring of Wickham-Crowley's findings and shows that the cases support both theories to different extents. The analyses offer strongest support to the agrarian structure hypothesis, as four of the six cases strongly support it while the remaining two cases offer more limited support. For the moral economy hypothesis, on the other hand, only two cases offer strong support, with four offering mixed support.

Table 3.1 Wickham-Crowley's use of pattern matching for economic theories of rebellion in Latin America

	Cuba	Venezuela	Guatemala	Colombia	Peru	Bolivia
Agrarian Structure	Support	Support	Support	Mixed	Mixed	Support
Moral Economy	Support	Mixed	Mixed	Mixed	Mixed	Support

Source: Wickham-Crowley, 1993

Because Wickham-Crowley analyzes several countries in Chapter 6 of *Guerrillas and Revolutions in Latin America*, his analysis includes a comparative component. Still, inter-case comparison is very limited in this chapter, and it focuses on testing whether or not theoretically derived hypotheses are supported by different cases, through qualitative and quantitative assessment and the comparison of regions within a single country. In this way, the insight provided by the analysis is not derived from comparing the six countries; it is derived from within-case analysis.

Primary Within-Case Methods

Causal narrative, process tracing, and pattern matching are techniques for gathering, analyzing, and synthesizing diverse evidence in order to gain insight into the research question. The evidence that the secondary within-case methods analyze, however, is usually produced by different methods, as within-case analysis employs a methodological division of labor. Wickham-Crowley's *Guerrillas and Revolutions in Latin America* (1993), for example, uses statistical comparison of different regions within a country and historical methods for evidence to test theories through pattern matching. I refer to these data producing methods as **primary within-case methods** because they precede secondary within-case methods and provide the data secondary within-case methods ultimately analyze.

Comparative-historical researchers commonly employ primary within-case methods personally to gather data for their analyses. More frequently, however, they gather evidence from secondary sources without using the primary within-case methods themselves. In the case of the latter, the primary method is hidden from the comparative-historical analysis but remains an integral component of it because the analysis depends on the method for data. Although primary within-case methods have received only limited attention in comparative-historical analysis, they are absolutely fundamental to any within-case analysis; there can be no analysis without evidence, and primary within-case methods provide the latter. For this reason, comparative-historical researchers cannot ignore them and, in fact, must strive to use them to produce new evidence into research questions. Indeed, comparative-historical researchers must pay equal attention to the generation of evidence and the analysis of evidence, although the latter presently dominates the research tradition.

Any method that offers evidence about the phenomenon under analysis can be used as a primary within-case method. Different analyses, for example, have used evidence from linguistic methods (Diamond 1992), ethnographic methods (Geertz 1968), archeological methods (Diamond 1997), and game-theoretic methods (Schickler 2001). In the pages that follow, I do not attempt to describe all of the primary methods used by comparative-historical researchers for within-case analysis. Instead, I review a few examples, selecting both the most popular primary within-case methods and less common methods that help to highlight their diversity.

Historical Methods

Historical methods are used primarily by historians and deal with gathering data, assessing their reliability, and presenting the findings in a narrative. They are *easily* the most common primary within-case method used in comparative-historical analysis. Indeed, Skocpol's (1979) use of causal narrative and Rueschemeyer, Stephens, and Stephens's (1991) use of process tracing both depend almost exclusively on historical methods for data and insight. At times, comparative-historical researchers use historical methods to gather and assess data. More frequently, however, they simply use the historical narratives of others—usually historians—as sources of data and insight. Both Skocpol (1979) and Rueschemeyer, Stephens, and Stephens (1991), for example, depend almost completely on historical narratives from secondary sources for their data (see Chapter 7 for potential problems with relying on secondary sources for data).

Similar to both causal narrative and process tracing, a **historical narrative** takes a narrative form. It differs markedly from both, however, because it does not explore the causes of phenomena. Rather, researchers employ historical narrative for descriptive purposes, that is, to document what happened and what the characteristics of a phenomenon were.

Because the goal of comparative-historical analysis is causal analysis, comparative-historical researchers use historical narratives as a source of evidence to feed into their research questions. For example, causal narrative commonly depends on historical narrative to describe the characteristics of a social phenomenon and subsequently analyzes how this social phenomenon is either shaped by or shapes another.

Although comparative-historical researchers depend heavily on historical narrative for data, they usually do not present historical narratives in their analysis. The historical narratives are generally either broken down and incorporated into the analysis or simply referred to. In either case, researchers use historical narratives as a source of data, and the researchers analyze this data through a secondary within-case method to build their arguments.

At times, however, comparative-historical researchers incorporate historical narratives into their analyses, and the historical narratives comprise a large part of the actual analysis. This might occur when there is disagreement in the historical literature, prompting the researcher to use historical narrative explicitly to document what happened and the characteristics of the phenomena under question. Similarly, it might also be used to revise preexisting historical understandings. Lustick's *Unsettled States, Disputed Lands* (1993) offers an example of a work using historical narrative to assess competing historical narratives. The book analyzes ethno-nationalist separatist movements in Ireland, Algeria, and the Palestinian Territories, with an eye on the causes of state expansion and contraction. For his case study of Ireland, former British Prime Minister William Gladstone's support for Irish independence was vital to his explanation, but different historical analyses offer opposing views. As a result, Lustick uses historical methods to gather, assess, and present data in order to assess Gladstone's position. The end result is a historical narrative assessing the different views and describing the development of Gladstone's support for Irish independence. In so doing, Lustick is able to justify his choice of historiography, and he subsequently uses the data from his historical narrative for the larger analysis.

Comparative-historical researchers might also include distinct historical narratives in their analyses when there are no or only incomplete preexisting histories on the subject. In this situation, a researcher uses historical methods to gather and assess data and presents the findings in a historical narrative. The data and insight from the historical narrative are subsequently used by the secondary within-case method for the overall analysis. Steinmetz's *The Devil's Handwriting* (2007) offers an example of a comparative-historical analysis that explicitly uses historical narrative as a primary within-case method in this way.

Steinmetz's book investigates what shaped "native" policy in colonies and focuses on three former German colonies—Southwest Africa, Samoa, and Qingdao—that experienced very different native policies. Through a comparative-historical analysis, Steinmetz finds that four mechanisms affected native policy: (1) precolonial discourses or representations, (2) competition between colonial officials, (3) identification of the officials with the colonized, and (4) the responses of the colonized. Of these, Steinmetz focuses primarily on the impact of precolonial discourses and representations of the colonized on native policy. In order to analyze the impact of precolonial discourses, he must note the discourses and representations of different colonized peoples and explore how they affected subsequent policy. He uses two chapters to accomplish this task for each of his three cases: the first uses historical methods to review evidence and describe precolonial discourses and representations, and the second uses causal narrative to analyze how these discourses and representations affected native policy. The three chapters that explicitly use historical methods as their sole within-case method offer detailed analyses of the main sources of precolonial discourses and representations of subsequently colonized peoples. Specifically, Steinmetz analyzes the discourses and representations presented by missionaries, explorers, academics, authors, and artists. The narratives are historical and not causal because they seek simply to document what the discourses and representations were, not the factors that caused them. Without documenting the discourses and representations, Steinmetz could not have completed the subsequent analysis exploring how discourses affected native policy for the simple reason that he could not gauge their impact without analyzing what they were.

Internal Comparison

Historical methods are easily the most common primary within-case method used by comparative-historical researchers, and many works use historical methods as their sole primary within-case method. Of the remaining primary within-case methods, **internal comparison** is among the most common. It involves either comparing the subcomponents of a whole with one another or comparing the whole with itself at different periods of time. Notably, internal comparison uses the same techniques as other types of comparison (see Chapter 5 for a review of types of comparison). Internal comparison is analytically distinct from other comparative methods, however, because other comparative methods pursue nomothetic insight through inter-case comparison whereas internal comparison pursues ideographic insight into a particular case by comparing either the same case at different periods of time or subcomponents of the case. Comparison of the same case over time helps the researcher to analyze how the case transformed and to highlight potential causes of change, and comparison of subcomponents of the case allow one to understand better the characteristics of the case. Importantly, not all analyses that compare subcomponents of a case are internal comparisons. When subcomponents of a larger entity are the unit of analysis and when researchers compare them to gain general insight into the subcomponents, the comparison is not an internal comparison.

It is useful to consider examples showing how researchers use internal comparisons to offer case-specific insight. Goldstone's (1991) analysis of the determinants of the English Revolution provides one example. He uses causal narrative as his secondary within-case method, but he depends heavily on internal comparison to supplement the causal narrative by offering insight into the determinants of the revolution. For example, he compares England to itself over a two-hundred and fifty-year period in an effort to explore transformations that caused the English Revolution. For this, he operationalizes three variables—fiscal distress, elite competition, and mass mobilization potential—for every decade between 1500 and 1750 and describes how population pressure contributed to each. In turn, Goldstone combines all three variables into a single aggregate indicator of pressure for political crisis and plots the data graphically over the entire period. One can therefore analyze the graph to see whether the aggregate variable changed over time in England and was related temporally to the revolution. As shown in Figure 3.4, Goldstone finds that pressure for political crisis began increasing rapidly during the second half of the sixteenth century and peaked during the 1640s, just when the English Revolution occurred. Thereafter, pressure for political crisis declined rapidly.

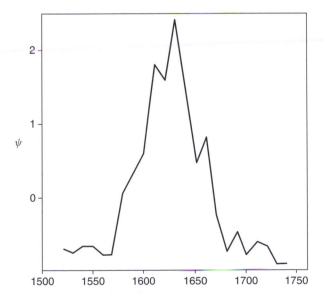

Figure 3.4 Goldstone's timeline of pressures for crisis in England (Goldstone 1991, 144)

All in all, his use of internal comparison provides a type of time-series analysis offering evidence that population pressure contributed to the English Revolution through its impact on fiscal distress, elite competition, and mass mobilization potential.

Besides simply using a graph, Goldstone also uses formal statistical methods for a separate time-series analysis that explores the causes of state fiscal distress in England between 1500 and 1750. He uses the statistical analysis to test the impact of inflation and an inflexible tax system on state fiscal crisis in England over time and finds strong and positive relationships, offering evidence that both inflation and inflexible tax systems contributed to the revolution.

Several comparative-historical analyses also use internal comparison to explore internal variation among subregions. As described above, Wickham-Crowley (1993) uses internal comparison as a primary method in this way. Specifically, he explores internal variation in countries to test theories, thereby using internal comparison as a means of pattern matching. Ziblatt's *Structuring the State* (2006) offers another example of a comparative-historical analysis that uses internal comparison to explore internal variation. In particular, he analyzes state building in Italy and Germany to investigate why the former developed a unitary state while the latter developed a federated state. His main argument revolves around the preexisting infrastructural power of the subunits that ultimately became part of Italy and Germany: weak subunits in several parts of Italy promoted a unitary structure, powerful subunits in Germany promoted a federated structure, and path dependence reinforced both state structures over time. Like Goldstone, Ziblatt's analysis is based on causal narrative but depends on internal comparison to show how Piedmont was the only region in Italy with considerable political development prior to unification, whereas the remaining six regions had very limited political development (2006, 84–6). The internal comparison, therefore, supplements other data presented in the causal narrative and is incorporated into the causal narrative to strengthen his claim that Piedmontist nationalists pursued a unitary state because ineffective regional government severely impeded the construction of a federated state. In contrast, Ziblatt's internal comparisons of Germany offer evidence that all regions had relatively high levels of political development—making a federated state possible—and he integrates these findings into his causal narrative on state formation in Germany (2006, 113–18).

Additional Primary Within-Case Methods

Both historical methods and internal comparison are among the most common primary methods used for within-case analysis. Many other techniques are also used to produce data, however, including interviews, content/textual analysis, and game theoretic methods. This section reviews several of them—none of which are very common within the research tradition—to give an idea of the variety of methods that can be used by researchers as primary within-case methods.

Network Analysis

Similar to comparative-historical analysis, **network analysis** is a separate research tradition with its own theories and methods, and such methods are most often used by researchers to offer independent insight into social phenomena. Network analysis has slowly begun to infiltrate comparative-historical analysis, but when used in comparative-historical analysis it is generally used as a primary within-case method. The methods of network analysis can focus on any sort of actor, including individuals and large corporate bodies. Most commonly, however, it is used to analyze individuals. As noted in Chapter 1, the analysis of individuals is quite rare within comparative-historical analysis largely because the research tradition focuses on structural analyses. Even when focusing on individuals, however, network analyses make structural explanations of social phenomena. Specifically, they focus on how the structure of the network affects the outcome. Burt's (1992) work on structural holes helps to highlight the inherent structuralism of network analysis. Burt named a particular network structure in which one actor has ties to multiple actors but the latter lack any ties among themselves. The single actor that joins the unconnected actors, in turn, is positioned at a structural hole. Burt offers evidence that this network structure is a major source of power for those actors positioned at structural holes. Specifically, actors who are positioned at structural holes are able to monopolize information and resource flows among the non-connected actors, exploiting the dependence of the other actors on them by making demands on the non-connected actors in exchange for transferring information and resources. They can also increase their power by playing non-connected actors off against one another. In this way, structural holes are a means of power, and this power is derived from structure—specifically, one's position in a network—rather than individual characteristics.

Gould (2003) describes two main types of network analysis. The first is the connectivity network. This type of analysis analyzes networks and notes their particular structures, with a focus on the density of ties and ties that span different network nodes. Researchers pursuing this type of analysis consider the overall structure of connections among actors. Alternatively, positional methods focus on how network structures create positions for the actors. So, based on their position within the network structure, an actor might be a leader or a follower, a broker or an isolate. Burt's (1992) structural holes offer an example.

The work of Roger Gould provides notable examples of network analysis. Gould employs methods of network analysis to help explain historical episodes of collective mobilization. For example, he analyzes the Paris Commune of 1871 and finds that militia recruitment patterns affected cross-neighborhood contacts and that these contacts were important means of mobilization during the insurrection (Gould 1991). In order to understand why the insurrection occurred where it did, it is therefore instructive to look at the network structure of militia recruitment.

In his analysis of the American Whiskey Rebellion of 1794, Gould (1996) analyzes what caused elites to mobilize for or against the rebellion. The Whiskey Rebellion was caused by the federal government imposing a tax on whiskey production; many producers strongly opposed the law, stating that most of their whiskey was for personal consumption, not for sale. His network analysis of elites helps to highlight factors that contributed to the different positions taken by them. He finds that elites with network ties to the federal government were generally strongly opposed to rebellion. In contrast, those whose patronage networks were reduced because of the imposition of a federal system of government were much more likely to favor rebellion. Ultimately, his argument focuses on both material interests—as some elites benefited from federalism while others were hindered by it—as well as identity, with those elites who were connected to the federal government gaining a stronger national identity than the isolated elites.

In order to arrive at this conclusion, Gould maps out the networks of elites and categorizes their network positions. For this, he gathers data and maps out networks of patron-client relations for the elites in three counties. Figure 3.5 reproduces his network analyses for one county—Washington County. Based on these diagrams, he is able to operationalize variables for individuals and subsequently use statistical methods to explore whether these network variables are related to participation in the rebellion. One important variable measures whether a member of the elite is part of the patron-client network. Thus, if a member of the elite from Washington County is not found on Figure 3.5, he is coded as 0 but he is coded as 1 if he is part of the network of patron-client relations. Another variable measures whether a patron within the patron-client network shares a client with an elite member with ties to the federal government. Using the network map reproduced in Figure 3.5, Gould analyzes whether a patron shares a client with another patron, and he is able to operationalize the variable because he also has data on which patrons have ties to federal office. Using this data, he finds that elites who were not part of patron-client networks and elites who shared a client with a patron with ties to the federal government were much more likely to participate in the Whiskey Rebellion.

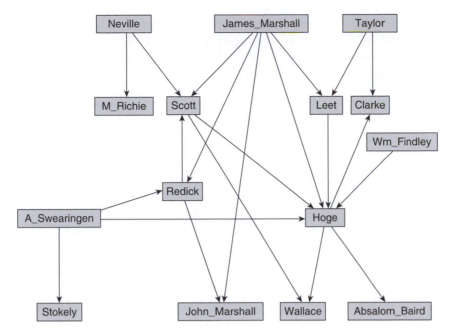

Figure 3.5   Political network of Washington County, 1789-93
(Gould 1996, 417)

© Gould, R., *American Journal of Sociology* 102: 2 (1996) University of Chicago.

Notably, Gould uses methods of network analysis as an independent comparative method, not as a primary within-case method for comparative-historical analysis. In the case of the latter, researchers would use the evidence derived from the network analysis to inform their case studies, and the case studies would be based on a secondary within-case method and would employ additional primary within-case methods for more evidence into the cases. Few comparative-historical analyses have used methods of network analysis in this way.

Saxenian's *Regional Advantage* (1994) offers one example. In it, she incorporates network analysis into her causal narrative. She offers a comparative-historical analysis of the IT communities of Boston and Silicon Valley that explores how the latter ultimately became the dominant IT region in the United States of America despite the early advantages of the former. She finds that the different network structures between high-tech industries help explain the different outcomes. In Boston, high-tech industries conformed to the dominant business model, with hierarchical and closed corporations; in contrast, the networks were less hierarchical and possessed many more ties between corporations in the Silicon Valley. The cross-corporation ties found in Silicon Valley, in turn, proved to be very important bases of information on cutting-edge technologies, allowing businesses to have low-cost access to the most important element of technological development. Moreover, such ties facilitated cooperative relations between firms, allowing firms to specialize in particular areas rather than trying to produce multiple technologies.

GIS *(Geographic Information System)*

Like methods of network analysis, **GIS (Geographic Information System)** is another method that can be used as a primary within-case method. GIS is a visual technology that merges cartography with statistics to map differences between geographic regions. The use of GIS might simply help to visualize geographic similarities and differences within a case instead of presenting them statistically or through a narrative—as Wickham-Crowley (1993) and Ziblatt (2006) do. It is also able to highlight geospatial factors, so the method offers important advantages for analyzing the causal impact of geospatial elements such as concentration or distance, neither of which is easily captured through statistics.

Because many comparative-historical researchers consider geospatial factors, it can be a valuable method to add to the research tradition's methodological toolkit. It is relatively new, however, and has yet to firmly establish itself as a common primary within-case method in the tradition. Herbst's *States and Power in Africa* (2000) offers one example of a comparative-historical analysis that uses GIS. In his book, Herbst explores reasons for the historical weakness of states in sub-Saharan Africa and focuses on the impact of human geography. Specifically, he believes low population densities and dispersed populations afflict much of Africa and pose severe risks to constructing efficient systems of state control and extraction. As part of his analysis, Herbst employs GIS to create maps of sub-Saharan African countries that depict elements of their human geography. Figure 3.6 reproduces six GIS maps used by Herbst. Each map depicts variation in population density across the regions of a country. Herbst uses the maps to classify each country as having human geographies that hinder state building, as they show how the populations are concentrated in some regions and dispersed throughout much of the territory, thereby hindering the construction of efficient systems of state control and extraction.

Herbst's use of GIS as a primary within-case method is incomplete, however, because he does not actually use the GIS analysis as a source of evidence for within-case analysis. Instead, he simply highlights the diverse human geographies present in sub-Saharan Africa and suggests they have an impact on state building. For him to use GIS as a primary within-case method, he would need to incorporate it into case studies

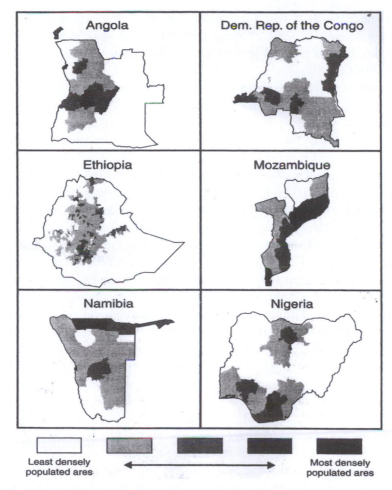

Least densely
populated ares ←——————————→ Most densely
populated ares

Figure 3.6 The use of GIS to analyze countries with difficult political
geography (Herbst 2000, 148)

and use it as evidence. In particular, he must analyze the presence and
strength of a country's state and show how differences in both are related
to the political geographies highlighted in the maps.

Methodological Pluralism: Diamond's Work on Development

Historical methods, internal comparison, network analysis, and GIS
show some of the diverse primary within-case methods that researchers
can use for comparative-historical analysis. However, there are many

additional methods that comparative-historical researchers employ to generate evidence. One example that helps to highlight some of this diversity is Jared Diamond's work on the determinants of the rise of the West (1992, 1997).

In his work, Diamond investigates the central and classic comparative-historical question: how did Western Europe emerge as a global economic and political powerhouse? To answer the question, he exploits numerous primary methods for evidence. Like most comparative-historical researchers, he uses historical methods in different case studies, such as of the Maori conquest of the Chatham Islands and the Spanish conquest of Peru (1997: 53–81). These cases offer evidence that certain technological advantages underlay the rise of the West, with domesticated animals, weaponry, and diseases being notable examples.

For additional evidence, Diamond uses other primary within-case methods. Most notably, his research question forces him to analyze factors that lack written historical sources, and he therefore turns to other methods that allow him to gain insight into his question. In an essay entitled "Horses, Hittites, and History," for example, he (1992) uses the methods of comparative linguistics to explore what enabled a group of people to conquer a large area with millions of people and establish the Indo-European language family. Because this event occurred in prehistoric times, the normal sources of historical insight are not available. Linguistic methods, however, offer some evidence into this question. For example, one can explore which modern language is most related to the proto-Indo-European language. One can also explore which phenomena have common root words throughout the Indo-European languages, suggesting that the word spread through the conquering group who established Indo-European languages across much of Europe and western Asia. Similarly, one can see which phenomena lack common root words—suggesting that the Indo-European conquerors did not have words for those phenomena.

Through a linguistic analysis, Diamond notes that the conquering group that spread the Indo-European language family appears to have originated on the Russian steppes. For example, he notes that Lithuanian is the contemporary language conforming to the proto-Indo-European language most closely. He also shows that the Indo-European language shares common roots for technologies derived from animal husbandry (including horse, cow, plow, wheel, and harness) but lacks common roots for the first crops grown by settled agriculturalists. He therefore concludes that—contrary to a popular hypothesis—intensive agriculture did not empower the Indo-European speakers to conquer much of Europe and Asia, as they do not appear to have possessed settled agricultural technologies. In contrast, the common linguistic roots of horse, harness, wheel, etc. suggest that the conquerors possessed these technologies—a cluster of new technologies that proved a very effective means of conquest in human history and that, Diamond concludes, helps to explain how the Indo-European language group spread through such a large dispersed area.

In addition to linguistics, Diamond also uses evidence derived from archeological methods for his analysis, although—like his linguistic analysis—he depends on secondary sources for the data. He notes that archeological evidence places the domestication of the horse on the Russian steppes slightly before the spread of the Indo-European language group, thereby offering evidence that supports the linguistic evidence. Diamond also uses archeological evidence to analyze the origins and spread of the main efficient crops and domesticated animals that humans exploit for settled agriculture. He finds that the most important crops and domesticated animals were not evenly dispersed throughout the world but were highly concentrated in the Fertile Crescent. He concludes therefore that the presence of efficient crops and animals that could be domesticated is the most important factor that helps to explain why settled agriculture first emerged in the Fertile Crescent. Similarly, Diamond also uses archeological evidence to analyze the speed at which crops spread from the Fertile Crescent to other regions, another factor that helps to explain the rise of settled agriculture. He finds that the most important crops originated in the Middle East but were able to spread relatively rapidly westward to Europe and eastward to Asia. In contrast, the crops were not able to spread to the Americas because of their geographic separation, and they penetrated Africa only partially and at a much slower rate because the continent's north–south axis affected plant germination and survival. According to Diamond, this helps to explain the more limited technological development in the Americas and Africa and the greater technological development of the Eurasian continent.

Summary

Within-case methods are the dominant method of comparative-historical analysis. They take diverse forms and can analyze diverse topics. Most notably, some methods are secondary within-case methods, which are the main methods guiding the within-case analysis, and some are primary within-case methods, which provide evidence that is subsequently analyzed through the use of secondary within-case methods. There are three main secondary within-case methods, all of which employ similar techniques but pursue different types of insight. Causal narrative is the most common secondary within-case method and reconstructs causal processes in an effort to highlight causal determinants. Process tracing, on the other hand, explores mechanisms linking particular elements of the causal process. Finally, pattern matching tests theories.

These secondary within–case methods depend on diverse primary within–case methods for evidence. Historical methods are the dominant primary within–case method used in comparative-historical analysis, and nearly all comparative-historical researchers use them. Internal comparison is also a common primary method and offers insight by either comparing a case over time or comparing subcomponents of the case. Other types of primary within–case methods include—but are not limited to—methods of network analysis, GIS, linguistic methods, archeological methods, game theoretic analysis, and ethnographic methods. Although most work on within-case methods has focused on secondary within–case methods, primary within-case methods should not be overlooked because they offer evidence and the latter is absolutely vital to any social scientific analysis. One of the best ways to improve comparative-historical analysis is therefore for comparative-historical researchers to use primary within–case methods more frequently and to employ a greater variety of them.

Glossary

Causal narrative: A secondary within-case method that commonly guides the within-case analyses of comparative-historical analysis. It uses narrative analysis to explore the causes of particular phenomena.

GIS (Geographic Information System): A method that allows researchers to map different levels of a phenomenon geospatially. Within the social sciences, GIS is used to show how social relations vary geospatially and allows researchers to improve their analyses of social processes with geospatial dynamics. GIS can be used as a primary method for within-case analysis.

Historical narrative: A narrative description of the characteristics of a social phenomenon. Different from causal narrative, it attempts to describe, not explain, the phenomenon. Historical narrative is commonly used in history and is an element of historical methods. It is used in comparative-historical analysis principally as a primary within-case method.

Internal comparison: A common primary within-case method used in comparative-historical analysis that uses comparison to increase insight into a particular case. It either compares the same case over time to see how changes in independent variables are related to changes in dependent variables or compares regions of the case to gain a better understanding of its internal dynamics.

Mechanism: A mechanism is commonly referred to as a "black box" that explains a causal relationship or sequence. The black box links a cause and an outcome and suggests that the cause induces transformation in a way that generates the outcome. Thus, a mechanism is the transformative action through which the cause produces the effect.

Narrative: A sequential account—or story—of an event or series of events that organizes material chronologically to provide an overview of either what happened or the characteristics of a particular social phenomenon. Narratives are commonly used for within-case analysis.

Network analysis: A type of social analysis that considers the impact of network structures on social processes. Diverse methods are used for network analysis, and these methods can serve as primary within-case methods for comparative-historical analysis.

Pattern matching: A secondary method that guides within-case analysis. It allows researchers to use case studies to test theories. It therefore differs from the other two secondary within-case methods because it does not necessarily explore causal processes.

Primary within-case methods: Methods used to generate evidence for within-case analysis, the latter of which is subsequently analyzed by another method to answer the research question. Primary within-case methods are used for all within-case analysis and include diverse methods: historical methods, internal comparison, methods of network analysis, GIS, ethnographic methods, linguistic methods, and archeological methods.

Process tracing: A secondary within-case method that commonly guides the within-case analyses of comparative-historical analysis. Like causal narrative, it explores causal relations, but process tracing differs because it is much more focused: it focuses on mechanisms that link particular elements in a causal sequence. Moreover, while causal narrative is focused on ideographic explanation, process tracing commonly explores mechanisms that are general across a larger set of cases.

Secondary within-case methods: Methods used for within-case analysis to analyze evidence produced by primary within-case methods. In this way, secondary within-case methods guide the overall analysis but depend on other primary within-case methods for evidence. Causal narrative, process tracing, and pattern matching are three types of secondary within-case method.

4

Within-Case Methods and the Analysis of Temporality and Inter-Case Relations

As described in Chapter 3, within-case methods offer important insight into the determinants of particular social phenomena. In so doing, they do not simply offer snapshots of individual cases that focus on internal processes; rather, they are well suited to analyze cases historically, thereby analyzing temporal sequences and transformations over time. Moreover, within-case methods are able to analyze a case in relationship to other cases, noting how such relationships shape the characteristics and processes of the case. The ability to analyze the impact of temporality and inter-case relations, in turn, offers important advantages that make within-case methods valuable. This chapter reviews the ways within-case methods can analyze the causal impact of temporality and inter-case relations. In so doing, it moves beyond reviewing the types of within-case methods and considers how researchers can employ within-case methods to analyze ways in which temporality and inter-case relations shape social processes.

Within-Case Methods and Temporality

Causal narrative, process tracing, and pattern matching are the secondary within-case methods used in comparative-historical analysis. They are also the within-case techniques that constitute the "history" of comparative-historical methods because all three depend heavily on historical narrative, analyze historical phenomena, and are well suited to analyze diachronic processes—that is, processes that occur over time. Recently, social scientists have focused considerable attention on how time shapes social processes and the subsequent need for **diachronic analysis** to understand the causal process better. Because within-case methods are able to analyze sequential processes that unfold over time, they are advantaged at providing insight into the causal impact of time. Most notably, researchers can employ within-case methods to analyze the causal impact of time in six different ways: establishing causal order, analyzing causal processes that occur over time, analyzing non-linear processes, exploring asymmetric processes, considering period effects, and investigating path-dependent processes. Importantly, within-case methods do not automatically highlight these temporal characteristics; researchers must be aware of them and purposefully employ within-case methods to analyze the potential influence of temporality.

Causal Ordering

One of the most common and simplest ways researchers use within-case methods to analyze temporal processes is to establish causal order. While simple, such evidence provides important insight into causal relationships, and numerous causal claims have been rejected by subsequent evidence showing that the supposed effect preceded the supposed cause. In addition, the temporal ordering of events offers evidence regarding the direction of causation. Indeed, one common critique of statistical analysis is that they fail to establish causal order, as an independent variable might be determined by the dependent variable instead of the reverse. So, a statistical analysis might find that agrarian backwardness and state breakdown are related but be unable to provide insight into the direction of causation. However, through a causal narrative analyzing sequence, Skocpol (1979) was able to provide strong evidence that agrarian backwardness was a cause of state breakdown in eighteenth-century France, not the reverse.

Sometimes, establishing causal order through a narrative analysis can be quite difficult. This is particularly the case when there is no clear temporal ordering and when both factors appear to reinforce one another. For example, effective states might promote economic development, but economic development might promote effective states. Thus, a narrative analysis of the impact of states on economic development might have difficulty analyzing the direction of causation in a country that has both effective states and impressive economic development. Still, within-case methods can address these problems by going back in time to see whether the country developed an effective state before or after the onset of rapid economic expansion. Moreover, within-case methods help to highlight causal mechanisms, which provide insight into the direction of causation as well as the potential of an elective affinity—a situation where two factors simultaneously promote one another.

Covariation Over Time

Within-case analysis usually goes further than simply establishing causal order. For example, it commonly provides a type of time-series analysis, where a researcher analyzes the covariation of factors over time. In so doing, within-case methods can provide a temporal analysis showing that a change in one factor promoted a change in another. In her analysis of the Russian Revolution, for example, Skocpol (1979) notes that the revolt of 1905 largely failed because the Russian state—although weak—had the capacity to quell the rebellion. In contrast, it was militarily impotent after its total defeat in World War I, and this opening allowed the Russian Revolution ultimately to succeed. As this example shows, such pseudo-time-series analyses do not employ formal statistical methods to test relationships between variables over time. Rather, they use a narrative to describe the covariation of the variables, provide a table showing the covariation of the variables, or both. Importantly, they also usually describe mechanisms underlying the relationship, something that allows greater confidence that the covariation highlights a causal process.

Most comparative-historical analyses are similar to Skocpol's because they use causal narrative for a pseudo-time-series analysis, but others use formal statistical methods. For example, Goldstone's (1991) *Revolutions and Rebellions in the Early Modern World* (see the section on internal comparison in Chapter 3) offers a time-series statistical analysis to offer insight into the factors that contributed to the English Revolution. Although capable of highlighting within-case covariation, statistics has great difficulty highlighting causal mechanisms. As a result, Goldstone and others who use time-series analyses as part of their comparative-historical analysis incorporate it into the within-case analysis and use the latter to explore causal mechanisms underlying the statistical findings.

Non-Linear Temporal Processes: Threshold Effects

Over the past two decades, researchers have made a concerted effort to use within-case methods to do more than simply explore causal ordering and covariation over time. In particular, they note that complex causal processes frequently do not occur in a linear fashion and that within-case methods can help overcome this problem by focusing on temporal elements of processes. Pierson (2003), for example, notes that only a few social processes occur rapidly, suggesting that **synchronic analysis**, which analyzes a phenomenon at one point in time, is generally ill-suited to social scientific analysis. Some of the slower processes have causes that take a long time to spark a change in the outcome, and some have outcomes that take a long time to occur. In both cases, the relationship between the cause and the outcome is not linear, and there is a considerable lag between them.

Threshold effects provide a particular example of causes that do not have a linear impact on the outcome. In such an instance, an increase in a causal variable has little or no impact on the outcome until it reaches a particular level, at which time the outcome variable transforms rapidly; and if a researcher takes a short-term perspective, he or she will be more likely to miss the importance of the causal variable because previous transformations had little or no impact. Within-case methods can do more than explore linear causal processes, however; they are extremely well suited to the analysis of processes that occur in a non-linear fashion because of causes or effects that take a long time to occur. Their advantage lies in their ability to highlight causal processes and mechanisms, and then move either forwards or backwards in the causal chain to show how the causal impact of one variable on another took a long time to materialize.

Goldstone (1991) takes this approach in *Revolution and Rebellion in the Early Modern World*. He analyzes the impact of population growth on revolutions in England, France, the Ottoman Empire, and Ming China and finds that all four revolutions were preceded by a long period of steady population growth. Such growth, in turn, created pressures that increased in a non-linear fashion, thereby creating more and more stress that the rulers began to have more and more difficulty coping with. In the end, the revolutionary pressures caused by sustained population growth finally could not be contained and were unleashed, resulting in state breakdown and revolutionary change. Goldstone notes that a simple focus on population growth would not provide much causal insight into the process, as growth was steady for long periods prior to the revolution. Yet, by using within-case methods to analyze long-term change, he offers evidence that threshold effects underlie the impact of population on revolutions.

Asymmetric Processes

Within-case methods are also well-suited to analyzing **asymmetric causal processes**. Lieberson (1985) divides all causal processes into symmetric and asymmetric processes. The outcome of a symmetric causal process returns to the previous state once the cause has been removed. So if economic recession causes an increase in theft rates, and the causal process is symmetric in nature, theft rates will return to normal once the recession ends. Alternatively, once an asymmetric causal process begins, it creates or transforms structures in ways that perpetuate the process—even after the initial causal conditions have been removed—meaning that theft rates would remain elevated even after the end of the recession.

Asymmetric causal processes can be difficult to analyze because the causal impact of a factor is not constant. Within-case methods, however, are able to analyze asymmetric processes because they focus on diachronic processes and are able to highlight mechanisms. Indeed, asymmetric causal processes must be analyzed diachronically in order to show how a factor caused an outcome and how, in turn, this outcome is able to reproduce itself once the cause is removed. In addition, the ability to reproduce itself usually takes time and involves additional steps in the causal sequence. Such an analysis must focus on the mechanisms that originally caused the outcome as well as the mechanisms that reproduced it once the initial cause was no longer present. Within-case methods are also well suited for analyzing asymmetric causal processes because such processes commonly involve institutions, and within-case methods are ideal for institutional analysis. Most importantly, they can analyze how a factor promotes institutional genesis as well as mechanisms that promote institutional reproduction after the removal of the original cause.

Weber's *Protestant Ethic and the Spirit of Capitalism* offers an example of how within-case methods can be used to analyze an asymmetric causal process. Weber suggests that capitalist development is an asymmetric process because one of the initial conditions contributing to its rise—the Protestant ethic—was not necessary for its continued development since, once established, capitalism shaped individual norms and cognitions and thereby created "mechanical foundations" for a spirit of capitalism that took over once the Protestant ethic weakened (1905/1992, 181–2). Several comparative-historical analyses of colonial institutional legacies also highlight asymmetric causal processes (Charrad 2001; Kohli 2004; Lange 2009; Mahoney 2010). They show how colonialism interacted with local conditions and promoted particular economic and political institutions. Once created, these institutions were able to reproduce themselves without colonial backing. As a result, the institutions created during colonialism commonly persisted, with only minor transformations, after independence.

Period Effects

Comparative-historical researchers also analyze how history matters because of **period effects**. That is, the time at which a process occurs can have great bearing on that process. Most notably, technologies, institutions, and ideas change over time and have important effects on a number of social processes. As a consequence, processes can differ dramatically depending on the period in which they occur. Within-case methods, in turn, are able to analyze period effects because they can explore the causal impact of diverse factors. Moreover, an analysis of period effects is necessarily diachronic because it follows a causal sequence showing how time affects a causal determinant and how this causal determinant subsequently affects the outcome.

Ertman's *Birth of the Leviathan* (1997) offers an example of a comparative-historical analysis that notes the impact of period effects. The book explores the causes of different configurations of states and regimes in Early Modern Europe and finds that the time of onset of intense warfare had a major impact on the form of the state. In particular, rulers who entered intense international warfare prior to 1450 generally pursued patrimonial strategies of state building because there was a lack of expert personnel for the administration and legal institutions. Conversely, those countries that first engaged in intense international competition after 1450 had alternative options for state expansion. The rapid expansion of university education, for example, created a much larger pool of expert candidates. As a consequence, a more meritocratic and rule-based state structure was possible. In addition, late state-builders were able to observe the strategies of earlier state builders and adopt the most successful elements.

Path Dependence

Like asymmetric processes and period effects, **path dependence** is also a temporal concept suggesting that the causal impact of factors can vary over time. It posits that there are periods of flux during which a factor can have a greater impact on a process because there are openings for change. In contrast, at other times the social environment is much more stable and has factors that reinforce this stability, thereby making major change more difficult. Since the 1990s, path dependence has received considerable attention, and comparative-historical researchers have increasingly used causal narratives to analyze path-dependent processes (see Collier and Collier 1991; Mahoney 2000a, 2001b; Pierson 2003).

Path dependence has two central components. The first is a critical juncture, or period "when the presence or absence of a specified causal force pushes ... a single case onto a new political trajectory that diverges significantly from the old" (Slater and Simmons 2010: 888). It is at this period that a causal factor can have a large and long-lasting effect because permissive conditions allow for greater agency and change (Soifer Forthcoming). The second component involves the long-term reinforcement of the process that began during a critical juncture, in ways that prevent radical change. This might occur when a critical event sparks a causal sequence that reinforces itself in ways that prevent either the return to earlier conditions or the pursuit of options that were feasible at an earlier time. In addition, the outcome can be reinforced over time by constant causes that were put in place during the critical juncture. Most commonly, reinforcement occurs through four different general mechanisms. The first is through the rational-choice mechanism. Through this mechanism, processes become locked in because the cost of radical change is much greater than that of maintaining the present social relations. Thus, once a federated system of government is built, the cost of transforming current organizations along a more centralized line can help maintain this structure. Second, path dependence can be reinforced by the power mechanism. That is, powerful interests frequently have a stake in the status quo and exert their power to prevent change. In the case of a federated system of government, this structure empowers regional authorities who, in turn, frequently use their power to oppose centralizing reforms. The third mechanism is cognitive. It occurs when actors have cognitive "blinders" that impair their ability to perceive alternatives, thereby locking them into the status quo. So, if federated government strengthens regional identities, it helps create cognitive frameworks that perpetuate the structure. Finally, path dependence can be reinforced through norms. This can occur when individuals perceive the status quo as normatively desirable and therefore act in ways that perpetuate it. Thus, if an educational system socializes students to believe that a federal system of government is highly desirable, norms can promote the maintenance of a federated system.

Within-case methods—especially causal narratives—are well-equipped to analyze path-dependent processes. A causal narrative allows one to trace a causal sequence, analyze factors that cause some periods to be critical periods of change, and to explore mechanisms that reinforce and reproduce outcomes. For this type of analysis, causal narratives inherently focus on three periods and the sequences linking all three: pre-critical juncture, critical juncture, and post-critical juncture. For the first, researchers document the preexisting period and note the trajectory of change that preceded the critical juncture. One important reason for documenting pre-critical juncture conditions is because path dependence suggests that the critical juncture initiates a period of rapid change that breaks from the past. If this is the case, it is clear that one must document the pre-critical juncture period. The analysis of the second period—the critical juncture—focuses on the critical changes that occurred during this period, with an eye on permissive conditions that made change possible and the ways the critical juncture parted from the previous trajectory (as documented in the pre-critical juncture period). Frequently, researchers describe the different possibilities for change that could have occurred during the critical juncture and explore why change occurred in one way rather than another. The purpose of this is, generally, to provide evidence that the critical juncture is a period during which processes had the potential to change in a variety of ways. Finally, the analysis of the post-critical juncture period documents the trajectory of change that occurred after the critical juncture and explores how the critical juncture instigated this new trajectory. In addition, researchers usually also analyze factors that reinforce trajectories over time.

Although path dependence might be relevant for any number of social processes, comparative-historical scholars have applied it most commonly to institutional change. Such works recognize that institutions commonly reproduce themselves over long periods of time, suggesting that periods of institutional genesis or radical reform are critical junctures initiating path-dependent processes. One notable example is Mahoney's *The Legacies of Liberalism* (2001b). This book starts by recognizing the diverse and long-standing regime outcomes in Central America, with Guatemala and El Salvador having military-authoritarian regimes, Honduras and Nicaragua having traditional dictatorial regimes, and Costa Rica having a democratic regime. Through a causal narrative of all five cases, he concludes that their different regime trajectories were the outcomes of different liberalizing reforms that were implemented in each country between 1870 and 1920. These reforms attempted to restructure political and economic institutions along liberal lines and faced stiff opposition from traditional elites.

According to Mahoney, the liberalizing reforms succeeded to different extents and, when they were successful, took different forms. He finds that Honduras and Nicaragua began liberal reforms but that these reforms were aborted because of internal pressure and external intervention. As a result, the traditional-style dictatorships were maintained and continued as the dominant regime type. Alternatively, in Guatemala and El Salvador, the liberal reformers attempted to implement the reforms as quickly as possible and built a militarized state in an effort to do so. The pace and extent of the reforms also aggravated class relations and increased inequalities. Both a militarized state and class inequalities, in turn, promoted military-authoritarian regimes. Finally, Costa Rican liberal reformers implemented more gradual reforms which neither exacerbated class conflict nor required a militarized state for their implementation. In this way, the more gradual reforms helped to create an institutional setting that supported a democratic regime.

Notably, Mahoney claims that his findings are path-dependent because the liberal reform period was a critical juncture during which the trajectory of each country's regime type was begun. In particular, he suggests that the decisions of liberal elites to implement either radical or gradual reforms had highly significant consequences for the future because of their impact on political and economic institutions. These institutions, in turn, reinforced the regime trajectories and created long-term differences of regime type in Central America.

Overall, Mahoney's account of Central America provides strong evidence that time, sequence, and rate are influential and must be considered by researchers in their causal analyses. He suggests that the reform period was a critical period during which the regime trajectories of countries were in flux and could have gone in different ways. After the reform period, on the other hand, the institutional environment helped lock in the different regime types. As a consequence, the impact of elite decisions on regime type was much more influential during the reform period than afterwards. If we want to understand why there is such diversity in Central America, Mahoney therefore suggests that we need to consider this influential period and how it helped lock each country into different regime trajectories.

Chibber's *Locked in Place* (2003) offers another path-dependent analysis. Chibber compares state-led economic development efforts in India and South Korea after World War II and concludes that the decisions of political elites to pursue different economic policies—import substitution industrialization (ISI) in India and export-led industrialization in South Korea—caused the countries to commence different trajectories of economic development. He also notes that Indian officials realized a decade after their ISI policies began that such policies were failing. He finds, however, that they were unable to shift to export-led policies—despite an effort to do so—because the ISI policies strengthened capitalist elites who were opposed to a shift in economic policy and because the implementation of ISI created divisions within the state that limited the effectiveness of export-led reforms. He therefore concludes that this ineffective policy remained locked in place for two more decades. In turn, the strength of the capitalists and the ineffectiveness of the state prevented officials from pursuing export-led policy at this time, thereby causing subsequent liberalizing reforms that sought only to limit state economic management, not change the form of such management.

In general, path-dependent analyses such as Mahoney's and Chibber's are very difficult to complete. Most notably, they require analysis of a social process over a long period of time—something that is difficult for one case let alone multiple cases. In addition, in order to show that there was a critical juncture that could have begun different trajectories, a researcher must have evidence showing that different options were possible, which can require evidence about the options that were weighed by political decision-makers during the critical juncture. Further, when attempting a comparative analysis of critical junctures, scholars can only make strong claims about critical junctures causing differences between cases either when no significant difference is present in the cases prior to the critical juncture or by documenting how these differences did not affect how the critical juncture occurred. Notably, both Mahoney and Chibber recognize that structural factors help to explain why political elites made the decisions that they did (differences in class relations among Central American countries and differences in the type of foreign investment in India and South Korea). In this way, neither book suggests that the whims of political elites were the sole cause of different trajectories; rather, they argue that structural factors had considerable bearing on the decisions made during critical junctures, thereby making the junctures less critical. Along these lines, Slater and Simmons suggest that critical antecedents, which "shape the choices and changes that emerge during critical junctures," usually play important roles in path-dependent processes (2010, 887).

Within-Case Methods and Inter-Case Relationships

Despite their name, within-case methods need not simply explore cases as independent entities in isolation from others. Instead, they are well equipped to analyze the relationships a case has with other cases and the impact these relationships have on the case. The ability to analyze cross-case relations, in turn, is extremely important because—contrary to common statistical assumptions—cases in the real world are very rarely completely isolated from one another and because inter-case relations commonly have large effects on the cases. As a consequence, one cannot simply analyze the processes and characteristics internal to the case; one has to analyze the interaction of the case with other cases as well.

A focus on inter-case relationships is particularly important for all social analysis, including comparative-historical analysis. This is because social relations link diverse social actors and these interactions can have great effect on the internal characteristics and processes of the social actors. For example, one actor might either coerce or assist another actor, and such inter-relationships can have a strong bearing on the internal processes and characteristics of the actors. Thus, both the Russian and American-led occupations of Afghanistan have had considerable effect on Afghan society, and one cannot gain an understanding of contemporary Afghan society without considering the impact of external intervention. Inter-case relations can also be influential when they are a means of diffusion. Ideologies, institutions, and technologies can all spread from one case to another and, in so doing, have great transformative effects wherever they go. The potential impact of diffusion, in turn, can cause considerable problems for statistical analysis, as such analysis assumes case independence and has difficulty analyzing the impact of diffusion. This is commonly referred to as the **Galton problem**, after Sir Francis Galton, who first noted that diffusion can cause gross inaccuracies in statistical analyses.

Although comparative methods—especially large-N comparison—are ill equipped to consider inter-case relationships, within-case methods—especially causal narrative—have an analytic advantage for this sort of analysis. As Rueschemeyer and Stephens (1997) note, an analysis of causal sequences is able to consider factors and processes internal to the case as well as factors and processes external to the case. Indeed, in tracing a process, a researcher can easily consider both internal and external elements. Thus, an analysis of capitalist development can consider the impact of local factors and external factors, as well as interactions between the two.

A focus on internal and external elements of processes is vital, as both can be very influential. If, for example, an analysis focuses solely on internal elements of processes, it can overlook important determining factors. Similarly, if an analysis focuses on external factors, the researcher can overlook how internal factors had considerable consequence. Finally, the local context commonly has a mediating effect on external effects, meaning that researchers must consider the interactions between both.

Although important for all social analyses, inter-case relationships are particularly important for comparative-historical analysis because comparative-historical analysis focuses on large-scale processes involving big units of analysis, with national states being the most common example of the latter. Over the past several centuries, in turn, national states have become the dominant form of political organization and community, and the scope and intensity of inter-state relations has increased exponentially. Indeed, in an era of globalization, researchers cannot avoid analyzing the impact of global relations. As a result, comparative-historical researchers have paid considerable attention to the causal impact of inter-case relations. Indeed, the early researchers of comparative-historical analysis's second generation paid great attention to the impact of inter-case relations, and this focus has been institutionalized in the research tradition, making inter-case relations a common concern of comparative-historical researchers.

Within comparative-historical analysis, there are two primary ways researchers deal with inter-case relations: one focuses almost exclusively on the impact of inter-case relations, and the other explores the impact of both inter-case relations and internal factors. Tilly (1984) refers to the first as "encompassing comparisons." Scholars making encompassing comparisons analyze cases within a larger "structure or process and explain similarities or differences among those locations as consequences of their relationships to the whole" (1984, 125). Notably, encompassing comparisons are not really comparisons—they are within-case analysis focusing on the causal impact of inter-case relationships. A more appropriate name, therefore, is encompassing analysis.

Within comparative-historical analysis, the first works that focused on inter-case relationships were written as critiques to both Marxist and structural functionalist theory. Both meta-theoretical perspectives considered social change as inevitable and driven by internal processes. Because of the latter, they failed to consider the impact of inter-case relations on social change. Modernization theory, a theory of social development that was popular during the 1960s and 1970s, offers an example. Like Marxist theory, it suggests that all societies pass through the same stages of development. Passage through these stages, according to the theory, is inevitable and driven by internal processes. Numerous modernization theorists therefore analyzed Africa, Asia, and Latin America and suggested that their underdevelopment was only temporary and that they would pass through the stages of development more quickly if the countries' leaders implemented policy that replicated the experience of more developed countries.

By the late-1960s and early-1970s, numerous scholars severely criticized this view for disregarding the impact of international context. These scholars were generally left-leaning, although they also criticized Marx for disregarding the influence of international context. Their views are known now as dependency theory and world-systems theory, and their main point is that Western countries became dominant in an international state system that did not severely constrain their subsequent transformations. Indeed, the international system at the time of the rise of the West offered an opportunity to conquer and exploit diverse regions of the world for the material benefit of Western countries. While benefiting the core countries, non-Western peoples found themselves continually exploited by the dominant Western countries and faced extreme impediments to development. Therefore, these scholars claimed, the fundamental developmental challenges faced by the Global South are not internal failures to modernize but international constraints.

Anthropologist Eric Wolf exemplifies this view in his *Europe and the People without History*. In the introduction, he proclaims:

> The central assertion of this book is that the world of humankind constitutes a manifold, a totality of interconnected processes, and inquiries that disassemble this totality into bits and then fail to reassemble it falsify reality. Concepts like "nation," "society," and "culture" name bits and

threaten to turn names into things. Only by understanding these names as bundles of relationships, and by placing them back into the field from which they were abstracted, can we hope to avoid misleading inferences and increase our share of understanding. (1982, 3)

Wolf's subsequent analysis is divided into three parts: he describes diverse modes of production in the world in 1400, analyzes Europe's efforts to extract wealth from the rest of the world thereafter, and describes the global division of labor under European-dominated capitalism. All in all, the analysis describes how European interference transformed diverse regions of the world and how Europe was also transformed in this process.

The most famous comparative-historical researcher using encompassing analysis is Immanuel Wallerstein. Wallerstein began his research exploring social change in sub-Saharan Africa. Following the dominant research traditions of the 1960s, this work focused on internal factors. Eventually, however, he came to the conclusion that an analysis that focuses on internal factors overlooks very important determinants of social change. Like Wolf, he concluded that Europe incorporated Africa and other regions of the world into a global political and economic system. He described Europe as the core, with the coercive and economic means of subordinating Africa, Asia, and other regions of the global periphery. Besides the dominant core and the subordinate periphery, he recognizes that some regions fall between the two extremes—into what he refers to as the "semi-periphery". His overall theory of core exploitation of the periphery is now popularly referred to as world-systems theory.

Wallerstein has written extensively on the world system, but his most notable body of work is his four-volume *The Modern World-System* (1974, 1980, 1989, 2011). In this work, Wallerstein does not analyze individual cases, per se; rather, he analyzes the world system as a whole, exploring the position individual cases have within it and the impact their position has on social change. In this way, his analysis is—as Tilly's terminology suggests—extremely encompassing. The first volume explores the construction of the world system during the seventeenth and early eighteenth century, and the subsequent volumes consider the expansion and transformations of the world system over the following three centuries. Ultimately, Wallerstein's work highlights that a focus on inter-case relations is important for two reasons: diffusion has been a dominant process in world history, with capitalism and states being powerful institutions that have spread from Europe to other regions of the world, and, most importantly, one's position within the global economy and state system has great bearing on how social change occurs.

Instead of focusing on the totality of cases and their manifold interrelationships, other comparative-historical scholars differ from Wallerstein and other practitioners of encompassing analysis by focusing equally on units and their relations with other units. Skocpol's *States and Social Revolutions* (1979) offers one notable example. Skocpol is interested in explaining social revolutions and focuses largely on internal factors and processes. At the same time, she notes that external factors played very important roles—particularly in state crises and breakdown. She therefore suggests the need for a "Janus-faced" analysis that focuses on both internal and external factors (1979, 32). More specifically, her analysis focuses on the interaction of the two, as the internal mediates the impact of the external. For example, her analysis of state breakdown in France focuses on internal processes dealing with agricultural production, external processes such as international warfare, and how both combined to create a severe financial crisis contributing to state crisis and breakdown (see Figure 3.2 in this volume).

Such a Janus-faced analysis is much more common in comparative-historical analysis than an encompassing analysis. Indeed, even comparative-historical analyses that focus on internal processes usually consider the impact of inter-case relations. Thus, Ertman's (1997) analysis of political development in early-modern Europe considers the impact of international warfare and the diffusion of institutions; Kohli's (2004) analysis of economic development in the Global South considers the impact of colonialism on state institutions; Chibber's (2003) analysis of economic development considers the international diffusion of policy (but notes that such diffusion can be a long and uncertain process given internal conditions); Weyland (2009) explores how revolutions spread from one country to another in 1848; Rueschemeyer, Stephens, and Stephens (1991) and Mahoney (2001b) both consider how international diffusion and relations shape democratization; and Gorski (2003) notes that the Protestant Revolution and cross-country movements of different Protestant sects had important effects on state building in Early-Modern Europe.

Given the frequency at which comparative-historical researchers consider inter-case relations, it might come as a surprise that Goldthorpe (1997) criticized comparative-historical methods for having difficulty analyzing them. This critique, like many other critiques of comparative-historical methods, is based on a misunderstanding of what the methods of comparative-historical analysis actually are. Specifically, Goldthorpe suggests that the main method of comparative-historical analysis is Millian comparison and notes that such comparisons assume "that nations can be treated as units of analysis, unrelated to each other in time and space" (1997, 10).

Goldthorpe is correct in his critique of Millian comparison, as it has difficulty analyzing inter-case dependence on its own (see Chapter 5). Still, Skocpol (1979) uses Millian comparison to analyze international threat, showing that even Millian comparison can explore the impact of external factors. More importantly, there are several additional methods within the comparative-historical toolkit, and many of these are well suited to the exploration of inter-case relationships. Narrative comparison, for example, is able to analyze complex inter-case relationships among multiple cases. Process tracing can explore mechanisms through which external factors shape internal processes. Of all methods, however, causal narrative is probably the most appropriate for exploring the impact of inter-case relationships. Indeed, as Rueschemeyer and Stephens (1997) note in their rebuttal of Goldthorpe, causal narrative is able to consider the case within its international context and explore causal sequences leading to the outcome. These causal sequences, in turn, are able to consider how the international context affects internal processes. Indeed, nearly all of the analyses described above use causal narratives to analyze the impact of inter-case relationships.

So, within-case methods—despite the name—allow comparative-historical researchers to explore the causal impact of inter-case relations. However, these methods do not automatically consider the potential impact of inter-case relations, so comparative-historical researchers must continue to recognize the potential importance of inter-case relationships and purposefully use the methods to explore their potential impact. Such an analysis can be quite demanding, as it requires that researchers have considerable understanding of within-case processes, inter-case processes, and the impact each has on the other. The large and insightful body of work within the comparative-historical research tradition that explores the impact of inter-case relations, however, suggests that the difficulties of using within-case methods to analyze the causal impact of inter-case relations are not prohibitive.

Summary

Similar to Chapter 3, this chapter considers how within-case methods are used in comparative-historical analysis. However, while Chapter 3 focuses on the within-case techniques used to gather and analyze data, this chapter considers two ways within-case techniques can be employed to provide particular and important insight. First, it notes how within-case methods are well-equipped to analyze historical processes. Second, it recognizes that within-case methods are able to analyze the potential causal impact of inter-case relationships. This ability to analyze a case over time and in relationship to other cases is vital to social scientific analysis because both time and external factors shape social processes in important ways.

Glossary

Asymmetric causal process: A causal process that does not return to the original state after the cause has been removed. Igniting a paper with a match is an example, as removing the match from the paper will not return the paper to its unburned form. In the social world, asymmetric causal processes commonly involve institutions, as they usually reproduce themselves and rarely disappear once their causes are removed.

Diachronic analysis: An analysis that considers how a causal process unfolds over time. Causal narratives are able to make diachronic analyses.

Galton problem: Named after the nineteenth-century British polymath, Francis Galton, who famously criticized a comparative anthropological analysis showing a statistical relationship between economic and familial institutions across a wide range of societies. The author suggested the relationship was driven by functional needs, but Galton criticized this finding, claiming that it could also be caused by cultural diffusion among societies. The Galton problem therefore refers to potential error caused by overlooking the effect of inter-case relations and focusing simply on the impact of internal factors. The Galton problem is especially relevant for statistical analysis, which commonly assumes the independence of cases.

Path dependence: A type of process in which an initial decision or event locks the process into a particular pathway. It has two key components: a critical juncture, which is a period of flux when the decision or event occurs, and the reinforcement of the process, which perpetuates the pathway begun during the critical juncture. Path dependence suggests that there are periods of flux during which a factor can have a greater impact on a process because there are openings for change. Alternatively, at other times, the social environment is much more stable and has factors that reinforce this stability, thereby making major change more difficult and reducing the causal impact of a factor.

Period effects: Variation in the effect of one factor on another that is caused by the different periods in which the causal process occurred. It suggests that different historical contexts mediate the impact of causal determinants, causing factors to have different effects in different historical contexts.

Synchronic analysis: An analysis that analyzes a phenomenon at one point in time.

Threshold effect: Radical change that manifests suddenly when a critical limit—the threshold—is crossed.

5

The Comparative Methods of Comparative-Historical Analysis

According to the renowned comparative historian Marc Bloch (1953), "there is no true understanding without a certain range of comparison" (42). Although Bloch's claims have subsequently been ignored by many of his fellow historians, comparative-historical researchers embrace Bloch's claims and—as the name implies—actively employ comparative methods alongside within-case methods. Just as there are numerous types of within-case methods, there are also many types of comparisons employed by comparative-historical researchers. In this chapter, I describe the main types and subtypes of comparison used in comparative-historical analysis (see Figure 5.1).

The first major type of comparison used by comparative-historical researchers is large-N comparison. As its name implies, this type of comparison analyzes several cases, anywhere between thirty and several

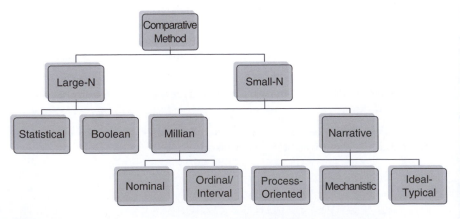

Figure 5.1   Types of comparison in comparative-historical analysis

hundreds—or even thousands. It operationalizes variables and explores the relationships between them, and these relationships offer independent insight into the research question. The two main subtypes of large-N comparison are statistical comparison and Boolean algebra.

The second major type of comparison is small-N comparison, which is easily the most common type of comparison used in the research tradition. As the name implies, small-N comparisons analyze fewer cases than large-N comparisons—usually between two and ten cases. Unlike large-N comparison, small-N comparison offers little or no independent causal insight and is necessarily combined with another method. There are two subtypes of small-N comparison, each of which can be divided into further subtypes. Millian comparison is similar to large-N comparison because it operationalizes variables and explores relationships among a small set of cases. The two subtypes of Millian comparison are nominal and ordinal/interval comparisons. Narrative comparison is the second subtype of small-N comparison. It differs fundamentally from Millian comparison because it uses narrative to compare factors and does not explore relationships between variables. The three major subtypes of narrative comparison are process-oriented, mechanistic, and ideal-typical comparisons.

Notably, there are also comparative-historical analyses that use medium-N comparison. I do not include them in my scheme, however, because there are no comparative methods that are specific to medium-N comparison. Rather, medium-N comparisons employ one or more of the comparative methods associated with either small-N or large-N comparison.

Large-N Comparisons within Comparative-Historical Analysis

In comparative-historical analysis, an increasing number of researchers employ either statistical comparison or Boolean algebra, but both remain quite rare. Both types of **large-N comparison** operationalize variables, test relations between independent and dependent variables among a large number of cases, and offer independent insight via inter-case comparison. The ability to produce independent insight is a result of the large number of cases analyzed by large-N comparison and is the most important factor that separates large-N comparison from small-N comparison. Along with these commonalities, however, statistical comparison and Boolean algebra differ in a number of ways, including the number of cases they analyze, whether they take a deterministic or probabilistic view of causation, and whether they use a configurational approach.

Statistical Comparison in Comparative-Historical Analysis

There are a number of subtypes of statistical comparison, yet all share a number of basic elements. As a matter of convenience, I lump them together and focus on their commonalities. The fundamental characteristic that defines all statistical methods is the operationalization of variables and the testing of relationships between them among a large number of cases. In operationalizing variables and testing relationships, statistics attempts to approximate controlled experiments by using natural variation among cases to explore whether certain variables are systematically related to one another. The basic assumption of statistical methods is that strong relationships between variables provide evidence—albeit inconclusive—of a causal relationship. Spurious relationships can and do occur but, at the very least, statistical methods pinpoint factors with a heightened possibility of being causally related. So, if population density is strongly and positively related to revolutions, statistical methods offer evidence that the two might be causally related.

Statistical methods are unique among the various comparative methods used within comparative-historical analysis because they formally estimate causal effects. For this, statistical methods average the relationships between variables among a set of cases and calculate coefficients showing either how a change in one variable is associated with a change in another or how a change in one variable is associated with a change in the risk of a particular outcome. For example, an analysis might find that an increase in secondary school enrollment rate of ten percent is associated with an increase in GDP growth of one percent. Similarly, an analysis might find that an increase in secondary school enrollment rate of ten percent among authoritarian regimes increases the risk of democratic onset by twenty percent. Notably, these examples suggest a linear relationship between variables, where an increase in education by x is always associated with an increase in the dependent variable—either economic growth or the risk of democratic onset—by y. Statistical methods are also capable of investigating non-linear relationships as well. Thus, a statistical analysis might find that a unit increase in secondary school enrollment rate has a relatively large impact on GDP growth or democratization when the overall level of education is low but a relatively small effect when the level of education is already high.

Statistical methods are probabilistic. As a result, statistical findings do not suggest that the causal effect applies to all cases. Rather, they assume that the social world is complex and suggest that it is simply more likely that a case with characteristic x will experience outcome y when x and y are related.

Statistical methods have several important strengths. Most notably, they offer a powerful means of general insight, as they explore relationships across a large set of cases. Therefore, researchers pursuing nomothetic explanations commonly use statistical comparison. Moreover, standard multivariate statistical techniques allow researchers to test simultaneously the relationships between several independent variables and a dependent variable. As a result, statistical methods are well suited for multi-causal explanations and for testing competing theories. Statistics also allows researchers to estimate causal effects. Finally, statistical methods are extremely formalized, with set rules about appropriate procedures and the interpretation of results. Such formalization, in turn, makes statistical analyses easy to replicate.

In addition to these strengths, statistical methods have weaknesses. Most notably, statistical findings generally offer very little insight into whether relationships are causal or spurious because statistical methods do not analyze actual causal processes. Similarly, they offer little or no insight into mechanisms. Moreover, the accuracy and validity of the statistical findings are always open to question for two additional reasons. First, the results of statistical analyses depend on the models selected by the researcher, and there is no set procedure for selecting the most appropriate model. As a consequence, different statistical analyses of the same dependent variable commonly generate different results. Second, statistical analysis is based on numerous assumptions, and these assumptions are rarely met. Most notably, statistical methods assume unit homogeneity, the absence of any systematic relationship between the independent variables included in the model and any other factors that are related to the dependent variable but are not included in the models, the ability of interaction terms included in the models to capture all interaction effects among the independent variables, and the lack of case interdependence (Wallerstein, M. 2000).

Despite their popularity in nearly all social scientific disciplines, researchers from the comparative-historical tradition use statistical methods only rarely. There are two principal reasons for the historic unpopularity of statistics within comparative-historical analysis. First, the logic of within-case analysis is very different from statistical analysis, and within-case analysis has been the most prominent method of comparative-historical analysis. On the other hand, small-N comparisons are easily combined with within-case analysis and are therefore the most common comparative methods used by comparative-historical researchers. Second, comparative-historical researchers usually analyze fewer than ten cases and rarely analyze enough cases to use statistical comparison. Researchers who use statistical methods for comparative-historical analysis usually circumvent the small-N problem in one of two ways: by using panel data for a time-series analysis of the cases or by expanding the set of cases of the comparative analysis beyond the set analyzed in the within-case analysis.

Although rare for these reasons, statistical comparison is used by an increasing number of comparative-historical researchers to provide insight into causal determinants. Huber and Stephens's *Development and Crisis of the Welfare State* (2001) is one notable example. The book analyzes both the causes of welfare state development and the factors that promoted welfare-state retrenchment during the 1980s and 1990s. Although the authors also depend heavily on small-N comparison, their main comparative method is statistical. They use cross-national time-series statistical methods to explore the correlates of both welfare state expansion and retrenchment among all democratic welfare states. This particular method gains insight from both comparing different cases and comparing the same case over time. For example, the statistical analysis on welfare state expansion finds that different factors are strongly related to welfare state development, including a left-leaning cabinet, a centralized constitutional structure, and female labor force participation. The analysis therefore highlights general relationships and, thereby, offers insight into potential determinants of welfare state development.

Boolean Comparison

Comparative-historical researchers—and social scientists more generally—have only recently begun using Boolean algebra, and its growing (but limited) popularity is largely the result of Ragin's (1987, 2000) methodological work on qualitative comparative analysis (QCA) and fuzzy-sets. Like statistics, Boolean algebra provides generalizable insight by operationalizing variables for a set of cases and comparing them. It differs fundamentally in the way it compares them, however. Instead of analyzing the relationships between variables, Boolean algebra analyzes which configurations of causal variables produce positive and negative outcomes. In this way, it focuses on which configurations of causal factors are related to the outcome instead of analyzing the relationships between each causal factor and the outcome. Moreover, Boolean algebra explores necessary and sufficient causes, not linear relationships between variables, and it does not estimate causal effects. Although popularly known as Boolean algebra, I refer to this method as **Boolean comparison** in order to highlight that its insight is derived from inter-case comparison.

Ragin (1987) calls his first Boolean techniques "qualitative comparative analysis" (QCA). He refers to the method as qualitative because—like within-case methods—it takes a more holistic approach that focuses on how the configuration of factors shapes the outcome. At the same time, QCA's insight comes strictly from the comparison of cases, so it is hardly a within-case method. To make comparisons, QCA uses binary data measuring the independent and dependent variables. The researcher then constructs a "truth table," which shows every possible combination of the independent and dependent variables and the number of cases that possess each configuration of variables. Based on this information, the researcher is able to see which configurations produce positive outcomes and which configurations produce negative outcomes. As originally formulated by Ragin, QCA uses **deterministic comparative logic**. As a result, QCA only concludes that a certain configuration of independent variables is causally related to an outcome when all cases with the same configuration of independent variables have the same outcome.

To clarify how Boolean comparison works, Table 5.1 provides a hypothetical truth table on revolutions. Within the table, there are three causal factors that are considered in the analysis: state collapse (A), economic crisis (B), and population pressure (C). These independent variables and the dependent variable measuring revolution are dichotomous, with 1 representing the presence of the factor and 0 representing its absence. One can, therefore, look at the table and see which configurations are associated with revolutions and which are not. Notably, the table is simplified for presentation purposes, as a researcher will rarely have a table in which all cases with the same configuration of independent variables share the same outcome.

The table shows that three of the eight configurations are associated with revolutions: state collapse and population pressure; state collapse and economic crisis; and state collapse, economic crisis, and population pressure. Besides providing insight into the causal impact of configurations of

Table 5.1 Hypothetical truth table of revolutions

A	B	C	Outcome	Frequency
1	0	1	1	6
1	1	0	1	5
1	1	1	1	3
1	0	0	0	2
0	1	0	0	9
0	0	1	0	6
0	1	1	0	3
0	0	0	0	4

variables, the method is very different from standard statistical methods because it helps highlight necessary and sufficient causes through comparison. When a particular causal factor is present in every positive outcome, the analysis offers evidence that it is a necessary condition for the outcome. In the hypothetical truth table above (Table 5.1), state collapse (A) is present in every positive outcome, suggesting that it is necessary for revolution. The method also helps highlight sufficient conditions when the presence of a particular causal factor is always linked to a positive outcome. In the truth table above, state collapse (A) is associated with revolution in three of the four configurations. The table therefore suggests that it is not sufficient—a revolution requires either economic crisis (B) or population pressure (C) in addition to state collapse.

Ragin's more recent work, *Fuzzy-Set Social Science* (2000), is based on the same logic as QCA. **Fuzzy-set methods** modify QCA by allowing non-dichotomous scorings of the variables and incorporating a **probabilistic comparative logic** instead of a deterministic logic. He also creates a statistical program that can analyze the data and provide the p-values of the different configurations of independent variables. Different from standard statistics, however, these p-values highlight the probability that an independent variable or configuration of independent variables is a necessary or sufficient cause of the outcome.

Both types of Boolean comparison can only be used when several cases are under analysis, making it a type of large-N comparison. Yet, considerable knowledge is commonly needed to score the variables of each case because very few preexisting Boolean data sets exist, and this constrains the number of cases that can be analyzed through Boolean comparison. Moreover, Ragin emphasizes the need to limit the set of cases analyzed through Boolean comparison to promote case homogeneity. As a consequence of both of these issues, Boolean comparisons usually analyze fewer cases than statistical analyses and commonly are medium-N analyses with between fifteen and thirty cases.

Along with the number of cases under analysis, the number of independent variables used for Boolean comparisons is also more limited than in statistical comparison. Because the number of possible configurations among independent variables increases exponentially, they can get out of hand with more than half a dozen independent variables. As a consequence, researchers using this method must pay considerable attention to the relevance of causal factors and only include those that appear most influential. The method can, therefore, be inappropriate for causal processes that appear to be dependent on a large number of factors.

Boolean comparison has several analytic strengths and weaknesses. Like statistics, Boolean comparison is well-suited for pursuing nomothetic explanations, although the fewer number of cases that can be analyzed using Boolean comparison makes the method somewhat less advantaged than statistics in this regard. Boolean comparison also shares the greatest weakness of statistics: a very limited ability to analyze causal processes directly. Different from statistics, Boolean comparison is well suited to explore necessary and sufficient causes and to explore the causal impact of configurations of variables. It is disadvantaged relative to statistics, however, because it cannot estimate causal effects and can only include a more limited number of independent variables in its models.

Wickham-Crowley's *Guerrillas and Revolution in Latin America* (1993) offers one of the earliest works using Boolean comparison. He uses Boolean comparison only in the final chapter and employs it as a final synthesis and concluding analysis of the previous chapters. In particular, he scores the independent variables analyzed in the previous chapters and checks which configurations of variables are related to two dichotomously scored dependent variables: peasant support for revolutions and successful revolutions. For his analysis of peasant support, he analyses twenty regions within Latin America and includes four causal variables: agrarian structure, agrarian disruption, rebellious cultures, and peasant linkages. This Boolean analysis finds that many configurations of variables produced strong peasant support and provides evidence that all four factors can contribute to it. For his Boolean analysis of revolutionary success, Wickham-Crowley analyzes twenty-eight cases and includes five causal variables: guerrilla attempts, peasant/worker support, guerrilla military strength, patrimonial praetorian regime, and loss of US support of government. He finds that all five variables were present in cases with successful revolutions. In contrast, none of the unsuccessful revolutions had more than three of the five factors. All in all, the analysis provides strong evidence against monocausal explanations of both peasant revolutionary support and revolutionary success, and suggests that several factors—in combination with others—contribute to them.

Mahoney's *Colonialism and Postcolonial Development* (2010) offers another example of a comparative-historical analysis that employs Boolean comparison. The book explores the impact of colonialism on long-term development and focuses on the fifteen Spanish colonies on the American mainland, noting the considerable variation in development among this group. Mahoney's main method is causal narrative. He begins by providing a narrative analysis of Spanish colonialism in the Americas during two different periods of colonialism—mercantilist and liberal. Next, he uses brief causal narratives to analyze each of the colonies during both the mercantile period and the liberal period.

Although most of the insight from *Colonialism and Postcolonial Development* comes from causal narrative, Mahoney also uses Boolean comparison. In particular, he uses the data from his narrative analysis to make Boolean comparisons at the end of each analytic chapter. These comparisons serve two primary purposes. First, it can be extremely difficult for readers to process the findings of fifteen different case studies, and Boolean comparison offers a neat way of summarizing the findings of the causal narratives. Second, the Boolean comparisons offer a relatively simple and quick means of comparing all of the cases, thereby providing comparative insight into the research question.

Mahoney uses Boolean comparison in four instances: to explore the determinants of the level of colonialism during the mercantile period, to explore the relationship between mercantilist colonialism and levels of development, to explore the determinants of the level of colonialism during the liberal period, and to explore the determinants of postcolonial development. In Table 5.2 I have reproduced one of Mahoney's tables in order to show how he uses Boolean comparison. This table is from his analysis of the cause of levels of colonialism during the mercantilist era and includes complex indigenous society, significant mineral wealth, and proximity to imperial capital as the three main independent variables, which he scores as full member (1), partial member (0.5), or non-member (0). He scores the dependent variable

Table 5.2 Determinants of center, semiperipheral, and peripheral colonies: mercantilist era

Country	(A) Complex indigenous society	(B) Significant mineral wealth	(C) Near empire capital	A& (B v C)	(Y) Colonial center
Argentina	0.0	0.0	0.0	0.0	0.0
Bolivia	1.0	1.0	0.5	1.0	1.0
Chile	0.0	0.5	0.5	0.0	0.0
Colombia	1.0	0.5	0.0	0.5	0.5
Costa Rica	0.5	0.0	0.0	0.0	0.0
Ecuador	1.0	0.0	0.5	0.5	0.5
El Salvador	1.0	0.0	0.0	0.0	0.0
Guatemala	1.0	0.0	0.5	0.5	0.5
Honduras	0.5	0.0	0.0	0.0	0.0
Mexico	1.0	1.0	1.0	1.0	1.0
Nicaragua	0.5	0.0	0.0	0.0	0.0
Paraguay	0.0	0.0	0.0	0.0	0.0
Peru	1.0	1.0	1.0	1.0	1.0
Uruguay	0.0	0.0	0.0	0.0	0.0
Venezuela	0.5	0.0	0.0	0.0	0.0

Source: Mahoney 2010, 116

similarly, with 1 designating membership to the colonial core, 0.5 designating membership to the colonial semiperiphery, and 0 designating membership to the colonial periphery.

Through the comparative analysis, he finds that all former colonies that received scores of either 0.5 or 1 on the dependent variable received scores of 1 on complex indigenous society, suggesting that it was necessary for a moderate level of colonialism. In order for cases to have a score of 1 on the dependent variable, however, he finds that either significant mineral wealth or proximity to the imperial capital must have a score of 1. Alternatively, when either significant mineral wealth or proximity to the imperial capital are 0.5, the dependent variable is also 0.5; and, if both significant mineral wealth and proximity to the empire are 0, the dependent variable is also 0. The Boolean comparisons, therefore, offer evidence that a complex indigenous society was necessary for more intensive colonialism but that the latter also required either mineral wealth or proximity to imperial capitals.

Small-N Comparisons within Comparative-Historical Analysis

Comparative-historical researchers usually compare only a few cases and are therefore unable to use either statistical or Boolean comparison. **Small–N comparison**, in turn, is well adapted to maximize the insight that can be gained from a small number of cases and has a much stronger affinity with within-case analysis. As a result, small-N comparison is much more common in comparative-historical analysis and is viewed by some as the only real comparative method within the comparative-historical toolkit.

Unlike large-N comparison, comparative-historical researchers rarely use small-N comparison for independent comparative insight for the simple reason that small-N comparison offers little or no independent insight. Instead, researchers usually combine small-N comparison with within-case methods, an issue discussed in considerable depth in Chapter 6. The combination of small-N comparison and within-case methods is usually so complete that it can be difficult to separate the two. Similarly, the insight of small-N comparison and within-case analysis cannot be easily separated, as both are commonly intertwined within the same narrative and strengthen one another.

Although small-N comparison can offer nomothetic insight when combined with within-case methods, the insight offered by small-N comparison is usually much more circumscribed, and researchers using small-N comparison rarely make very broad claims based on small-N findings; rather, they usually consider scope conditions that limit the generalizability of their findings. One reason for this tendency is that small-N comparisons are also commonly used to highlight differences. Moreover, their combination with within-case methods usually forces researchers to pay greater attention to detail. Finally, small-N comparisons analyze only a few cases, and this numeric limitation hinders broad nomothetic explanations. For these three reasons, researchers using small-N comparison almost always make much weaker nomothetic claims than researchers who use large-N comparison.

There are two main subtypes of small-N comparison, each of which can be further divided into multiple subtypes. Narrative comparison is the most common type of small-N comparison, although methodologists have largely ignored it. In contrast, Millian comparison has been a topic of heated debate within comparative-historical analysis, with some claiming that it is the main method used by comparative-historical researchers and others claiming that it is a worthless technique.

Narrative Comparison

Narrative comparison differs from all other types of comparison used by comparative-historical researchers because it does not analyze relationships between variables. This is because the entities it compares are not measured numerically and are compared through a narrative analysis—hence the name *narrative* comparison. Narrative comparison is widely used by comparative-historical researchers but largely ignored by methodologists, possibly because it is perceived as part of the within-case analysis. Mahoney (2000b) and Rueschemeyer and Stephens (1997) are exceptions in this regard, as both recognize narrative comparison as a powerful source of insight (although Mahoney calls it causal narrative and Rueschemeyer and Stephens refer to it loosely as comparing historical sequences).

Like all types of comparison, narrative comparison can be an initial means of generalizing causal arguments, although it is relatively disadvantaged in this regard. It is advantaged over all other comparative methods, however, because it can offer many of the same benefits of narrative analysis—such as taking a more holistic account, comparing the actual sequences leading to the outcomes, and noting the influence of events (see Abbott 1990, 1992, 1995; Mahoney 1999, 2000b; Rueschemeyer and Stephens 1997). Considering the first benefit, narrative comparison is able to compare holistic phenomena, not variables measuring one element of a phenomenon. For example, a narrative comparison is able to consider complete institutional structures instead of a single characteristic of institutions. Further, narrative comparison can analyze processes and events, allowing researchers to explore actual causal processes and highlight the most influential factors in the processes.

Given the fundamental differences, it is helpful to consider how the different sorts of comparison are used to analyze the same topic. A variable-oriented comparative study of the impact of religion on state building, for example, would likely explore whether the religious composition of a country is related to state effectiveness, thereby showing a correlation between the segment of the population of a particular religion and the strength of the state. Along these lines, LaPorta et al. (1999) make a cross-national statistical analysis and find that certain religions are associated with more or less effective political institutions. Such an analysis can be problematic both because the independent variable might not capture the aspect of religion that affects state building and because data on state effectiveness are generally quite poor (especially for historical cases).

Gorski (2003) uses narrative comparisons in *The Disciplinary Revolution* to explore this same issue in Early Modern Europe but in a much more detailed fashion that allows him to compare more causally relevant factors. First, he uses narrative comparison to compare elements of religious doctrines that might affect self-discipline and following authority, noting that the Calvinist creed had the most powerful disciplining elements. He also uses narrative comparison to compare different processes and mechanisms affecting state building. Specifically, he notes how three events—the Papal Schism, the Protestant Reformation, and precisionist revolutions—promoted greater venality among Catholic countries than Protestant countries and thereby facilitated state bureaucratization in the latter relative to the former. Finally, his narrative comparisons consider aspects of states—such as institutional structure and organizational capacity—that are not easily measured numerically. Thus, Gorski's narrative comparisons are much better able to highlight causally relevant factors than imprecise variables because of their greater attention to detail, and their focus on processes and mechanisms. In this way, their insight does not come from simply highlighting a relationship; it usually highlights actual processes and mechanisms.

Narrative comparison is also quite distinctive because researchers commonly use it to gain both nomothetic and ideographic insight, whereas all other comparative methods are used almost exclusively for nomothetic insight. As a comparative method, narrative comparison offers insight into multiple cases and can, therefore, be a source of nomothetic insight. Different from large-N comparison, however, narrative comparison usually makes much more limited general claims, as it has difficulty making nomothetic explanations based on the comparison of a few cases. Gorski, for example, does not compare all world religions at all periods but focuses on a few European countries during a particular period. As a result, his findings offer direct insight into how religion affected state building in Early Modern Europe but not beyond this region or time period (although they can only be used to guide subsequent analyses of religion and state building in other regions and time periods). Narrative comparison's greater attention to detail also limits nomothetic insight, as detailed comparisons inevitably highlight differences as well as similarities. Gorski's narrative comparisons, for example, highlight incongruence preventing broad nomothetic claims. Although disliked by those attempting nomothetic explanations, highlighting incongruence is very valuable because it helps prevent overgeneralizations. Along these lines, Reinhard Bendix, a master of narrative comparison, claimed that "comparative analysis is a weapon to be wielded against closed theories of history, as well as grand deductive theories" (1984, xiii). In addition, highlighting differences helps pinpoint additional causal factors affecting the cases, something that strengthens the within-case analysis and thereby contributes to ideographic explanations.

As noted above, narrative comparisons are advantaged over large-N comparisons because they are able to make more detailed comparisons that offer greater insight into causal processes, but they also have disadvantages. For example, narrative comparisons require considerable time and effort, as a researcher must gather and assemble considerable data. Relatedly, narrative comparisons—almost of necessity—analyze a small number of cases. This is not only because of the time and effort that they require, but also because it is very cumbersome to make narrative comparisons for more than a few cases. The smaller number of cases, in turn, limits the nomothetic insight that can be gained from narrative comparison. Finally, narrative comparison depends on within-case methods and offers little or no independent insight. As a consequence, it cannot be used as a sole method of analysis.

Based on the object of comparison, comparative-historical researchers employ three main subtypes of narrative comparison: process-oriented, mechanistic, and ideal-typical comparisons. Each type of narrative comparison helps strengthen the within-case analysis. They also offer different analytic benefits. Process-oriented comparison is advantaged at exploring diverse factors causing similarities and differences and is, therefore, ideal for exploratory analyses that consider a broad array of potential causes. Mechanistic comparison, on the other hand, is much more focused and offers insight into mechanisms and the contextual factors affecting mechanisms. Finally, ideal-typical comparison combines elements of the previous two, as it can be used to explore similarities and differences but focuses on particular factors. It is also the most theory dependent, requiring that researchers have developed ideal types that offer insight into the research question.

Process-Oriented Comparison

Process-oriented comparison is a common subtype of narrative comparison. To use it, researchers must highlight causal processes for multiple cases and subsequently compare the processes to explore similarities and differences. Process-oriented comparisons are, therefore, usually matched with causal narratives. When researchers make process-oriented comparisons to explore similarities among cases, they frequently attempt to show how the cases share key elements of the causal process and to highlight factors that promote their similar outcomes. Because all processes are unique, the comparisons can highlight only general commonalities that contributed to similar outcomes, not identical processes. When researchers use process-oriented comparisons to highlight inter-case differences, on the other hand, they usually compare cases with similar starting points but different outcomes. In this way, process-oriented comparison contrasts processes leading to different outcomes in order to highlight the factors that caused the cases to diverge.

The primary analytic role played by process-oriented narrative comparison is offering insight that improves the strength of the within-case analyses. Regardless of whether they highlight similarities or differences, process-oriented comparisons implicitly rely on **counterfactuals**. That is, the researcher weighs the evidence from the within-case analysis and considers what would have happened if a case was similar to or different from another case in one or more ways. The comparisons, therefore, force researchers to go through the mental game of considering the causal impact of a factor and what could have happened if this factor had been present or absent. Similarly, the comparison of different processes can help highlight key similarities and differences that appear causally relevant. Once highlighted, the researcher is then able to explore whether these similarities and differences are causally relevant through within-case analysis.

Process-oriented comparisons generally have a broad focus. They are therefore the most appropriate form of narrative comparison when the researcher does not have a particular focus, something that is common among exploratory analyses. Because they are well-paired with causal narrative, they also are well-suited for analyses that use the latter as their secondary within-case method. Within this broad focus, researchers can further focus on diverse elements of processes, including sequencing, interactions and configurations, exogenous factors, and critical events.

One book that provides examples of process-oriented comparison is my *Lineages of Despotism and Development* (Lange 2009), in which I explore the developmental legacies of British colonialism and make several different process-oriented comparisons between four different former British colonies: Botswana, Guyana, Mauritius, and Sierra Leone. The purpose of each comparison is to highlight similarities and differences in processes that led to similar and dissimilar outcomes and, therefore, to increase insight gained from the within-case analysis. For example, I make process-oriented comparisons of Mauritius and Guyana in order to highlight factors that explain their different outcomes despite their similar origins: both cases had very similar political, economic, and social environments up until the early 1950s, but their developmental trajectories diverged at that time. In turn, the process-oriented comparison of the two highlights different processes leading to independence as the key to their divergent trajectories. In Mauritius, the colonial government and the most powerful party collaborated and combined their efforts to strengthen the state and provide public goods. In Guyana, on the other hand, the colonial government removed the strongest party from power because of its anti-colonial and Marxist rhetoric, and this event led to conflict between the colonizers and colonized—thereby impeding state reforms and expansion. At the same time, the conflict created a strong rift between Afro- and Indo-Guyanese, and this conflict hindered state building and reform even further. Thus, the process-oriented comparison highlights different state transformations as an important cause of the divergent trajectories of Guyana and Mauritius and helps pinpoint the causes of these different state transformations.

In the book, I also employ process-oriented comparisons to explore potential factors promoting similar outcomes. For example, I use a process-oriented comparison of Mauritius and Botswana to explore how Botswana was able to avoid the more negative developmental legacy commonly associated with indirect rule. The comparison highlights that Mauritius and Botswana experienced very similar political reforms during the transition period and that the reforms in Botswana undermined its indirect form of rule and created a relatively unified, large, and bureaucratic state in a relatively short period of time. A process-oriented comparison with other directly and indirectly ruled colonies, in turn, shows that such extensive and successful reforms were very rare among indirectly ruled colonies and quite common among directly ruled colonies, suggesting that the late colonial reforms were an important factor underlying the superior developmental performance of directly ruled colonies, as well as Botswana's rather unexpected developmental improvements.

Although process-oriented comparison is a type of narrative comparison, some researchers have attempted to formalize the technique in different ways that make it a comparison of operationalized variables. Abbott (Abbott and Forrest 1986; Abbott and Tsay 2000), for example, has written extensively about optimal matching—which uses techniques first developed for studying sequences of DNA—to analyze sequences in social processes. This technique requires the coding of sequences and then allows researchers to compare them—either over time or between cases—to explore similarities and differences. For example, Abbott and Hrycak (1990) analyze the sequences in the careers of a sample of eighteenth-century German musicians and find that there were a limited number of sequential routes that led to the top positions. Although optimal matching could be used by comparative-historical researchers, it has not been used for comparative-historical analysis to date because of the costs associated with learning the technique as well as its more limited applicability to comparative-historical analysis. Concerning the latter, comparative-historical researchers generally focus on more macro-level processes, and such processes can be quite difficult to code for optimal matching. In addition, optimal matching simply focuses on sequences, but most comparative-historical researchers use process-oriented comparisons to analyze several additional aspects of social processes.

Mechanistic Comparison

Ultimately, my process-oriented comparison of Mauritius, Guyana, Botswana, and other former British colonies highlights state-centered mechanisms that help to explain the diverse developmental legacies among former British colonies. Indeed, most process-oriented comparisons highlight causal mechanisms. These comparisons are not **mechanistic comparisons**, however, because process-oriented comparisons focus on processes more broadly and consider how processes unroll to gain insight into mechanisms. Alternatively, mechanistic comparisons explicitly focus on mechanisms linking causes and outcomes; thus, mechanisms— not processes—are compared. Most commonly, mechanistic comparison explores whether the absence or presence of mechanisms helps to explain similar or different outcomes among multiple cases. Mechanistic comparisons also frequently analyze contextual factors that shape mechanisms, exploring either how similar contexts promote the presence or absence of a mechanism or how different contexts cause the presence of the mechanism in one case but not another. For those who believe that mechanistic analysis must pay close attention to context (see Falleti and Lynch 2009), mechanistic comparisons are therefore vital.

Similar to process-oriented comparison, mechanistic comparison helps to strengthen within-case analysis. Important analytic differences exist between the two, however. Relative to process-oriented comparison, mechanistic comparison is generally used when researchers are more interested in nomothetic explanations. This is because causal processes are unique, but mechanisms are bits of mid-level theory that can usually be applied to numerous cases. Analyses using mechanistic comparisons are also usually less exploratory and much more focused than analyses using process-oriented comparisons.

Comparative-historical researchers have made mechanistic comparisons for some time, but such comparisons have become more common and explicit in recent years. One reason for their growing prominence is that comparative-historical researchers have placed more and more importance on mechanistic analysis. Relatedly, the rise of process tracing as a within-case method explicitly focuses on discovering causal mechanisms, and the method therefore privileges mechanistic comparison.

Charles Tilly's comparative-historical work pays considerable attention to mechanisms, and many of his comparative-historical analyses make mechanistic comparisons; *Contention and Democracy in Europe, 1650–2000* (2004) provides a notable example. It analyzes the competing historic trends of democratization and de-democratization in several countries, focusing on the Netherlands, Iberia, France, the British Isles, and Switzerland. His main argument is that democratization is inherently a contentious process and one that depends on three things: the segregation of categorical inequalities from public politics, the integration of trust networks into public politics, and the expansion of the breadth and complementarity of state–society relations. One major finding, in turn, is that the construction of powerful states promotes all three in different ways.

Despite his pursuit of general insight into democratization processes, Tilly notes that no two countries democratize in the same way, and sets out to explore the different ways countries have arrived at similar points. For this, he begins by outlining different mechanisms that can promote the three main determinants of democratization. Notably, he recognizes six mechanisms that can promote the segregation of categorical inequalities from public politics, eight mechanisms that help integrate trust networks into public politics, and seven mechanisms that promote state–society relations (Tilly 2004, 18–20). (To give an idea of what his mechanisms are like, Table 5.3 reproduces part of Tilly's own table and lists the six mechanisms that can promote the segregation of categorical inequalities from public politics.) For the remainder of *Contention and Democracy in Europe, 1650–2000*, Tilly uses case studies to highlight these twenty-one mechanisms in action and to show how

Table 5.3 Tilly's mechanisms segregating categorical inequalities from public politics

1 Dissolution of governmental controls (e.g., legal restrictions on property holding) that support current unequal relations among social categories; for example, wholesale confiscation and sale of church property weakens established ecclesiastical power.
2 Equalization of assets and/or well-being across categories within the population at large; for example, booming demand for the products of peasant agriculture expands middle peasants.
3 Reduction or governmental containment of privately controlled armed forces; for example, disbanding of magnates' personal armies weakens noble control over commoners.
4 Adoption of devices that insulate public politics from categorical inequalities; for example, secret ballots, payment of officeholders, and free, equal access of candidates to media forward formation of cross-category coalitions.
5 Formation of politically active coalitions and associations cross-cutting categorical inequality; for example, creation of region-wide mobilizations against governmental property seizures crosses categorical lines.
6 Wholesale increases of political participation, rights, or obligations that cut across social categories; for example, governmental annexation of socially heterogeneous territories promotes categorically mixed politics.

Source: Tilly 2004, 18

they affect democratization. Of greater interest here, he also uses narrative comparison to explore similarities and differences among the cases. Although also analyzing processes, these comparisons differ from process-oriented comparisons because of their more explicit focus on causal mechanisms.

As a percentage of the total book, the mechanistic comparisons made by Tilly are very limited; however, one can see that Tilly constantly made mechanistic comparisons while completing the entire analysis. In his most elaborate mechanistic comparison, Tilly compares France and the British Isles (2004, 164–7). Through this comparison, he highlights four key mechanistic similarities. First, he notes that democratization occurred very differently in each place, with political change driven by revolutionary breakthroughs in France but a more gradual, step-by-step expansion in the British Isles. Despite these differences, the comparison highlights similar processes and mechanisms that pushed the countries toward democratization. For instance, the comparison highlights the state's containment and reduction of private armies as an influential mechanism limiting categorical inequalities. Second, Tilly finds that the destruction of patronage networks created opportunities for more encompassing trust-networks that are integrated into public politics. In both cases, the demise of the nobility and the growth of bourgeois and working classes facilitated this process. Third, Tilly highlights how both France and Britain experienced shifts in political identity from more parochial and particular to more encompassing and cosmopolitan. Finally, he notes that religion promoted de-democratization in both cases by strengthening categorical inequalities in public politics, with Catholics being excluded in the British Isles and Protestants being excluded in France.

Tilly employs the comparisons to help highlight common mechanisms, thereby showing how seemingly different processes were, in actuality, driven by similar mechanisms. In this way, the mechanistic comparisons do not provide new insight into the research question, and primary causal insight is gained through within-case methods. The comparisons remain valuable in two ways, however. First, they restate more clearly and forcefully findings from the within-case analysis. Second, they demonstrate that the mechanisms hold across cases and, therefore, show that the mechanisms are not particular to one case. Similar mechanistic comparisons between other cases do the same and allow Tilly to create a strong argument for his theory of democratization.

In addition to comparisons that focus on mechanisms, Tilly also compares contexts and notes how they affect mechanisms. I refer to these as **contextualizing mechanistic comparisons**. He pays most attention to the strength of states and finds that they have important effects on the three categories of mechanisms. For example, he compares Spain, Portugal, France, and Great Britain and notes that rapid democratization was possible in all four because it occurred at a time when powerful states were already present (2004, 238). He contrasts these cases with post-revolutionary and post-cold-war Russia and finds that the country's much more limited state capacity obstructed the three general democratizing mechanisms (238). Ultimately, these contextualizing comparisons are process tracing in reverse: instead of starting with a relationship and then searching for mechanisms underlying it, contextualizing comparisons begin with mechanisms and then show how the presence and strength of the mechanisms depends on certain factors, thereby inferring that there should be a relationship between the contextual factor (that is, state strength) and the outcome (that is, democratization).

Tilly's contextualizing mechanistic comparisons—and contextualizing comparisons in general—help to highlight factors that shape the presence and strength of mechanisms. Within-case analysis can also highlight scope conditions, but contextualizing comparisons force researchers to consider more rigorously how different environments affect the mechanisms.

Ideal-Typical Comparison

Ideal–typical comparison is the final subtype of narrative comparison. As its name implies, researchers use it to explore the extent to which cases conform to ideal types. Such comparisons help to pinpoint causal determinants in two ways: the ideal type serves as an heuristic device by highlighting what needs to be explained and the ideal type itself offers hypothetical explanations of patterned action.

As mentioned in Chapter 2, ideal types were first employed by Max Weber in his effort to find an appropriate middle-position between the extremes of ideographic and nomothetic analysis. He believed that attempts to discover abstract covering laws are doomed to fail because they lose touch with reality and provide little or no insight into real-world events. Most importantly, they ignore variation in social phenomena, something that must be explained by social scientific analysis. Alternatively, however, Weber disagreed with extremely historical analysis that portrays every event as unique. He felt that this type of analysis fails to acknowledge that social processes can occur in similar ways and have similar causes. Ideal types, he believed, allow social scientists to use abstract concepts like covering laws in a way that allows the researchers to see both similarities and differences among cases, both general trends and particular characteristics.

According to Weber, an ideal type is "formed by the one-sided accentuation of one or more points of view and by the synthesis of a great many diffuse, discrete, more or less present and occasionally absent concrete individual phenomena, which are arranged according to those one-sidedly emphasized viewpoints into a unified analytical construct" (Weber 1904/1997: 88). In this way, ideal types are abstractions of reality—that is, ideas—that overemphasize one element of a phenomenon and ignore all other elements, even if the other elements have important effects on the phenomenon. Despite being mental constructs, one does not create ideal types simply through thought experiments. A researcher must have a thorough knowledge of the social phenomenon under question in order to know the common characteristics and patterns of the phenomenon, as the ideal types must capture and accentuate these common features.

For an ideal-typical comparative analysis, one first analyzes the extent to which the cases conform to one or more ideal types. This step therefore involves a comparison of the cases with the ideal type. Next, the researcher investigates the factor or group of factors that cause cases to conform to ideal types to different extents. As part of this analysis, researchers also compare their cases both to see differences in the extent to which they conform to the ideal type and to explore causes of similarities and differences. Ideal-typical comparison, therefore, commonly involves a double comparison between case and ideal type and between cases.

Weber's work is overflowing with ideal types. Most notably, his most celebrated work, *Economy and Society* (1922/1968), lays out diverse ideal types governing a great variety of social relations. Among his most famous are his ideal types of social action. He believed individuals act for a multitude of reasons and created four ideal types that capture distinct reasons for action. First, instrumental-rational action occurs through a cost-benefit calculation in order to fulfill the needs of the actor. value-rational action, on the other hand, is action that is guided by a value or set of values. As such, it involves people acting rationally in ways that follow their values. Weber's third ideal type is affective action, or action that occurs simply out of feelings, attachments, and emotions. Finally, traditional action involves action that occurs through habit. Similar to affective action, traditional action occurs almost automatically without an individual thinking about how to act.

Weber noted that it is difficult—if not impossible—to find a real case of social action that conforms completely to one of his ideal types. In reality, social action usually conforms only partially to an ideal type—and it usual for it to partially conform to multiple ideal types simultaneously. For example, a vengeful act can be affective to the extent that anger motivates it, instrumental-rational to the extent that the perpetrator considers and plans an appropriate retributory act, value-rational to the extent that the form of retribution is planned in a way that conforms with dominant values, and traditional to the extent that it follows a precedent.

Since Weber, ideal types have only rarely been used in comparative-historical analysis (although typological theory and analysis approximates it in some ways [see Collier, LaPorte, and Seawright 2012]). This is something of a paradox because Weber is nearly universally celebrated as the most brilliant and influential comparative-historical researcher and theorist of all time, and because social scientists recognize Weber's ideal types as the most important and ground-breaking element of his work. Thus, in his work on Weber's methods, Kalberg (1994) laments that Weber's thoughts are very much alive but his methods neglected and unused. One reason for this paradox is, simply, that many researchers do not understand what ideal types actually are, as they are taught in courses on social theory instead of social methods. For those researchers who do understand what ideal types are, an ideal-typical analysis is a time-consuming undertaking, as it requires considerable effort to create ideal types and to provide an ideal-typical analysis.

Given the scarcity of recent works making ideal-typical comparisons and the exceptional work of the creator of ideal types, Weber's own work offers the best examples of ideal-typical comparisons in action. His interest in the impact of religion on capitalist development is probably his most famous work making ideal-typical comparisons. This body of work extends beyond *The Protestant Ethic and the Spirit of Capitalism* (1905/2001) to include several additional analyses of the world's major religions and their impact on economic action. The findings of this body of work are quite complex and cannot adequately be presented in a few paragraphs. Here, I present a grossly simplified summary that focuses on his use of ideal types.

The ideal type of social action that Weber focuses on for these works is value-rational action, and he considers how different religious values shape economic activities. In *The Protestant Ethic and the Spirit of Capitalism*, Weber develops a more specific ideal type of value-rational action: the Calvinist. This Calvinist ethic promoted two types of economic action that, according to Weber, helped promote capitalist development: hard work and the reinvestment of profits. Weber's Calvinist ideal type combines both and emphasizes work for work's sake.

Within *The Protestant Ethic and the Spirit of Capitalism*, Weber compares different religions to the Calvinist ideal type and, in turn, compares Calvinism with Catholicism and other Protestant sects. He shows that his Calvinist ideal type of economic action was powerful among Calvinists, weaker among other Protestant sects, and weakest among Catholics. Comparison is, therefore, used to highlight the different extents to which religions conform to the ideal type. In showing that other Christian sects do not conform to the ideal type as closely as Calvinism, Weber offers evidence that the Calvinist ethic might have contributed to capitalist development. However, this evidence is weak, and the comparison of the religions with the ideal types therefore plays more of a role in formulating hypotheses.

In order to look into these findings/hypotheses further, Weber completed subsequent analyses of Confucianism and Taoism in China, and Buddhism and Hinduism in India. These analyses were focused on the impact of the religions on capitalist development. Weber found that some religions were more favorable to capitalist development than others but that the Calvinist ideal type of economic action was absent from all, as no other religious creed promoted a hard work ethic and the reinvestment of profits through value-rational action. All together, his work therefore raises the possibility that the Calvinist ethic contributed to the rise of capitalism in Western Europe and New England.

Millian Comparison

Millian comparison is a type of small–N comparison with affinities to both large–N comparison and narrative comparison. It is similar to narrative comparison because it compares only a few cases, thus making it a type of small–N comparison. Alternatively, Millian comparison is closer to large–N comparison in other aspects. For one, it is possible to complete a Millian comparison without within-case analysis. Moreover, and most notably, it operationalizes variables and explores relationships. According to one of the first researchers to discuss the methods of comparative-historical analysis, Millian comparison is "the mode of multivariate analysis to which one resorts when there are too many variables and not enough cases" (Skocpol 1979, 36).

According to Mahoney (1999), Millian comparison is divided into two distinct types: nominal and ordinal. **Nominal comparison** operationalizes variables dichotomously, generally accepts a deterministic comparative logic, and therefore parallels Boolean comparison. They are hardly identical, however, as Millian comparison only rarely takes a configurational approach. Alternatively, **ordinal comparison** operationalizes variables along a scale with at least three scores (low, medium, and high) and explores the covariation of independent and dependent variables. For this, they employ a probabilistic comparative logic. Notably, a researcher could also make interval-level Millian comparisons using continuous data, but such comparisons are very rare because the complex concepts compared through Millian comparison usually lack interval-level data.

Although comparative-historical researchers use both nominal and ordinal comparisons, Mahoney notes that it is inappropriate to combine nominal and ordinal comparisons in the same analysis. This is because only nominal comparison uses deterministic standards, and the latter are more stringent than probabilistic standards. Authors cannot justify using a more stringent standard in one instance but a more lax standard in another. If nominal comparisons are used probabilistically instead of deterministically (something that is possible but rare), however, the use of both ordinal and nominal comparison in the same analysis is not a problem.

Both nominal and ordinal Millian comparisons conform to the comparative methods outlined by John Stuart Mill. In particular, researchers have attempted to use his methods of agreement, difference, and concomitant variation, with the first two using nominal comparison and the latter using ordinal comparison. The **method of agreement** compares independent and dependent variables, with all variables measured nominally. It can only offer insight when all independent variables but one differ, with the method highlighting the common variable as the causal determinant. Thus, if one case has causal factors A B C D, another case has the causal factors a b c D, and both share the outcome Z, then the method highlights D as the cause of Z. Mill's **indirect method of difference** is a variation of the method of agreement that includes a second step. After using the method of agreement to highlight a common cause, the researcher analyzes additional cases without the outcome to see whether or not the factor that was highlighted previously through the method of agreement is absent. If it is present, the findings of the first step must be rejected.

Contrary to the method of agreement, the **method of difference** compares cases with different nominally-scored dependent variables. According to Mill, the method offers insight only when all of the independent variables but one are similar among a set of cases, and the comparative method therefore highlights the one difference as the cause of the dissimilar outcomes. Thus, for a case with the outcome Z with causal factors A B C D and another case with the outcome z with the causal factors A B C d, the method highlights D as the cause of their divergent outcomes.

Finally, the **method of concomitant variation** explores whether the dependent variable varies according to the level of one or more independent variables. Thus, if the independent variables A1 B1 C1 produce Y1 (where the letter designates the variable and the number its level), and if the independent variables A1 B1 C2 produce Y2, the method shows how an increase in C is associated with an increase in Y. And, if one were to add a third case with the independent variables A1 B2 and C2 with outcome Y3, the method provides insight that both B and C shape the outcome. Different from the two previous methods that require nominal-level variables (i.e., one or zero), the method of concomitant variation requires ordinally scored variables in order to see whether an increase in an independent variable is associated with an increase in the dependent variable. Because a real-world analysis using this method very rarely produces relationships with a perfect correlation, the method of concomitant variation accepts a more probabilistic view of causation. In this way, the method approximates a standard statistical analysis for a small set of cases whereas the other Millian methods are more similar to Boolean comparison.

Several early comparative-historical methodologists focused on Millian comparison as the main method of comparative-historical analysis. Skocpol, for example, was a pioneer in the methods of comparative-historical analysis and stressed the centrality of Millian comparison (see Skocpol 1979; Skocpol and Somers 1980). This view coincides with and was influenced by Przeworski and Teune's (1970) and Lijphart's (1971, 1975) methodological work, both of which were very influential in comparative politics in the 1970s and 1980s and suggested that comparison is the basis of insight in comparative-historical analysis. Over the past two decades, however, this view has been increasingly critiqued. Goldstone (1997), for example, notes that Mill himself recognized that his methods of agreement and difference are not appropriate for the social sciences because they are deterministic, and nearly all social phenomena cannot be analyzed deterministically because they have multiple causes and can arrive at the same outcome through different combinations of causal determinants (see Mill 1843/1949). Moreover, insight from the methods of agreement and difference requires that the cases are either completely the same except in one way or completely different except in one way—and both situations are extremely rare in the social world. Finally, if the method of concomitant variation is simply statistics with a small-N, the comparative insight gained from such an analysis is little or nothing because of insufficient degrees of freedom.

For these reasons, Goldstone is correct in concluding that Millian comparisons are not the main source of insight in comparative-historical analysis. That said, Millian comparisons can provide valuable insight *when combined with within-case analysis*. For such a combination, Millian comparisons supplement within-case methods in one of two ways. First, and most commonly, Millian comparisons are frequently used in an exploratory fashion to highlight factors that appear causally relevant. Then, within-case methods are employed to analyze whether the factors highlighted in the comparative analysis are actually influential. This can be a powerful combination, as mechanistic insight from the within-case analysis provides insight into whether the relationships established through Millian comparisons are causal. The second strategy is the reverse, with Millian comparison following within-case analysis. Such a strategy uses Millian comparisons to explore whether any of the causal factors highlighted in multiple within-case analyses help to explain the outcome across cases. If they do, the comparisons—in combination with the insight provided by within-case methods—offer general insight for a larger set of cases.

The small number of cases analyzed by Millian comparison is a source of both strength and weakness. Considering first the strengths of Millian comparison, the small number of cases allows researchers to operationalize variables through qualitative assessments of the evidence and thereby analyze complex phenomena that cannot be analyzed through large-N comparative methods because of the absence of an appropriate data set. Indeed, Millian comparisons rarely compare phenomena that are easily operationalized. Common examples of complex phenomena that are compared through Millian comparison include institutions, ideologies, discourses, and policies. At the same time, however, the small number of cases analyzed by Millian comparison places a severe limit on the independent insight that can be gained through Millian comparison. This can be a major problem because the method attempts large-N style comparisons to highlight relationships but does not usually have sufficient degrees of freedom to offer any independent comparative insight. As a consequence, Millian comparisons should never be used as the sole method of analysis, and—as described below and in Chapter 6 more thoroughly—comparative-historical researchers combine Millian comparison with within-case methods, using the latter to bolster the insight provided by the Millian analysis.

Millian comparison has both advantages and disadvantages relative to narrative comparison. Millian comparison compares variables, not processes, ideal types, or mechanisms. As a result, it has much more difficulty offering direct insight into causal processes. Relative to narrative comparison, however, Millian comparison is better able to guide subsequent within-case analyses by highlighting relationships for the within-case analyses to explore. Along these same lines, Millian comparison is also advantaged when highlighting relationships among a set of cases. Because of the latter, Millian comparison offers more nomothetic insight than narrative comparison.

One example of a work using Millian small-N comparsion is Charrad's *States and Women's Rights* (2001). Charrad analyzes Algeria, Morocco, and Tunisia and explores causes of variation of family law, with family law in Tunisia supporting women's rights the most, family law in Morocco supporting women's rights the least, and family law in Algeria falling between the two, although closer to Morocco. Her method of comparison conforms most closely to Mill's method of difference, although it shares some elements with Mill's method of concomitant variation. (Her dependent variable and the independent variable measuring state centralization are both measured ordinally, something that conforms to Mill's method of concomitant variation.) Charrad uses Millian comparison primarily to set up her subsequent analysis, and the latter comprises the overwhelming majority of the book. In particular, she notes in the introduction that all three countries were very similar in many important ways: they have kin-based tribal societies, are Islamic, are located in the same region, and all experienced French colonial rule. In contrast, she notes that they differ in one important way: they had different histories of state formation, especially with regard to state centralization. The comparison, therefore, highlights one factor that might account for the variation among the three cases.

The remainder of the analysis supplements this finding through comparative case studies of the three countries. Charrad begins the empirical analysis with a section showing strong historical, cultural, and institutional similarities among all three cases. This is followed by two related sections.

The first offers a historical analysis showing how the states in the three countries developed in different ways. This section focuses on the influence of both precolonial factors and French colonialism. She finds that the three states emerged from colonialism with different extents of centralization and control over social relations: the Tunisian state was very centralized, the Moroccan state was very decentralized, and the Algerian state was slightly more centralized than the Moroccan state. To arrive at these ordinal-level measurements of state centralization, Charrad uses narrative analysis to describe the institutions, thereby showing how researchers commonly combine Millian comparison with narrative analysis, using the latter (in part) to operationalize complex variables.

After highlighting differences in state institutional structure, Charrad's next section uses causal narrative to help to highlight ways in which state structure affected family law and women's rights in the three cases. This section conforms to process tracing, as it explores and highlights mechanisms underlying variation in state centralization and family law. She finds that decentralization empowered tribes, and the latter fiercely protected their male-dominated culture. As a consequence, the states in Morocco and Algeria ultimately depended on tribes for support and, therefore, protected their legal interests. In contrast, the Tunisian state effectively destroyed any remnant of tribal autonomy during the independence process, reforming the family law system in order to weaken the political power of tribes even further and thereby bolster their own power. Thus, Charrad finds evidence that the relationship highlighted through Millian comparison is causal and driven by struggles for power between central states and regional tribes.

As this example shows, Charrad uses the method of difference neither in a deterministic way nor as a source of independent insight. Rather, she uses the method to highlight one factor that might cause variation and employs additional methods to explore whether this relationship is causal. Charrad's work, therefore, shows how comparative-historical analysis gains insight from the combination of Millian comparison and within-case analysis. Most notably, Millian comparison operationalizes variables and shows relationships, within-case methods offer evidence that the relationships are causal, and together they offer explanations for a set of cases.

Summary

This chapter reviews the types of comparative methods used in comparative-historical analysis and highlights a great variety of comparative methods within the research tradition. Large-N comparison compares variables and offers independent insight by highlighting relationships among a large number of cases, but these relationships offer little or no insight into particular processes and mechanisms. The main goal of large-N comparison is nomothetic insight, or insight that can be applied to a larger set of cases. The two subtypes of large-N comparison are statistical and Boolean. Neither is very common in comparative-historical analysis, but the popularity of both is increasing because more and more comparative-historical researchers—especially political scientists—pursue nomothetic explanations. Statistical and Boolean comparisons differ markedly because the former focuses on the causal effects of particular independent variables whereas the latter explores whether configurations of independent variables are necessary or sufficient causes.

Narrative comparison and Millian comparison are the two main subtypes of small-N comparison. Millian comparison is similar to large-N comparison because it operationalizes and compares variables to explore relationships. Such comparisons follow the logic of John Stuart Mill's three methods of comparison, although they rarely if ever conform to them completely. Narrative comparison uses narratives—not variables—to compare complex social phenomena. It allows researchers to pay considerable attention to detail; makes possible a more holistic analysis; helps to pinpoint influential factors contributing to inter-case similarities and differences; and is able to analyze processes, mechanisms, and ideal types. The latter three, in turn, are important means of insight into causal processes, making narrative comparison an important means of causal insight.

Although small-N comparisons are able to offer explanations that apply to a larger set of cases, they are ill-suited to offering extremely nomothetic explanations because the limited number of cases severely limits the generalizability of their findings. Researchers pursuing highly nomothetic explanations should therefore use large-N comparison. A second key disadvantage of small-N comparisons is that they rarely offer independent insight and must, therefore, be combined with other methods. At the same time, one must note that these weaknesses also have their benefits: the common use of small-N comparison has forced researchers to use both comparative and within-case methods, thereby pushing them to grapple simultaneously with the general and the particular, and keeping them from getting lost in either the overly abstract or overly particular. This advantage—as well as the common interest among comparative-historical researchers to pursue a balance of nomothetic and ideographic explanations—helps to explain the relative popularity of small-N comparison in the research tradition.

Small-N comparison, therefore, requires a multi-method analysis. Comparative-historical researchers who use large-N comparison also commonly combine it with other methods even though large-N comparison offers independent insight. Combining methods is therefore a common element of comparative-historical analysis, and Chapter 6 explores how comparative-historical researchers combine methods.

Glossary

Boolean comparison: A type of large-N comparison more commonly referred to as Boolean algebra that was developed for social scientific analysis and popularized by Charles Ragin. It differs from statistical comparison in two key ways: it analyzes how the configurations of independent variables are related to the dependent variable among a set of cases, and offers insight into necessary and sufficient causes of the outcome.

Contextualizing mechanistic comparison: A particular type of mechanistic comparison that simultaneously compares mechanisms and contextual factors of multiple cases to explore scope conditions affecting causal mechanisms.

Counterfactual: Within social scientific analysis, a heuristic device used for within-case analysis that considers what would have happened if some aspect of a case had been different. It forces the researcher to consider the causal effect of factors but does not offer the researcher a way of assessing what really would have happened if the factors were different.

Deterministic comparative logic: A type of logic used for comparative analysis to assess the validity of general propositions. It suggests that a general proposition is proved invalid when one or more cases do not conform to the proposition.

Fuzzy-set methods: A type of Boolean comparison that can use either nominal-, ordinal-, or interval-level data and that does not analyze relationships deterministically.

Ideal-typical comparison: A type of narrative comparison developed by Max Weber that compares cases with ideal types.

Indirect method of difference: A more rigorous variation of the method of agreement that includes a second step. After using the method of agreement to highlight a common cause, the researcher analyzes additional cases without the outcome to see whether or not the factor that was highlighted previously through the method of agreement is absent. In this way, the indirect method of difference offers a check on the findings derived from the method of agreement.

Large-N comparison: A type of comparative method that gains independent insight by comparing multiple cases. Such analyses compare at least fifteen cases and explore whether independent variables are related to dependent variables. Statistical and Boolean comparisons are the two main large-N methods used in comparative-historical analysis.

Mechanistic comparison: A type of narrative comparison that compares mechanisms.

Method of agreement: A comparative method developed by John Stuart Mill that highlights a common cause among cases when the cases share the same outcome and have different scores for all of the independent variables but one. The method therefore highlights the sole similar independent variable as the common cause. The method of agreement is a common methodological strategy employed for nominal comparison.

Method of concomitant variation: A comparative method developed by John Stuart Mill that explores covariation between independent and dependent variables among a small number of cases. It applies the logical of statistical analysis to small-N analysis without actually using formal statistical methods. The method of concomitant variation is the main methodological strategy employed for interval comparison.

Method of difference: A comparative method developed by John Stuart Mill that highlights a cause of divergent outcomes among cases. The method highlights the cause of divergence when all of the independent variables but one are the same. The method therefore highlights the sole dissimilar independent variable as the cause of difference. The method of difference is a common methodological strategy employed for nominal comparison.

Millian comparison: A type of small-N comparison used in comparative-historical analysis and named after John Stuart Mill. It operationalizes variables for a small number of cases and explores relationships. Millian comparisons therefore apply large-N techniques to small-N comparison. The three main types of comparison discussed by Mill are the method of agreement, the method of difference, and the method of concomitant variation.

Narrative comparison: A type of small-N comparison commonly used in comparative-historical analysis. It is the sole comparative method that does not operationalize variables. Instead, it uses narratives to compare phenomena that cannot easily be operationalized numerically. Process-oriented, mechanistic, and ideal-typical comparisons are three types of narrative comparison.

Nominal comparison: A type of Millian comparison that measures data at the nominal level—that is, as either present (1) or absent (0)—and explores relationships between independent and dependent variables. Within comparative-historical analysis, it is generally used deterministically. Both the method of agreement and the method of difference use nominal comparison.

Ordinal comparison: A type of Millian comparison that measures data at the ordinal level—that is, on a scale with at least three points—and explores relationships between independent and dependent variables. It approximates statistical methods and is used for probabilistic analysis. The method of concomitant variation uses ordinal comparison.

Probabilistic comparative logic: A type of logic used for comparative analysis to assess the validity of general propositions. It suggests that a general proposition is not necessarily invalidated when one or more cases do not conform to the proposition. Instead, it considers a proposition valid when, on average, cases conform to the proposition. Statistical comparison uses probabilistic logic.

Process-oriented comparison: A type of narrative comparison that compares processes and sequences.

Small-N comparison: A type of comparative method that gains insight by comparing between two and ten cases. Such comparisons usually cannot offer independent insight and are therefore combined with other methods. Narrative and Millian comparison are the two main types of small-N comparison.

6

Combining Comparative and Within-Case Methods for Comparative-Historical Analysis

Comparative-historical methods are different from nearly all other major methodological traditions in the social sciences in that they are inherently mixed and combine both within-case and comparative methods. In addition, as described in Chapters 3 and 5, there are several types of comparative and within-case methods employed by comparative-historical researchers, and researchers very frequently use multiple types of comparative and within-case methods in a single analysis.

Although the previous chapters began to discuss the mixing of methods, this chapter brings these elements together and provides an overview of how comparative-historical researchers combine methods. It describes three combinatorial strategies that increase analytic insight: methodological triangulation, methodological complementarity, and methodological synergy. The chapter focuses primarily on combining comparative and within-case methods and describes the strengths of different methodological combinations.

Comparative-Historical Methods: A Review

Before considering how methods are combined in comparative-historical analysis, it is useful to review briefly the main comparative-historical methods described in Chapters 3 and 5. Table 6.1 lists the methods and their primary strengths and weaknesses.

Causal narrative is a detective-style within-case method that explores the causes of a particular social phenomenon. It has a superior ability to provide insight into causal determinants. Thus, if a researcher really wants

Table 6.1 Methodological strengths and weaknesses within comparative-historical analysis

Method	Strength	Weakness
Causal narrative	Offers causal insight into particular phenomena; Able to analyze complex processes and concepts	Findings are not generalizable
Process tracing	Offers insight into causal mechanisms; Offers causal insight into particular phenomena	Findings are not generalizable; Disadvantaged for exploring large and complex processes
Pattern matching	Able to test theories	Does not necessarily offer insight into causal processes
Statistical comparison	Generalizable; Estimates causal effect; Tests competing theories	Does not analyze actual processes; Difficulty analyzing complex concepts; Uncertainty due to broken assumptions and potential spuriousness
Boolean comparison	Generalizable; Configurational; Insight into necessary and sufficient causes	Does not analyze actual processes; Only able to analyze a few independent variables; Difficulty operationalizing complex concepts
Millian comparison	Parsimonious; Able to compare complex concepts	Offers little independent insight
Narrative comparison	Able to analyze processes and compare complex phenomena; Offers considerable insight into causal determinants	Offers no independent insight; Offers relatively limited nomothetic insight

to know the determinants of a particular phenomenon, this is the most appropriate method. There are three reasons for its superior ability to shed insight into internal validity: its ability to consider the causal impact of multiple factors, to analyze complex processes, and to take a holistic approach. These characteristics, in turn, make causal narratives appropriate for either an exploratory analysis or an analysis that focuses on the causal impact of particular factors. If internal validity is the main strength of causal narrative, external validity—or insight into general processes within a larger set of cases—is its greatest weakness. Given the focus on particular causal processes, the method has difficulty providing nomothetic insight on its own.

Process tracing is similar to causal narrative but is more focused, as it explores causal mechanisms linking potential causes and outcomes instead of general processes involving a multitude of factors. It has many of the same advantages and disadvantages of causal narrative. Because it is more focused, however, process tracing is less able to analyze complex causal processes involving many factors. Relative to causal narrative, process tracing is therefore less appropriate for exploratory studies and analyses of multiple causal determinants. At the same time, process tracing's more limited focus heightens its ability to discover mechanisms and thereby to uncover more generalizable insight. It can also promote a more parsimonious analysis.

Pattern matching is a technique that explores whether a case conforms to one or more theories. Because theories make multiple predictions and because an individual case can test all predictions, a single case can offer insight into a theory through several data points, not just one. Pattern matching is a unique within-case method because it is more concerned with nomothetic insight than ideographic insight. Relative to the other within-case methods, it has a considerable advantage testing theories. It is disadvantaged, however, because it does not necessarily consider causal processes and commonly does not attempt to explain the determinants of particular cases. In this way, it is advantaged at testing theory but disadvantaged at explaining particular outcomes.

Along with these three within-case methods, comparative-historical researchers commonly employ four main comparative methods. Statistics is a broad comparative method that operationalizes variables, tests relationships between the variables, and estimates causal effects. It is able to establish relationships between variables and to estimate causal effects. In so doing, it provides a powerful means of testing competing theories and offers nomothetic insight. Because of the latter, social scientists who are interested in generalizable insight usually privilege statistical methods. Statistics is also advantaged because it is highly formalized and, therefore, easily replicable. As for disadvantages, statistics is usually unable to provide any insight into the particular processes of the cases under analysis. As a result, they offer limited causal insight and are commonly unable to stipulate whether a relationship is causal or spurious. Moreover, there is no way to specify the appropriate models for statistical analysis, and the results of statistical comparison depend on which model is employed. Finally, statistical analysis is based on several assumptions, and most statistical analyses break several of them, thereby problematizing the interpretation of the results.

Boolean comparison is a second type of large-N comparison. It operationalizes variables, categorizes cases based on their configurations of independent variables, and analyzes which configurations of independent variables produce which outcomes. Regarding the latter, Boolean comparison explores configurations of independent variables that are either necessary or sufficient causes of the outcome. Like statistics, it is also highly formalized and replicable and able to highlight relationships. More than statistics, it is able to consider the impact of configurations of variables instead of independent variables and, therefore, takes a more holistic approach. Analyzing configurations of variables comes with a cost, however: one can analyze only a few independent variables at a time. Similar to statistics, Boolean comparison also provides only limited ideographic insight, and is unable to provide insight into whether a relationship is causal or spurious.

Narrative comparison uses a narrative to compare complex phenomena for a small number of cases. It is very different from large-N comparison because it does not explore relationships between variables. Instead, it compares complex phenomena that cannot easily be operationalized, including processes, mechanisms, and ideal types. Relative to other types of comparison, narrative comparison has a superior ability to highlight causal determinants and analyze complex phenomena. Its two main disadvantages are an inability to offer independent comparative insight and a limited ability to offer nomothetic insight.

Millian comparison combines elements of large-N comparison and narrative comparison. Similar to large-N comparison, Millian comparison operationalizes variables and explores relationships between variables. Depending on whether the data are nominally or ordinally scored, such comparisons can either explore necessary and sufficient conditions or pseudo–statistical relationships. It is advantaged because the small number of cases allows researchers to gather data to operationalize complex concepts accurately and because it offers parsimonious results. On the other hand, however, the small number of cases impedes the ability of Millian comparison to offer any independent insight.

Methodological Combinations in Comparative-Historical Analysis

The purpose of combining methods is to increase insight into the research question. The underlying assumption is that all within-case and comparative methods are unable to offer conclusive insight into the research question but that the combination of evidence derived from multiple methods offers greater insight and, thereby, helps researchers to arrive at more accurate conclusions. Although very valuable for this reason, one must also recognize that combining methods comes at a cost. Most obviously, combining methods requires more time, data, and methodological skills. In addition, the combination of multiple methods can be cumbersome and limit analytic parsimony. Instead of a coherent story, an analysis using multiple methods can be disjointed. The lack of parsimony is particularly problematic when the findings of different methods do not concur. Given these costs and benefits, combining methods is most appropriate when the researcher goal is validity and understanding but least appropriate when the goal is parsimony, and when the researcher has limited time and resources.

Ultimately, the combination of methods can expand insight in three ways: methodological triangulation, methodological complementarity, and methodological synergy. The three strategies are not mutually exclusive, and researchers commonly employ multiple strategies simultaneously. They differ based on the extent to which the researcher attempts to integrate the methods, with methodological triangulation integrating them the least, methodological synergy integrating them the most, and methodological complementarity situated between these two extremes.

Methodological Triangulation

Methodological triangulation is a combinatorial strategy that involves using multiple methods independently to offer insight into the same research question. It compares the results of each method to see if they offer concurrent evidence. Thus, if multiple methods all provide insight pointing to the same conclusion, a researcher can have greater confidence in that conclusion. Alternatively, if the methods point to different conclusions, triangulation helps prevent the researcher from making incorrect conclusions that he or she might have made if only one method had been used. Given inherent problems with social scientific analysis, one could argue that no single method is able to generate conclusive evidence and that triangulation is, therefore, always beneficial. Although the name suggests the combination of at least three methods, I employ the term when two or more methods are combined in this fashion.

Methodological triangulation is a unique combinatorial strategy because it does not attempt to integrate the different methods in any way. That is, the insight from one method does not affect the insight from the other. As a result, the strategy does not privilege any method as particularly advantaged and does not attempt to supplement the findings of one with the findings of another. Quite simply, it uses different methods to produce different findings and compares the findings to see if they point to similar or different conclusions.

Many comparative-historical analyses combine methods to increase insight through triangulation. Paige's (1975) *Agrarian Revolution* offers an example. The book lays out a theory claiming that the structure of the agrarian economy is the most influential determinant of agrarian movements. His theory focuses on whether peasants earn their livelihoods from land or labor and whether land-owning elites earn their livelihoods from land or capital investments. He suggests that wage-earning peasants are more likely to participate in revolutionary movements than are peasants who earn their livelihoods from their control of land because they (a) are less risk-averse, (b) compete less with other peasants and are therefore more likely to form political organizations, and (c) are more interdependent and therefore have greater solidarity. Alternatively, the non-cultivating landowners who depend on land for their livelihoods instead of capital are more likely to promote agrarian revolutions because they (a) are economically weak and therefore depend on political restrictions to peasant land ownership, (b) are dependent on servile labor and are therefore opposed to the extension of political and economic rights to laborers, and (c) generally produce static products that create zero-sum conflicts with peasants. Thus, he predicts revolutionary movements when peasants are wage-earners and the non-cultivator landowners derive their income from land.

To test this theory Paige uses diverse methods, including inter-case comparison and within-case methods. His combination is an example of methodological triangulation because he does not privilege either comparative or within-case methods, using both to test his theory. Paige begins with a cross-sectional statistical analysis of 135 agricultural export sectors located in 70 countries in the world. He creates variables measuring agricultural organization and types of agricultural movements. Conforming with his theory, he finds that revolutions are most common in places with sharecropping and migratory labor estates, the two categories of agricultural organization that are characterized by wage-earning peasants and non-cultivating landlords who are dependent on land revenue.

After the statistical analysis, Paige turns to case studies of Peru, Angola, and Vietnam to explore whether particular histories of agrarian movements also support his theory. Within each case, the unit of analysis remains agricultural export sector, meaning that each country actually offers multiple cases. Ultimately, he uses diverse within-case methods as a means of pattern matching. Paige's case study of Peru offers a specific example. The country's agricultural organization is characterized by haciendas in some regions and plantations in others, and Paige's theory suggests that the former promotes agrarian revolts whereas the latter promotes labor reform movements. He begins with an analysis of the coastal region of Peru, focusing on sugar and cotton agricultural zones.

He describes how sugar production is dominated by plantation enterprises whereas commercial haciendas dominate cotton production. Then, using statistics to complete internal comparisons, he tests relationships between the sugar and cotton production and the type of economic movements, finding—as his theory predicts—that sugar production is strongly and positively related to labor movements and that cotton production is strongly and positively related to agrarian revolts. This comparison differs from his general statistical analysis because it uses internal comparisons to explore whether the subregions of two different units of analysis conform to his theory.

Paige's analysis of the mountainous region of Peru employs a similar strategy but also employs narrative analysis. Specifically, it uses internal comparisons to show general relationships that conform to Paige's theory and brief causal narratives to analyze particular subregions and to explore the processes leading to agrarian movements in these subregions. Similar to the previous analyses, they also support Paige's theory. In this way, both the comparative and within-case analyses point to the same conclusion, allowing Paige to use methodological triangulation to strengthen his conclusions.

Paige's example shows how researchers can employ methodological triangulation as a general strategy for the entire analysis. Researchers can also use it in a more focused manner to analyze specific parts of analyses. My *Educations in Ethnic Violence* (Lange 2012) employs triangulation in this more focused and limited way. The book begins with a statistical analysis exploring the relationship between educational expansion and ethnic violence. It highlights a strong and positive relationship between education and ethnic violence, although the findings are driven by countries that are ethnically diverse, non-wealthy, and possess political institutions with limited effectiveness. It is possible, however, that the relationship runs from ethnic violence to educational expansion, not the reverse: ethnic violence might increase inter-communal competition, heighten demand for education, and thereby promote educational expansion. To test the direction of causation, I run additional statistical analyses to see whether previous levels of ethnic violence are related to the subsequent expansions of education. These results fail to support claims that ethnic violence promotes educational expansion but are unable to rule out this possibility completely (one of the six models finds a positive relationship between previous ethnic violence and subsequent educational expansion).

For additional insight into the direction of causation, I exploit different within-case methods for the analysis of Sri Lanka, Cyprus, the Palestinian Territories/Israel, India, Canada, and Germany. First, and most basically, I use brief causal narratives to delineate the sequence of educational expansion and ethnic violence and find that episodes of ethnic violence generally follow periods of rapid educational expansion. Similarly, if the direction of causation runs from education to ethnic violence, one would expect that the educated play important roles in episodes of ethnic violence. Alternatively, one would not expect the educated to participate actively in ethnic violence if ethnic violence promotes educational expansion. I therefore use causal narrative to explore the roles educated individuals played in episodes of ethnic violence and find that the educated commonly play very influential roles in framing ethnic grievances, mobilizing violent ethnic movements, and participating in violence. Using counterfactuals, I conclude that ethnic violence would probably have been less severe and might not have occurred at all without the active and critical participation of educated elites. Finally, I employ process tracing to explore potential mechanisms, as mechanisms offer important insight into whether education contributes to ethnic violence. Through the multiple case studies, I highlight four mechanisms through which education contributes to ethnic violence, and process tracing therefore offers additional evidence that the causal arrows go from education to ethnic violence. Thus, neither statistics nor within-case methods offer conclusive insight into the direction of causation; yet both offer consistent evidence that education contributes to ethnic violence in particular contexts.

Methodological Complementarity

My methodological combination in *Educations in Ethnic Violence* (2012) conforms to triangulation to the extent that each method is used to offer independent insight. In some ways, however, I integrate the methods to exploit the strengths and limit the weaknesses of different methods. Most notably, statistical comparison cannot easily highlight the direction of causation because it offers little insight into causal processes and mechanisms. Narrative analysis and process tracing, in turn, has an advantaged ability to analyze processes and mechanisms and is, therefore, able to help make up for a weakness of statistics. In this way, the example also shares elements of a second combinatorial strategy commonly used in comparative-historical analysis: **methodological complementarity**.

Different from methodological triangulation, methodological complementarity does not treat the insight offered by each method equally. Instead, it uses a methodological division of labor that privileges one method for a specific insight and another method for another type of insight. That is, methodological complementarity recognizes the strengths and weaknesses of particular methods and purposefully combines methods that complement one another, thereby combining the strengths to limit the weaknesses. Relative to methodological triangulation, this strategy integrates the methods more thoroughly, as it exploits one method for one type of insight, another method for another type of insight, and combines all insight in an effort to offer a more complete picture of the phenomenon under analysis.

Several of the methods employed in comparative-historical analysis complement one another greatly, and the combination of methods in a way that maximizes complementarity is a major methodological advantage of comparative-historical analysis. Most notably, comparative and within-case methods have strengths and weaknesses that pair well to minimize their respective weaknesses. Given that comparative-historical analysis necessarily combines both methods, it is well positioned to employ methodological complementarity.

One notable strategy of methodological complementarity combines large-N comparison with either causal narrative or process tracing, thereby exploiting the nomothetic insight of the former and the ideographic insight of the latter. Statistical and Boolean methods, for example, offer very limited insight into actual processes, do not highlight causal mechanisms, and therefore have difficulty showing whether or not a relationship is causal. Both causal narrative and process tracing, however, are advantaged in their ability to analyze processes and discover mechanisms. By combining causal narrative, process tracing, or both with large-N comparison, the within-case methods help make up for the weaknesses of the comparative methods. Alternatively, the main weakness of causal narrative and process tracing is their limited ability to test the generalizability of their insight. The ability to test the generalizability of insight is, however, the main advantage of large-N comparison, so the combination of comparative and within-case methods limits the main weakness of the latter.

Lieberman's (2003) *Race and Regionalism in the Politics of Taxation in Brazil and South Africa* offers a notable example of a work that explicitly employs methodological complementarity. Lieberman explores factors affecting the capacity of states to collect taxes and analyzes two countries—Brazil and South Africa—with several similarities but a large discrepancy in state extractive capacity. Lieberman combines three main methods: causal narratives of both Brazil and South Africa, small-N comparisons of Brazil and South Africa, and a cross-national statistical analysis of 70 countries.

Lieberman begins his analysis using causal narrative and small-N comparison. Through this methodological combination, Lieberman offers evidence that constitutional definitions of the national political community and different levels of government centralization contributed to the different outcomes of South Africa and Brazil. Specifically, he finds that South Africa's racist definition of national community and its unitary system of government helped to overcome economic differences among whites and created greater national cohesion. As a consequence, the white elites were more willing to pay higher taxes. In Brazil, the non–racist definition of national political community and the federal system of government promoted greater regional and economic divisions, and such divisions reduced the willingness of individuals to pay taxes to the central government. Lieberman therefore concludes that different definitions of national political community and different state structures help to explain differences in state revenue effectiveness, promoting a "cooperative tax state" in South Africa but an "adversarial tax state" in Brazil (2003, 235).

In an effort to minimize the weaknesses of causal narrative and small-N comparison and to increase general insight, Lieberman follows the comparative case studies of South Africa and Brazil with a cross-sectional statistical analysis. For this, he codes a set of countries in two ways: whether countries possess inclusive or exclusive definitions of national political community, and whether countries possess federal or unitary states. The statistical results are unable to highlight processes and mechanisms but show that the definition of national political community and state structure are both strongly related to a country's tax revenue. In this way, the findings of the analysis using causal narrative and small-N comparison supplement the statistical findings by highlighting processes and mechanisms and, therefore, offer evidence that the relationship is causal. Alternatively, the analysis using causal narrative and small-N comparison offers very limited general insight, but the statistical analysis supplements them by offering evidence that the findings of the case studies are not unique to Brazil and South Africa.

Lieberman attempts to use statistics to generalize beyond the two cases analyzed through within-case methods and small-N comparison and to offer evidence that his small-N findings can be applied to a much larger set of cases. As such, he depends heavily on statistics for nomothetic insight and heavily on causal narrative and small-N comparison for insight into causal processes, showing a rather strict methodological division of labor that exemplifies methodological complementarity. Such a strategy is not without potential problems, however. Most notably, Lieberman uses two statistical outliers to offer insight into mechanisms, and both the small number of cases and their outlier status prevent him from making strong conclusions about whether or not the mechanisms highlighted in his case studies underlie the statistical relationships. Moreover, neither statistics nor causal narratives are guaranteed to produce valid results, so one cannot be overly confident in the results of either method. Methodological complementarity, however, inherently places considerable confidence in each method because—unlike methodological triangulation—it does not attempt to verify the findings with additional findings produced by a different method.

One way to help overcome these potential problems is to include more cases for the in-depth analysis. By adding more cases, inaccurate findings for any one case will have a smaller impact on the overall conclusion. Moreover, expanding the number of cases for in-depth analysis increases insight in the generalizability of the within-case and small-N comparative findings. A notable example of such a strategy is Rueschemeyer, Stephens, and Stephens's *Capitalist Development and Democracy* (1991), which notes a strong statistical relationship linking democracy to capitalist development and uses process tracing to analyze some thirty cases to explore mechanisms underlying the relationship. Given the large number of cases and the strong pattern present among them, the authors are able to offer considerable evidence into the generalizability of the within-case findings and can, therefore, be more confident that the mechanisms they highlight underlie the statistical relationship. Along with this notable advantage, however, increasing the number of cases analyzed through within-case methods has costs: it can limit parsimony, requires much more research, and can promote a repetitive analysis.

Methodological Synergy

Methodological synergy is a third way methods are combined in comparative-historical analysis to increase insight into the research question. It differs from the previous two methodological combinations in that the combination of methods actually improves the insight offered by one or both methods—unlike methodological triangulation and methodological complementarity, which simply combine the insight of different methods in different ways. At the extreme, one method is so dependent on the other that it offers no independent insight and can be difficult to disentangle from the other method. In this way, methodological synergy fuses methods in a way that strengthens them.

Methodological synergy commonly combines either causal narrative or process tracing with small-N comparison. Both types of small-N comparison—Millian and narrative—are unique methods because their insight depends on another method. They are usually combined with either causal narrative or process tracing because both within-case methods supplement small-N comparison by offering evidence that the patterns highlighted through small-N comparison are causal. In particular, the limited number of cases analyzed through small-N comparison usually places an extreme limit on the comparative insight it can provide; in most cases, no independent insight can be gained from small-N comparison. Yet, both causal narrative and process tracing offer case-specific evidence about the causes of social phenomena, and the combination of this case-specific insight with small-N comparison can offer strong evidence that allows researchers to explore common causal determinants across the set of cases. Thus, if a small-N comparison of four cases shows that the political exclusion of ethnic minorities promotes ethnic-based civil wars, the comparison offers little insight; when these comparisons are combined with four case studies that show how political exclusion promotes civil war, however, the comparisons offer much greater insight into the general impact of political exclusion on ethnic-based civil war.

Millian comparison is dependent on within-case methods in another way. Millian comparisons commonly compare very complex concepts that are difficult to operationalize. Within-case methods—usually historical narrative—are therefore used to describe the phenomenon in considerable detail and note its most important characteristics. Based on this narrative analysis, the phenomena under analysis can be operationalized along a nominal or ordinal scale for subsequent Millian comparison.

Although within-case methods can greatly improve the insight derived from small-N comparison, small-N comparison also generally strengthens within-case methods. Unlike small-N comparison, however, within-case methods are able to offer considerable insight in their own right. Small-N comparison helps strengthen within-case methods by forcing the researcher to consider counterfactuals about whether cases would be more similar or more different if one factor differed—something that pushes the researcher to consider the causal argument more rigorously. Second, small-N comparison helps to pinpoint additional causal factors and scope conditions. When one case study clearly highlights the causal relevance of one factor, small-N comparison forces the researcher to consider whether or not this factor was influential in another case. In so doing, it can improve the within-case analysis by prompting the researcher to analyze the impact of a factor that would have been overlooked without inter-case comparison. Further, if the factor does not prove influential, the comparison pushes the researcher to investigate scope conditions, multiple causation or other potential reasons for the difference.

Notably, small-N comparison makes possible these benefits, but ultimately causal narrative or process tracing offers evidence into causal determinants. That is, these small-N comparisons push the researcher to make new and possibly insightful considerations, yet within-case analysis offers evidence into whether the considerations are actually insightful. Similarly, whereas causal narrative and process tracing supplement small-N comparison and thereby expand the insight that can be gained from it, inter-case comparison is needed to explore whether the findings are generalizable across a set of cases. When combined, both within-case methods and small-N comparison can, therefore, strengthen one another in a synergistic fashion.

Skocpol's *States and Social Revolutions* (1979) offers an example of methodological synergy in which small-N comparison and causal narrative strengthen one another. In her methodological discussion of the work, Skocpol notes that her main method is Millian comparison. The centrality of the comparative method has subsequently been disputed, with Sewell (1996) and Mahoney (1999) suggesting that most of Skocpol's insight comes from causal narrative. Although their claims are correct, one cannot discount the insight gained from both Millian and narrative comparisons *through their combination with causal narrative*, as the comparisons strengthen the causal narratives and vice versa.

Skocpol's analysis of the causes of social revolution is divided into two chapters (Chapters 2 and 3), the first of which explores the impact of states on social revolutions and the second of which focuses on the impact of agrarian class structures. The chapter on the state begins with a causal narrative of France describing political conditions that promoted a revolutionary movement. After completing her analysis of France, she turns to China and uses causal narrative for a similar analysis of this case. The analysis of China differs from the French case, however, because it includes narrative comparisons with France. These comparisons focus on processes leading to revolutionary movements, help to pinpoint factors that contributed to the outcome, and offer insight into whether the revolutionary movements had similar or different causes (Skocpol 1979, 80–1). Ultimately, her combination of causal narrative and narrative comparison highlights three key similarities between France and China: both had administrations crippled by dominant class privilege, both experienced international pressure, and both experienced a political crisis caused by limited state autonomy from the dominant classes. In addition, although this comparative insight is of little value on its own, it offers considerably more insight when backed up with causal narratives, as an understanding of the processes increases confidence that the similarities highlighted through comparison are causal.

Next, Skocpol offers a causal narrative of the state and revolutionary crisis in Russia, and the narrative analysis also includes narrative comparisons of the case with those of France and China. This analysis highlights how Russia differed from the other two cases because dominant classes did not handicap the state, and the Russian state was therefore able successfully to implement modernizing reforms without provoking a revolutionary movement. In addition to highlighting how Russia differed from France and China in these ways, Skocpol employs narrative comparison to formulate counterfactuals and concludes that a Russian revolution might have occurred in the 1860s if the dominant classes had been more powerful (1979, 88). Because the findings for France and China do not hold for Russia, Skocpol is forced to consider scope conditions or additional causes. Ultimately, her within-case analysis of Russia—prompted in part by small-N comparison with France and China—highlights how Russia's utter defeat in World War I sparked a severe state crisis. In this way, small-N comparison helped push the within-case analysis to explore multiple routes to state crisis. These examples show how Skocpol is able to strengthen her within-case analyses through narrative comparison, as the comparisons raise counterfactuals that force her to consider her argument more thoroughly and direct the within-case analysis to explore additional factors.

In the final section of Chapter 2 in *States and Social Revolutions*, Skocpol uses both causal narrative and Millian comparison briefly to analyze two cases that avoided social revolutions—Japan and Prussia. These analyses show that neither case faced extreme international pressure leading to state breakdown or had a dominant class able to provoke a crisis over state modernization efforts. To do so, Skocpol uses insight gained from the previous within-case analyses and narrative comparisons that highlight international pressure and the power of the dominant class as determinants of social revolution. She then offers more abbreviated causal narratives that focus on these factors and describe how differences—such as the absence of a powerful landed class in Japan and its much more limited international pressure—helped to prevent social revolution. Embedded within this narrative analysis, in turn, are Millian comparisons that show a relationship between the two independent variables and social revolution, and these comparisons are dependent on narrative analyses for variable scores. We therefore see a purposeful sequence in Skocpol's methodological combination that moves from the particular to the more general: causal narrative describes causal processes in particular cases, narrative comparisons compare processes to highlight influential common factors, and Millian comparison explores relationships among a larger set of cases.

Skocpol's following chapter, on agrarian class relations, follows a similar methodological design: it begins with a causal narrative of France, her subsequent causal narratives of Russia and China also include narrative comparison to highlight similarities and differences between the cases, and she combines causal narrative and Millian comparison for more abbreviated analyses of cases that did not experience social revolution. This chapter differs from her Chapter 2, however, because it concludes with tables that summarize the main findings of all cases from both chapters. Although not explicit, the table provides the data needed to make Millian comparisons that explore variation between variables. Skocpol's table on political conditions includes columns on the lack of state autonomy, the structure of the economy, and international pressure; and together they offer a measure of the vulnerability of the state to social revolution. Skocpol's table on conditions for peasant insurrections includes columns for peasant autonomy and solidarity and landlord vulnerability, and together they offer a measure of peasant capabilities for insurrection. Skocpol's third and final table combines the information from the first two and shows how social revolutions require both state vulnerability and peasant capabilities. Although not statistical, the table therefore offers a pseudo-statistical analysis showing a relationship between political crisis, peasants, and social revolutions.

Notably, the insight of Skocpol's analysis is hardly derived strictly from this small-N comparison, as limited degrees of freedom prevent much if any independent insight. Instead, the causal narratives offer insight into particular revolutionary processes, and the narrative comparisons help pinpoint causally relevant factors. Then, Skocpol uses Millian comparison to summarize her findings and show a relationship among a set of eight cases. It is this relationship that forms the basis of Skocpol's more general findings about social revolutions, showing that her comparisons offer important insight *when combined* with the findings derived from other methods. Moreover, her narrative comparisons strengthened the within-case analysis by pushing it to consider counterfactuals, multicausality, and the causes of similarities and differences. The synergistic combination of small-N comparison and within-case analysis therefore strengthens Skocpol's findings.

The Value of Different Combinatorial Strategies

Given multiple within-case methods and multiple comparative methods, comparative-historical researchers can use many different combinatorial strategies. Each strategy, in turn, has particular strengths and is most appropriate for certain types of analysis. In this section, I review the advantages of the different methodological combinations as a guide to help researchers to choose which combination best suits their research goals.

Table 6.2 shows the nine possible combinations of the three main types of comparative method (large-N, Millian, and narrative) and the three main types of within-case methods (causal narrative, process tracing, and pattern matching). It lists the strengths of the different combinations as well as works that employ the combinations.

Because large-N comparison (whether statistical or Boolean) is advantaged at discovering nomothetic insight, the methodological combinations presented in boxes 1 through 3 are all relatively advantaged in this regard. Box 1 combines large-N comparison with causal narrative. It is probably the least common of the three because it combines a method specializing in nomothetic insight with a method specializing in ideographic insight. Researchers combining these methods can either build

Table 6.2 Combinatorial strategies for comparative-historical analysis

	Causal narrative	Process tracing	Pattern matching
Large-N Comparison	**Strength**: Check for spurious correlations; build and test theory 1 **Example**: Huber & Stephens 2001	**Strength**: Nomothetic insight 2 **Example**: Lange 2009	**Strength**: Theory testing; nomothetic insight 3 **Example**: Paige 1975
Millian Comparison	**Strength**: Theory building and testing 4 **Example**: Skocpol 1979	**Strength**: Theory building and testing 5 **Example**: Charrad 2001	**Strength**: Theory testing 6 **Example**: Luebbert 1991
Narrative Comparison	**Strength**: Internal validity; theory building 7 **Example**: Bendix 1978	**Strength**: Theory building 8 **Example**: Lieberman 2003	**Strength**: Theory testing 9 **Example**: Luebbert 1991

or test theory, with one strategy using causal narrative to build theory and large-N comparison subsequently to test it. One could also use causal narrative after the large-N comparison in order to explore mechanisms underlying the relationships. Process tracing is usually better suited for this second strategy, but causal narrative might be more appropriate in particular circumstances, such as when the large-N comparisons compare large and complex entities that could be linked by multiple mechanisms, when the researcher is particularly interested in exploring potentially spurious relationships, or when the large-N results are unclear or highlight multiple variables related to the outcome. Huber and Stephens (2001), for example, use rather abbreviated causal narratives after their statistical analysis primarily because the large-N analysis highlights multiple factors potentially affecting welfare states, and they therefore use causal narratives to offer a general causal assessment of different cases—one that simultaneously considers the impact of diverse causal factors.

Relative to all boxes, box 2 is particularly advantaged at offering nomothetic insight and is, therefore, the most appropriate combinatorial strategy for researchers interested in pursuing general explanations that apply to large numbers of cases. For this combination, the large-N analysis highlights relationships, and process tracing is subsequently used to explore mechanisms underlying the relationship. Different from box 1, this combination is more focused on discovering mechanisms that explain the relationship; and although particular causal processes cannot be easily applied to multiple cases, mechanisms are formulated for this very purpose.

Box 3 is also relatively advantaged at offering nomothetic insight but has a particular focus on testing theory. Indeed, it is the methodological combination that is best able to test theory, as both large-N comparison and pattern matching have strengths in this regard. Paige (1975) offers a particular example of this, as he uses a cross-sectional analysis to test his theory on agrarian movements and then uses pattern matching to test the theory on individual cases. The combination is particularly strong because the large-N analysis tests the theory across multiple cases, whereas pattern matching tests the theory more closely by analyzing the details of particular cases.

In addition to box 3, boxes 6 and 9 are relatively advantaged at testing theory because they also include pattern matching, which is the within-case method that is best at testing theory. Because neither methodological combination usually analyzes a large set of cases, however, they are disadvantaged at testing the generalizability of the theory relative to box 3. Although large-N comparison might be a more appropriate match with pattern matching when researchers desire nomothetic insight, Millian comparison is more appropriate when data for large-N comparison are unavailable. Box 9, on the other hand, is most capable of testing the details of theory across cases because narrative comparison focuses on processes, mechanisms, and contexts. Notably, one can easily employ both Millian comparison and narrative comparison with pattern matching, and Luebbert (1991) offers an example of a work that combines both with pattern matching in his analysis of how social class affected regime type in interwar Europe.

The remaining four boxes—4, 5, 7, and 8—are all relatively advantaged at theory building. Box 4, for example, combines Millian comparison with causal narratives. The causal narrative offers in-depth insight into the determinants of particular cases, something that is vital for building theory and making exploratory analyses. The Millian comparison, in turn, offers an initial test of the theories, showing how this combination allows researchers to explore whether the findings hold across a small number of cases. Box 5 is similar in this regard, as it too can build theory and test it across a small number of cases. It differs, however, because process tracing is much more focused on mechanisms and mid-level theory. Moreover, a researcher can only use process tracing when a relationship or apparent causal sequence has been established. As a result, Millian comparison is commonly used to establish a relationship, and process tracing is subsequently used to explore possible mechanisms underlying the relationship. Charrad's (2001) analysis of states and gender in the Maghreb is one example using this methodological combination.

Similar to box 5, box 8 also uses process tracing but combines it with narrative comparison. Because process tracing requires preestablished relationships or causal sequences, and because narrative comparison is poorly suited to highlighting relationships and necessarily follows the within-case analysis, this combination is most appropriate when the analysis also includes another method that highlights a relationship or causal sequence. Alternatively, it could simply refer to past works that establish a relationship or sequence. The combination of narrative comparison and process tracing is particularly advantaged for highlighting causal mechanisms and contextual factors that shape them.

Finally, box 7 combines narrative comparison with causal narrative. Similar to Millian comparison, narrative comparison can also be used to test theories across cases. Its greater ability to analyze processes, mechanisms, and interactions, however, make this combination more appropriate for building theory. Narrative comparison also offers important insight into the causal determinants of particular cases. Because ideographic insight is also a strength of causal narrative, this methodological combination is the ideal combination for researchers interested in internal validity.

Combining Multiple Within-Case and Comparative Methods

This chapter's previous sections focus on combining comparative methods with within-case methods, as this combination is a defining element of comparative-historical analysis. However, the examples also show that comparative-historical researchers commonly employ multiple within-case methods and multiple comparative methods within the same analysis. In this section, I briefly consider why and how researchers combine multiple within-case methods and multiple comparative methods.

Comparative-historical researchers commonly use several types of comparison in an effort to exploit the different advantages of each. As described previously, Skocpol's *States and Social Revolutions* (1979) uses both narrative and Millian comparisons. Even more, she integrates them, using process-oriented narrative comparison to highlight influential factors and Millian comparison to compare these factors across cases. The difference between process-oriented narrative comparison and Millian comparison can be very subtle, as they appear to consider the same thing, and Millian comparison commonly occurs in narrative form. Still, one must recognize that the process-oriented comparisons consider processes and compare them to highlight key similarities and differences that produce similar and different outcomes. Alternatively, the Millian comparisons do not consider processes and simply compare variables in order to explore relationships between variables. This combination is an example of methodological complementarity, as it exploits the ability of narrative comparison to highlight relevant factors and the ability of Millian comparison to explore relationships among variables.

One also sees this combination in Moore's *Social Origins of Dictatorship and Democracy* (1966). This classic analysis explores three paths to modernity: democratic, fascist, and communist. Moore focuses on the impact of the landed and peasant classes, and his book begins with chapter-length case studies of England, France, the United States, China, Japan, and India. Although these case studies make use of comparison, they rely primarily on causal narrative and describe the processes leading to their particular paths to modernity. In this way, the case studies are focused more on producing accurate analyses than on producing a general theory of modernization.

After his detailed analyses of the cases (an analysis that covers nearly four hundred pages), Moore provides a seventy-five-page comparative conclusion that helps to pinpoint factors contributing to the different pathways to modernity. The comparative analysis includes the cases analyzed in the previous chapters as well as Germany and Russia—two cases that Moore intended to include as case studies but ultimately excluded because of space constraints. The comparative analysis highlights the causal influence of (among other things) the strength of the landed elites, the presence of an alliance between the landed and bourgeois elites, the maintenance of traditional social relations among the peasantry, the persistence of royal absolutism, the presence of a vigorous independent class of town dwellers, ties between the peasantry and the landlords, and peasant cohesion. Moore's comparisons are Millian because they compare variables that can be measured either nominally or ordinally and highlight relationships (although Moore does not actually provide numerical scores for them and presents them through a narrative).

At the same time, Moore uses process-oriented comparisons to highlight these factors. Specifically, the within-case analysis overviews the processes leading to the particular outcomes of the cases, and Moore then compares these processes to highlight factors that appear to be influential. Once highlighted, in turn, he compares them among the cases, thereby exploring relationships between the variables and the outcomes among his small set of cases. This combination of process-oriented and Millian comparison appears quite logical for studies that employ Millian comparisons after within-case analyses: the within-case analysis lays out the particular processes, the process-oriented comparisons highlight influential factors, and the Millian comparisons explore whether there is a relationship between such factors and the outcomes among a set of cases.

Although less common than combining Millian and narrative comparisons, researchers also combine large-N and small-N comparison in the same analysis, and this is an even clearer example of methodological complementarity. As described above, Lieberman's *Race and Regionalism in the Politics of Taxation in Brazil and South Africa* (2003) relies heavily on both large-N and small-N comparisons. The book includes two chapters that analyze Brazil and South Africa through a combination of causal narrative and small-N comparison. These comparisons help highlight differences that appear to account for the different capacities of each state to collect revenue. Having highlighted the impact of race and regionalism through within-case analysis and small-N comparison, Lieberman then operationalizes both variables for a larger set of cases and uses statistical comparison to check whether the variables appear to affect other cases as well. Small-N comparison is, therefore, used to highlight causal determinants, and large-N comparison is subsequently employed to test the general impact of these factors among a larger set of cases.

Along with comparative methods, comparative-historical researchers also commonly employ multiple types of within-case methods. Indeed, as described in Chapter 5, within-case analysis always employs multiple methods, including at least one secondary within-case method and at least one primary within-case method. Most analyses combine multiple primary within-case methods in order to collect more evidence for the analysis. Some analyses also combine multiple secondary within-case methods. Most notably, researchers commonly combine process tracing and causal narrative. In fact, causal narratives usually include process-tracing elements, as causal narratives commonly highlight causal sequences and then explore mechanisms that help to explain the sequence. In such an instance, it makes sense simply to recognize the use of causal narrative, as process tracing is subsumed by it. In other instances, however, both causal narrative and process tracing are distinct and are combined to promote methodological complementarity; that is, to exploit their strengths and minimize their weaknesses. For example, the use of causal narrative in one or more cases might highlight a common relationship and a mechanism underlying it, and the analysis of subsequent cases might be guided by the findings of the causal narrative and simply use process tracing to explore whether the mechanistic findings apply to other cases. This sequential methodological combination allows researchers to exploit the ability of causal narratives to explore a variety of potential causes as well as the ability of process tracing to analyze particular causal mechanisms.

Pattern matching can also be combined with either causal narrative or process tracing. Such a combination usually privileges one over the other and uses the other to strengthen the dominant within-case method. For example, Paige's (1975) analysis of agrarian labor movements is primarily an example of pattern matching, as it sets out a theory and subsequently tests it in diverse ways. Cross-sectional statistics and internal comparisons are his main sources of evidence for pattern matching, but he also offers brief causal narratives that offer additional evidence in support of his theory. In such an instance, causal narrative must be viewed as part of the larger within-case analysis based on pattern matching.

In contrast, when either causal narrative or process tracing is dominant, pattern matching is used primarily as an initial check of the findings of the dominant within-case method. Here, either causal narrative or process tracing offers particular evidence and suggests a certain conclusion, and pattern matching is used to offer additional evidence for or against this conclusion. One work that uses pattern matching to supplement process tracing is Luebbert's *Liberalism, Fascism, and Social Democracy* (1991). The book explores how class structures and class coalitions affected regime development in Western Europe. He finds that a liberal-labor coalition prior to World War I institutionalized middle-class hegemony and promoted liberal democracy. Whether the remaining cases developed fascist or social democratic regimes, in turn, depended on whether the peasants aligned with the middle class (fascists) or the socialists (social democratic). The book is a rather disjointed example of process tracing because it does not follow the process in a single unified narrative. Instead, it goes through a step-by-step analysis that reviews all cases at one step before moving to all cases at a subsequent step in the process, forcing the reader to read segments of multiple chapters for the analysis of one case. Still, the work is an example of process tracing because one can clearly follow the process leading from class structure and alliance to regime outcome for each individual case.

As Mahoney (1999) notes, Luebbert employs pattern matching as part of his analysis. Specifically, he notes that Luebbert's arguments have implications for other social phenomena and that Luebbert subsequently uses within-case methods to analyze these implications empirically. For example, Luebbert's argument suggests that socialists in social democracies will not pursue particular policies because of their class alliance—they will not favor wealth distribution in rural areas or mobilize the rural proletariat—and subsequently tests these implications on the cases. When combined with his findings derived from process tracing (and small-N comparison), pattern matching offers additional support for his argument. In fact, because causal mechanisms are very difficult—if not impossible—to observe directly, pattern matching is commonly used to offer insight into mechanisms, as researchers make hypotheses about what should happen if a particular mechanism underlies a relationship and subsequently test these hypotheses empirically. In this way, pattern matching can be an integral part of process tracing (Mahoney 2012).

Summary

This chapter builds on the three previous chapters and explores how comparative-historical researchers combine methods to increase insight into the research question. It recognizes that combining methods offers considerable analytic benefits and describes three ways methods are commonly combined within comparative-historical analysis. First, methodological triangulation is a strategy that keeps each method separate and simply explores whether methods produce similar or different results. It assumes that all methods are limited and combines the insight from different methods to increase confidence in the findings. Secondly, methodological complementarity combines methods in a way that exploits a methodological division of labor. It recognizes the strengths and weaknesses of methods and uses one method for one type of insight and another method for another type of insight. Finally, methodological synergy combines methods in order to strengthen the insight that can be gained from the methods. It is most commonly used for methods that are unable to offer independent causal insight, Millian and narrative comparisons being the primary examples.

Sometimes it is not easy to identify which combinatorial strategy a researcher uses, and a researcher can employ multiple strategies simultaneously. Conceptually speaking, however, methodological triangulation, complementarity, and synergy differ according to the extent to which different methods are integrated. Methodological triangulation does not attempt to integrate methods; rather, it leaves them completely separate and simply weighs their different insight to arrive at a conclusion. At the other extreme, methodological synergy actively integrates multiple methods to improve the insight offered by one or both. Indeed, one method commonly offers no insight on its own—which is almost always the case for small-N comparison and explains why they are always combined with either causal narrative or process tracing. Methodological complementarity lies between triangulation and synergy, as it uses different methods to offer independent insight but exploits a methodological division of labor that uses one method to offer one type of insight, another to offer another type of insight, and combines both for a more complete picture. In this way, combining methods through methodological complementarity does not improve the actual insight offered by the methods, but the methods are actively combined to exploit the advantages of the different methods.

As its name suggests, comparative-historical analysis actively combines different methods, and the research tradition offers examples of all three strategies of methodological combinations. Most notably, comparative-historical researchers exploit methodological triangulation because of the complexity of the social phenomena under question, methodological complementarity to combine the nomothetic insight of large-N comparison with the ideographic insight of within-case analysis, and methodological synergy to strengthen small-N comparative analyses. An understanding of how comparative-historical researchers combine methods is, therefore, vital to understanding the analytic insight made possible by comparative-historical methods—something that has been greatly neglected in the methodological literature.

How one combines within-case and comparative methods has important effects on the analysis because different combinations are advantaged in different ways. For example, the combination of narrative comparison and causal narrative is most advantaged for ideographic insight, whereas the combination of large-N comparison and process tracing is most advantaged for nomothetic insight. Certain combinations are also more advantaged at either building or testing theory, with the combination of large-N comparison and pattern matching being particularly advantaged at the latter. For comparative-historical analysis, one's research goal should therefore inform one's combination of methods.

Glossary

Methodological complementarity: A strategy for combining different methods that employs a methodological division of labor recognizing that each method has advantages for producing particular types of insight. The methods are therefore combined in the same analysis, with one producing one type of insight and the other producing another type of insight.

Methodological synergy: A strategy for combining different methods that actively integrates the methods in order to increase the insight that one or multiple methods can produce. This strategy is most commonly used for both Millian and narrative comparison, as neither produces much—if any—independent comparative insight, but both can provide considerable insight when combined with within-case methods.

Methodological triangulation: A strategy for combining different methods that does not privilege any method and simply checks whether the methods produce concurrent results. If the results of the different methods support one another, the researcher is able to make strong conclusions. If the results of the different methods oppose one another, the researcher is unable to make a clear conclusion.

7

Data, Case Selection, and Theory in Comparative-Historical Analysis

In Chapters 3 to 6, I overview the methods that comparative-historical researchers use to analyze data and the ways the methods are employed to offer insight into the research question. The present chapter changes course by focusing on three more general methodological issues—gathering data, selecting cases, and theory—and considering the ways comparative-historical researchers address them.

Data and Comparative-Historical Analysis

Science ultimately involves gathering and analyzing data in ways that offer insight into the phenomena under investigation. In this way, data are the most central component of the scientific enterprise. This is true for the social sciences as well, and comparative-historical researchers must, therefore, carefully consider the data they analyze through within-case and comparative methods. Indeed, such is the importance of data that most methodological traditions pay close attention to how to gather data appropriately—and comparative-historical analysis is no different.

The word "data" is commonly associated with data set, or a collection of scored variables for a set of cases. For example, the World Development Indicators offers a data set for all countries in the world that includes variables on diverse indicators of development, ranging from per capita GDP to infant mortality rate. Statistical analysis requires data in the form of a data set, and comparative-historical researchers commonly use this type of data as well, especially when using large-N comparison. Most data used for comparative-historical analysis, however, come in different forms.

According to Brady and Collier (2004) and their contributors, qualitative researchers analyzing actual processes depend on **causal-process observations**, or CPOs, not data sets. They define a CPO as an "insight or piece of data that provides information about context, process or mechanism, and that contributes distinctive leverage in causal inference" (Seawright and Collier 2004, 277). A CPO is therefore evidence about what happened and why it happened the way it did. Notably, researchers sometimes gather CPOs from formal data sets. More commonly, however, they gather them from a variety of primary and secondary sources.

Data Sources

University courses on research design commonly categorize data as either primary or secondary. Most fundamentally, **primary data** are original sources of information about the phenomenon under analysis. In contrast, researchers gather **secondary data** from preexisting analyses that are based on either primary or secondary data. Comparative-historical analysis depends greatly on both primary and secondary data.

Because comparative-historical researchers analyze historical phenomena, they commonly use historical sources of primary data. These are the actual historical artifacts that offer insight into the past. Such data might take the form of archeological remains created during the period under analysis. Thus, a researcher exploring the means of livelihood in pre-Columbian Peru might perform archeological digs of past settlements to find physical remains that offer insight into how Peruvians lived prior to the Spanish conquest, and these physical artifacts are primary sources of data. Written sources are the most common type of artifact used by historians as primary data. Common sources include newspapers and other sources of print media, government documents, ledgers and account books, diaries and personal memoires, and letters of correspondence. So, a historian studying how Napoleon rose to power would use the memoires and correspondences of Napoleon and his close associates as primary data sources. Alternatively, a researcher studying popular culture in ninteenth-century London might use newspapers from that era as the main source of primary data.

The type of historical primary data one uses depends on different things, the most notable being the communication technologies that were available when the artifacts were generated. Thus, archeological data is a more important source of primary data in preliterate societies because written data sources are generally unavailable. Similarly, historians studying more recent phenomena can use primary data stored and accessed through electronic media, mainly recordings of television programs, radio programs, and interviews. For example, a researcher studying popular culture in inter-war London might use recordings of radio and television programs, commercials, and films as primary sources of data.

Although historical data can only be gathered from preexisting sources, social scientists are also able to generate their own primary data because they commonly explore contemporary processes. Surveys, interviews, and participant observation are the most common means of generating data about present conditions. Once the data generated from surveys, interviews, and participant observation are recorded, however, such data ultimately become a historical artifact that future researchers can exploit.

Like historians, comparative-historical researchers commonly have difficulty using interviews or surveys to gather data because they usually analyze phenomena that occurred long ago. As a consequence, there may be no one with first-hand knowledge of the phenomena under analysis still alive. For comparative-historical analyses that investigate more recent phenomena, however, interviews can be an important source of primary data (although surveys and participant observation remain largely irrelevant). Such interviews might gather information from someone who experienced or participated in the phenomena under question. Within comparative-historical analysis, institutional elites—such as politicians, military officials, or corporate executives—are the most common interviewees because they have first-hand knowledge of the phenomena under analysis. Researchers can also interview individuals with indirect insight into the phenomena, such as the children of deceased institutional elites or by collecting oral histories. In addition, researchers can interview academic experts who did not experience the phenomena at first hand but have studied it extensively and are a good source of information.

Although they gather primary data from historical sources and interviews, comparative-historical researchers usually depend most heavily on secondary sources for historical data. Secondary sources are usually empirical analyses that interpret and form conclusions based on data from other sources. Within comparative-historical analysis, preexisting historical analyses are the most common sources of secondary data, although comparative-historical researchers also commonly employ preexisting social scientific analyses as sources of secondary data.

Although it might seem clear-cut, the dividing line between primary and secondary data can be quite blurred. Within social scientific circles, for example, a researcher is commonly viewed as using secondary data when he or she does not collect their own survey or interview data but uses data gathered by someone else. This is arguably because the researcher is removed from the original data, as another researcher collected them and potentially transformed them in some way during the data collection process. Yet, to the extent that the researcher accurately recorded the phenomenon without adding a personal interpretation, this data should be considered primary data. Recordings of interviews are primary data because the data are not transformed by researcher interpretation, however, content analyses of the interviews that score interviewee responses offer secondary data because they are *interpretations* of the primary data.

Data Quality

The common use of both historical primary data sources and secondary data sources by comparative-historical researchers has drawn criticism from some, most notably sociologist John Goldthorpe (1991). Goldthorpe suggests that the dependence of comparative-historical researchers on both types of data has serious repercussions for the quality of their data. Further, because the quality of an analysis is only as good as its data, such claims have serious repercussions for the insight potentially gained from comparative-historical analysis.

The first element of Goldthorpe's criticism concerns the use of historical data. He claims that social scientists have an advantage over historians because they are not solely dependent on historical artifacts. In turn, he suggests they need to exploit this advantage because non-historical data is better for two reasons. First, one can gather more primary data when one analyzes contemporary phenomena because less has been lost over the years. Second, one can actually go out and create data through observation, interviews, and surveys. In creating their own data, in turn, researchers do not have to accept whatever data are available but can craft their data collection strategies to retrieve the data that offer the greatest insight into their particular research questions. Given these advantages, Goldthorpe suggests that comparative-historical analyses are inherently inferior to contemporary analyses of the same phenomenon and that researchers should not perform historical research when contemporary examples are present.

This critique raises an important point that comparative-historical researchers need to recognize. Mainly, one should not use historical data to gain insight into general research questions when contemporary data are available. Thus, if one wants to understand general factors that affect voter behavior, a researcher is better served to analyze present voter behavior than voter behavior in the 1890s, because more and better primary data are available for recent elections and because researchers can gather additional data about recent elections through interviews and surveys.

Goldthorpe's points are very commonsensical. If taken as a general rule, however, his critique goes too far. Most importantly, many—if not most—social scientific analyses cannot be dis-embedded from history, as processes occur over time. As noted in Chapter 4, analyses of social change lose considerable insight when they take a short-term perspective because both the causes and outcomes can take considerable time to occur. Thus, a synchronic snapshot of the present offers relatively little insight into the workings of a political system or economy compared to a diachronic analysis that traces their origins and transformations over time. This is particularly the case for more macro-level analyses of institutional formation and change; and institutional genesis commonly goes back centuries, meaning that institutional analyses commonly have no choice but to be very historical.

In addition, Goldthorpe openly privileges nomothetic over ideographic explanations, suggesting that the analysis of contemporary phenomena is able to offer nomothetic explanations. Yet, numerous researchers are interested in ideographic insight, and if a researcher is interested in the causes of capitalist development in the Netherlands and England, an analysis of the contemporary economy in the Netherlands and England will not offer much insight into this particular question. Similarly, some historical phenomena have important long-term consequences and, therefore, warrant special attention. Thus, if one wants to understand the origins of capitalist development, one cannot analyze contemporary countries that are undergoing a capitalist transformation because this process commonly involves the transfer of capitalism from one country to another. A historical analysis of the Netherlands and England would be much more appropriate because capitalism first developed there and then spread elsewhere. For these reasons, historical analyses are extremely important, and social scientists must continue to use historical data in order to complete them.

Along with his critique of using historical data, Goldthorpe also criticizes the common use of secondary data within comparative-historical analysis. This critique focuses on how secondary data can promote bias and has two related elements. First, secondary sources might offer different accounts of the same phenomenon. As a consequence, researchers are able to pick and choose between the secondary accounts that conform most closely to their theories. The result can be extremely biased analysis. Second, researchers manipulate and interpret data during the research process. These manipulations might produce erroneous findings, such as when a researcher uses inappropriate statistical techniques, and interpretations of data can produce biased and inaccurate results. Such bias is quite common because social scientists and historians accept particular theories, and their theoretical views affect their interpretations of the data. In extreme cases, researchers gather data and force them into a theoretical mold, thereby using theory to dictate the interpretation of the data rather than data to see if a theory holds. This issue is particularly problematic when the secondary source is far removed from the primary source, such as when the secondary source is an interpretation of an interpretation of an interpretation of the primary data. Indeed, just like a game of "telephone", the original message can be altered by each subsequent interpretation of the data, making the final message starkly different from the original.

The potential for erroneous results and researcher bias to enter the analysis in these ways is real and should be recognized and addressed by comparative-historical researchers. As all social scientists and historians know, one rarely—perhaps even never—concludes research without some data that conflict with the final conclusion. This occurs whether the researcher uses only primary data, only secondary data, or some combination of the two. Within history, for example, researchers are very concerned about the validity of primary data sources in an effort to make better conclusions in the face of conflicting evidence. Indeed, historiography is largely concerned about establishing the authenticity of primary data, the credibility of its sources, the reliability of the sources, and the exact meaning of the data (see Milligan 1979). Regardless of whether data is primary or secondary, researchers must recognize that some data are inaccurate and that all data must be interpreted, making the consideration of the quality of the data an important part of the research process. Along these same lines, researchers using the results of past social scientific analyses as data must consider the appropriateness of the data used by the analysis, its methods, and the interpretations of the researchers, in an effort to limit the use of erroneous or biased data.

Although history is very concerned with exploring data validity, Goldthorpe's main critique is that comparative-historical researchers are much less concerned about it and are, therefore, more likely to use inaccurate data for their analyses. This critique must be taken seriously but is not usually addressed by comparative-historical researchers because a thorough application of Goldthorpe's recommendation is frequently beyond the realm of possibility. Indeed, comparative-historical analysis commonly offers vast analyses of multiple countries over long periods of time. As a consequence, it might be impossible for researchers to use primary data for all or even most of their analyses, and it is usually impossible to assess critically the validity of all data. Even more, comparative-historical researchers commonly use the results of previous social scientific analyses, and it is commonly prohibitively time consuming to replicate these analyses in order to limit researcher error and bias. One conclusion might therefore be that comparative-historical analysis needs to be scaled down to more manageable projects so researchers can pay much closer attention to the validity of their data. In contrast, comparative-historical researchers often claim that there are both costs and benefits to large comparative-historical analyses, and the benefits of a broadly comparative and historical analysis cannot be disregarded. Most notably, the broad perspective of comparative-historical analysis allows researchers to explore how diverse social phenomena affect one another, to take a comparative perspective, and to explore how processes unravel over time.

Not surprisingly, most comparative-historical researchers believe the benefits of comparative-historical analysis are greater than the potential costs. Still, as Lustick (1993) notes, Goldthorpe's critique about bias is a potential problem and comparative-historical researchers should attempt to address it. According to Lustick (1993), the most basic way to address it applies to all social scientific researchers regardless of their method or data: researchers must be self-conscious about the data they use. This does not mean that researchers go through a long and laborious process exploring the validity of all data, but they should recognize that all data are potentially flawed and constantly consider whether the data they are considering using are accurate. Although simple, being self-conscious of potential data problems can go a long way towards limiting the use of erroneous and biased data.

A more specific strategy that addresses the issue of biased and inaccurate secondary data involves using primary data—something that removes potential researcher bias and error—and comparative-historical researchers are presently doing so more and more frequently. Given the overwhelming amount of primary research that is needed to complete a comparative-historical analysis, however, comparative-historical researchers usually depend heavily on secondary sources and must carefully choose when to perform primary research. One way to get the most out of primary data is to choose which elements of the analysis are most vital and most in need of primary data. One indicator of the need to use primary data is when multiple and competing accounts of the same phenomena exist. In this situation, primary data can be used to help decide which version is valid. Similarly, bias usually enters the analysis when there is a lack of data, forcing the researcher to fill in the blanks with educated guesses based on the data that are available. To avoid this, researchers should note the data holes that emerge when they are piecing together their arguments and subsequently gather primary data in an effort to fill them in.

Other strategies beyond primary data collection can also be employed to deal with contradictory secondary data. Most simply, researchers can address the issue of conflicting secondary data simply by noting the contradictions and explaining their rationale for accepting one version over another. Lustick (1993, 616) refers to this strategy as "triage." Given concerns about style and flow, such discussion is probably best addressed in footnotes. Although not removing the potential for bias, this strategy allows the researcher to explain their choice of data. Moreover, it highlights potential areas where researcher bias enters the analysis and thereby allows others to check and potentially critique the analysis. For example, Moore's *Social Origins of Dictatorship and Democracy* (1966) is commonly critiqued for its dependence on R.W. Tawney's work as Tawney's accounts differ from those of most historians but conform much more closely to Moore's theory. Moore openly invited this critique by noting the diversity of opinion and describing why he accepts Tawney's more unorthodox version. Thus, when a researcher recognizes diverse perspectives and justifies his acceptance of one view over others, this does not remove the possibility of bias entering the analysis. It does, however, highlight a potential problem with the analysis, thereby encouraging others to consider the validity of the analysis. From a knowledge accumulation perspective, this strategy is far superior to simply ignoring and thereby hiding areas where bias potentially enters the analysis.

To avoid criticisms such as those made against Moore, researchers can use different strategies for weighing the validity of competing claims. Most basically, researchers can explore whether there is general agreement in the literature and reject claims that are discounted by most specialists. Similarly, they can interview disinterested academic experts and ask them which secondary source is most accurate. A different strategy involves pinpointing places of divergence among secondary sources and considering the data on which the divergent claims are made. Thus, if one claim is not supported by evidence but another is, one should accept the claim that is supported by evidence. Finally, one can research the background and views of the authors of secondary sources and consider their potential biases. When a bias appears to be present and to affect the analysis of one source more than another, researchers should use the data from the source that appears least biased. So, when Moore accepts an unorthodox position that is necessary for his theory to hold for England, this offers evidence that bias has entered the analysis and that one should not accept Moore's claims.

None of these strategies is guaranteed to eliminate data bias. However, they help to limit biased research, and the goal of all social scientific research is an accurate analysis that offers insight into our social world. Researchers must, therefore, consider Goldthorpe's critique and strive to limit data problems.

Similarly, comparative-historical researchers should also be self-conscious about potential problems caused by using data from preexisting social scientific—as opposed to historical—analyses. When multiple analyses of the same phenomenon exist and produce competing findings, researchers must consider the causes of their different findings and accept those that appear most accurate. Because researcher error and bias can enter any social scientific analysis, ideally researchers should replicate past social scientific analysis instead of simply accepting their findings. Real-world constraints commonly prevent researchers from replicating all analyses that they draw on for data. A more realistic option is a two-part assessment of the analyses. The first step involves considering the appropriateness of the data and methods employed. The second involves considering the findings of the past analysis, making an individual conclusion based on them, and seeing whether one's interpretation of the results is the same as the author's. If either part of this assessment highlights potential problems, the researcher should either acknowledge this potential problem or attempt to rectify it.

Case Selection in Comparative-Historical Analysis

If a researcher employs within-case methods for a single case and simply pursues an ideographic explanation, she or he can select any case of interest. Once a researcher intends to use both within-case and comparative methods and is interested in pursuing more nomothetic explanations, however, appropriate cases for comparison must be carefully considered. Because comparative-historical researchers rarely pursue strictly ideographic explanations, case selection is an important element of research design for most comparative-historical researchers. In this section, I first review different strategies of case selection, going on to consider critiques claiming that case selection commonly produces biased comparative-historical analysis.

Strategies of Case Selection

For any researcher who intends to offer even the most limited nomothetic insight, the first step in case selection is to delimit the universe of cases for which the explanation potentially applies. This requires that the researcher designate the unit of analysis and consider which cases can be considered part of the same set. As Ragin (2000) notes, **set delimitation** is extremely important, as it can have a large impact on the findings. Moreover, subcategories of phenomena can have distinct causes, suggesting separate analysis is warranted. A researcher must therefore carefully consider how to define cases in an effort to promote case homogeneity.

After having decided the population of cases, researchers must next consider different factors that have considerable bearing on the subsequent research findings before finalizing case selection. Among the most important factors are the number of cases to be selected, data accessibility, characteristics of individual cases, inter-case comparison, and the position of the cases within the larger set of cases. These factors have the greatest impact on case selection strategies in comparative-historical analysis.

The Number of Cases

One very important consideration that all researchers must grapple with when selecting cases is simply choosing the appropriate number of cases to analyze. This decision can be a very difficult task because there are costs and benefits to adding each additional case, and these costs and benefits are commonly unknown at the beginning of the research process. It is, therefore, quite normal for researchers to modify their decisions about the number of cases after they have started research and gained a better idea of the costs and benefits of each additional case.

A researcher must weigh the costs and benefits of selecting different numbers of cases and decide what is most appropriate for the analysis. The main benefits of analyzing more cases are insight into a greater number of cases and thereby a greater potential to generalize. Moreover, when the phenomenon under analysis has distinct subcategories, additional cases allow researchers to explore similarities and differences among subcategories. Similarly, yet more generally, looking at more cases allows researchers to analyze greater variation, and variation allows researchers to explore scope conditions, ordering, and other factors shaping the phenomenon.

These benefits are extremely important and, therefore, suggest the need to expand the number of cases as much as possible. Unfortunately, expanding the number of cases comes at a cost. Most notably, it increases the amount of work and resources needed to complete the analysis. Further, given monetary, time, and publication constraints, an increase in the number of cases commonly causes a decrease in the depth of the within-case analyses. In this way, expanding the number of cases can affect internal validity, so researchers who analyze complex processes and want to get the cases right commonly analyze only a few cases. Another potential cost of expanding the number of cases is coherence and parsimony, both of which commonly diminish with each additional case. With more cases and greater variation, an analysis might very well highlight a number of very different processes, resulting in a situation where the researcher fails to have a coherent and parsimonious set of findings. Finally, the benefit of each additional case commonly diminishes when the findings simply parallel previous cases; an analysis of several cases with similar findings can be very repetitive.

Given the costs and benefits, researchers have to figure out the most appropriate number of cases given their goals. If the goal of the analysis is ideographic explanation, there is little reason to expand the number of cases. If the goal is nomothetic explanation, however, additional cases are needed—creating a situation in which the researcher must be ready to accept many of the costs of analyzing more cases. However, there are different strategies researchers can use to reduce some of the costs of analyzing multiple cases.

First, researchers can vary the depth of within-case analysis among cases. This option usually involves in-depth analyses of one or more cases followed by more abbreviated analyses of additional cases. The in-depth within-case analyses are used to explore and highlight causal processes, whereas the more abbreviated within-case analyses commonly explore whether the findings of the in-depth case studies can be applied to additional cases. A strategy of combining in-depth and abbreviated case studies reduces the time, resources, and effort needed to complete an analysis because the abbreviated case studies require less of all three. In addition, abbreviated analyses reduce the size of the analysis and thus repetitiveness. Considering their weaknesses, abbreviated case studies offer less evidence and detail and are, therefore, less insightful. And, because they apply previous findings to additional cases, they are commonly one-sided and have the potential to force a theory on a case instead of using the case adequately to test the theory.

A second strategy involves combining the in-depth analysis of a few cases with a large-N comparative analysis. This strategy also uses in-depth analysis of a few cases to highlight causal patterns and mechanisms, and employs large-N comparison to test the generalizability of the findings of the within-case analysis. This strategy is advantaged because it reduces repetition to a minimum while extending the findings to a maximum of cases. It has two main disadvantages, however. First, it requires the availability of appropriate data for a large-N analysis. Unfortunately, the findings of within-case analysis are often very complex and not easily modeled. As a consequence, it can be very difficult to test within-case findings through large-N comparison. Often, comparative-historical researchers must make an enormous effort to gather data and compile an appropriate data set. Second, yet related to the first point, one cannot be certain that the large-N findings actually are driven by the processes or mechanisms highlighted in the within-case analyses. This is particularly problematic when the relevant concepts are not accurately operationalized and when the researcher uses within-case methods to analyze only a tiny fraction of the set.

A third and final strategy is to combine the two previous strategies. In doing so, a few in-depth analyses offer insight into processes and

Comparative-Historical Methods

mechanisms, the statistical analysis shows general relationships among a large number of cases, and abbreviated case studies offer evidence that the processes and mechanisms highlighted in the in-depth case studies are present in a number of cases—thereby offering evidence that these processes and mechanisms underlie the large-N findings. In addition to these benefits, this combinatorial strategy requires considerable time, methodological skills, and resources and commonly limits parsimony.

Data Availability

No matter how many cases a researcher selects, all empirical analyses require data. When selecting cases, researchers must therefore consider whether appropriate data are available. If a case lacks sufficient primary and secondary data, the resulting analysis will be weak. If an equally appropriate alternative with more data exists, this alternative is a better option given the extreme importance of data in social scientific analysis.

Similarly, a researcher must consider whether he or she has the linguistic skills to gather data for particular cases or whether it is possible to rely on translators or collaborators—or to learn the language. If a researcher will have great difficulty gathering data because of language difficulties, researchers must select other cases that do not impose linguistic barriers. This problem can often be skirted around when a large secondary literature allows a researcher to access considerable secondary material. Given the importance of using primary sources, however, researchers must be wary of simply relying on secondary sources.

Case selection based on data availability is a practical reality but creates additional problems for researchers; in particular, it has the potential to bias analyses. For example, linguistic-based case selection can cause bias if language is correlated with other factors. Colonial legacies offers an example. Different studies have found that former British colonies have distinct development trajectories relative to the colonies of other former colonial powers. Therefore, a study that selects only former British colonies for linguistic reasons has a biased sample and should be wary of applying the findings to all former colonies. Similarly, if poverty limits the ability of people to generate and store data, data-based case selection can result in a set of cases in which wealthy cases are overrepresented and impoverished cases are underrepresented. Notably, potential bias caused by selecting cases with data availability need only be a concern for researchers who pursue nomothetic explanations for a set of cases but wish to base their explanations on a subset of cases.

When the selection of cases based on data availability appears to introduce bias, the researcher must simply weigh the options. If bias appears to be a serious problem, the researcher must be ready to sacrifice data availability for the appropriateness of the case and focus considerable attention on generating new data. Alternatively, a researcher who decides that bias is the lesser of two evils should discuss the potential for bias and be conscious of this possibility throughout the analysis.

Case Characteristics and Importance

The particular characteristics of cases can also affect case selection. For example, among the set of cases that could possibly be selected, one case might be commonly recognized as the most important, most typical, or purest. Eckstein (1975) refers to such cases as **crucial cases** and claims that they are particularly important for theory testing and theory building. For example, Algeria and Quebec might be considered crucial cases for an analysis of French settler colonialism given the sheer number of French settlers and the special interest of the French government in each. If neither of the cases were analyzed, one might therefore question the findings of the analysis because they ignore the most important cases of the phenomenon.

Cases might also be more appropriate for selection when they conform to particular categories or ideal types. This is the case when an analysis recognizes categories and explores similarities and differences between them. For example, a researcher using Esping-Andersen's (1990) three categories of welfare regimes to analyze the social effects of different regimes would be hard-pressed not to select the United States because it is the purest example of the liberal welfare state model.

Originality is another case characteristic that can affect case selection. Specifically, if a phenomenon emerges in one location and then spreads elsewhere, an analysis of the determinants of this phenomenon would offer greatest insight if it focuses on the original phenomenon, as subsequent examples of the phenomenon might simply be caused by diffusion. Thus, an analysis of the determinants of capitalist development might place special value on the places where capitalism first emerged—mainly the Netherlands and England.

Pairing Cases to Maximize or Minimize Commonalities

Besides the characteristics of a single case, case selection can also depend on how the characteristics of multiple cases match with one another. This consideration is most important for analyses that rely heavily on small-N comparison for insight. Most notably, researchers pay considerable attention to pairing cases when they employ small-N comparison in order to maximize insight gained from small-N comparison.

As described in Chapter 5, Millian comparisons are a subtype of small-N comparison and there are, in turn, three main types of Millian comparison: the method of agreement, the method of difference, and the method of concomitant variation. The paired characteristics of cases are particularly important for the first two. For the method of agreement, researchers must select cases with similar outcomes but only one similar independent variable score among the most relevant independent variables; the method is, therefore, used for highlighting common causes. For the method of difference, researchers must select cases with different outcomes and only one difference among relevant independent variables; the method is, therefore, used for highlighting factors that cause variation in the outcome. Chapter 5 notes that neither the method of agreement nor the method of difference is appropriate for social scientific analysis on its own but that both can be valuable when combined with within-case analysis.

Chapter 5 also notes that it is close to impossible to find cases that coincide perfectly with either the method of agreement or the method of difference. However, researchers can attempt to either maximize or minimize differences in ways that *approximate* the methods. For example, one variation of the method of difference involves the selection of cases with a different outcome but a similar score for an independent variable that a prominent theory suggests should promote the same outcome. Such a comparative strategy allows the researcher to test the theory, explore scope conditions, and investigate other potentially influential factors. Notably, attempts to maximize key similarities or differences do not apply solely to Millian comparisons. In addition, narrative comparisons commonly pair cases along these lines for the same reasons. For example, process-oriented narrative comparisons frequently pair cases with similar initial conditions but different outcomes, thereby employing narrative comparison to compare the processes leading to their different outcomes in order to highlight key determinants of their divergent paths.

Besides pseudo-Millian strategies that pair cases based on similarities and differences, some researchers also pair cases in order to ensure that the cases included in the analysis vary along key variables. Some choose cases that vary along the dependent variable, a strategy that allows researchers to explore what caused the different outcomes. Alternatively, some select cases based on variation in the independent variable. This latter strategy is championed by researchers who wish to apply statistical methods to comparative case studies, as they explore how a change in the focal independent variable affects the dependent variable. When a researcher considers the focal independent and dependent variables simultaneously, the strategy changes from selection based on pairing cases to selection based on case conformity to a larger set.

Case Conformity

Case selection based on case conformity is generally used when researchers use statistical methods to highlight whether cases conform to general patterns among a larger set of cases.[1] In addition, researchers can note past findings showing a general trend and select cases for their analyses based on the conformity of cases with the past findings. There are two main strategies of selection based on case conformity.

First, researchers often choose to select cases that conform to general patterns. For this, they usually use either **residuals** or scatterplots to identify **on-line cases**, or cases that conform to general relationships. This selection strategy is employed by researchers who pursue nomothetic insight, as on-line cases are most likely to be typical and therefore to offer more general insight. This case selection strategy is common among researchers who employ process tracing, as the selection of conforming cases offers an opportunity to explore mechanisms underlying general relationships.

An alternative strategy involves selecting cases that do not conform to large-N findings—or **off-line cases**. An analysis of off-line cases can offer different types of insight, although the researcher does not know what type of insight will be gained at the onset. First, it can serve as what Gerring (2007) refers to as an influential case, or a case that does not appear to conform to the general rule but does on closer inspection. That is, an influential case is an exception that proves the rule. For example, Ertman's *Birth of the Leviathan* (1997) analyzes Denmark, a case that Ertman suggests should have possessed a patrimonial constitutional state but was instead a bureaucratic absolutist state. His prediction was based on the fact that Denmark generally had relatively participatory local governments and experienced increased geopolitical competition rather late. Through his analysis of Denmark, Ertman ultimately supports his theory by showing that Denmark initially began to develop patrimonial constitutionalism—as his theory suggests—but was pushed off this pathway by the entry of German knights and their imposition of institutions that were similar to those back in Germany.

Influential cases can also highlight scope conditions that affect the process under analysis. For example, Lipset, Trow, and Coleman's *Union Democracy* (1956) analyzes an exceptionally democratic union in an attempt to test Michels's (1911/1968) iron law of oligarchy. The book offers strong support for Michels's theory by highlighting unique union characteristics that counteracted the mechanisms promoting the iron law of oligarchy and thereby allowed the union to organize and maintain a democratic system of governance.

Similarly, the analysis of off-line cases can help highlight additional factors that were not included as independent variables in the statistical analysis but that cause some cases to be outliers. Lieberman's *Race and Regionalism in the Politics of Taxation in Brazil and South Africa* (2003) offers an example (see the section on Methodological Complementarity in Chapter 6 for a more detailed discussion of the book). Lieberman begins by noting a strong relationship between per capita GDP and a state's capacity to gather revenue through taxation. Using a scatterplot showing this relationship, he highlights both Brazil and South Africa—two countries with very similar per capita GDPs but possessing states with very different capacities to gather taxes. He subsequently analyzes both cases using within-case methods and small-N comparison in an effort to highlight additional factors beside wealth that affect a state's taxation capacity. Ultimately, he highlights how ideas of national political community and the extent of state decentralization are two additional factors that affect a state's ability to tax.

Notably, analyses do not have to choose either conforming or outlying cases, as researchers might choose to select both. This mixed selection strategy is well suited for investigating mechanisms underlying general relationships but also allows researchers to investigate either scope conditions or additional causal determinants. The analysis of outlier cases also offers a check, as the analysis of the outliers can oppose, support, or qualify the findings of the other elements of the analysis.

Case Selection and Bias

Over the last two decades, there has been considerable debate about how case selection can bias analysis. Ultimately, there are two similar yet distinct arguments: first, some claim that selecting cases with extreme values on the dependent variable is unwise, as cases with extremely high or low dependent variable scores are usually outliers (Achen and Snidal 1989; Geddes 1991; King, Keohane, and Verba 1994). As a result, if the researcher estimates a causal effect based on the extreme cases, he or she incorrectly assesses the magnitude of the effect of the focal independent variable. The second argument is concerned with researchers who attempt to generalize based on their small-N analysis but do not estimate causal effects. It suggests that case selection causes bias when the cases are not representative. Although both critiques are commonly referred to as selection bias, I refer to the first as sampling error and the second as selection bias in order to distinguish between the two.

Sampling Error

Claims about the pernicious effects of **sampling error** in small-N analysis are influenced by the work of James Heckman (1976, 1979), a Nobel Prize winning economist who noted how biased samples can greatly affect statistical estimates of causal effects. Others, in turn, have taken this idea and applied it to non-statistical analyses, including comparative-historical analysis (see Achen and Snidal 1989; Geddes 1991; King, Keohane, and Verba 1994). These researchers suggest that sampling error can have a great impact on the findings of comparative-historical analysis when the cases under analysis do not conform to the natural variation of the entire set. This is particularly problematic when research-ers select extreme cases, something that is quite common in comparative-historical analysis. Extreme cases, according to this view, are less likely to be representative, so using them to calculate causal effects produces inaccurate estimates.

Although logical, the sampling error argument makes one major error: it assumes that comparative-historical analysis is based on the same logic as statistical comparison. As described in Chapter 3, this is rarely the case. Rather, within-case methods are the most important source of insight in comparative-historical analysis. To return to our detective anal-ogy, just as the detective's choice of which murder to investigate does not affect the validity of his or her findings about who committed the mur-der, a comparative-historical researcher's choice of case does not affect the insight about that case. This is because within-case methods investi-gate causal processes, highlight mechanisms, or test theories—or some combination of the three. None of these approximate cross-sectional statistics in any way because within-case methods piece together diverse evidence to understand what happened in particular cases. Most notably, the bias argument focuses on estimates of causal effects, and no within-case method attempts to estimate causal effects. Furthermore, extreme cases are likely to provide a heightened opportunity to highlight causal mechanisms, so the analysis of extreme cases might actually offer certain advantages. Thus, the sampling error argument does not affect within-case analysis in any way.

It remains possible, however, that the analysis of extreme cases can bias insight gained from cross-case comparison, and comparison is a vital method employed by comparative-historical researchers. Yet, most comparative-historical researchers do not estimate causal effects through their comparative methods. As a consequence, sampling error usually poses little problem. For example, narrative comparison does not attempt to estimate causal effects. Instead, it compares complex concepts, processes, mechanisms, and ideal types to improve our understanding of particular causal processes and increase insight into commonalities and differences among cases. Indeed, the main purpose of narrative com-parison is to inform and direct the within-case analysis—it supplements within-case analysis, which cannot be affected by sampling error. Finally, even the comparative insight gained from narrative comparison is dependent on the within-case analysis. That is, if narrative comparison highlights common concepts, processes, mechanisms, or ideal types, the comparisons are of very little value on their own; it is the within-case analysis that underlies the strength of narrative comparison. Further, these within-case analyses are based on showing mechanisms and processes, not relationships between variables.

Millian comparison differs from narrative comparison because it operationalizes and compares variables. It therefore employs pseudo-statistical analyses and can be affected by sampling error. However, Millian comparison very rarely offers independent comparative insight because of the small number of cases analyzed. As such, sampling error is practically irrelevant because a research design that uses Millian comparison as an independent method is already flawed and incapable of offering insight. When researchers combine Millian comparison with within-case methods, in turn, the great majority of insight is made possible by the latter. Indeed, when combined with within-case analysis, Millian comparison usually has one of two rather limited purposes: researchers either use Millian comparison to frame the subsequent analysis or make Millian comparisons at the end of the analysis to summarize the previous findings. Thus, the insight of analyses that use Millian comparison is derived primarily from within-case methods, and the Millian comparisons are not used to estimate causal effects, meaning that sampling error usually poses little problem to comparative-historical researchers employing Millian comparison.

Skocpol's *States and Social Revolutions* (1979) has been a target of proponents of the sampling error critique (see Geddes 1991). It is therefore helpful to use it as an example showing how sampling error has very little effect in comparative-historical analysis. As described in Chapter 3, causal narrative is Skocpol's most important basis of insight, and causal narratives are in no way affected by sampling error. She also uses narrative and Millian comparisons, however. The narrative comparisons are primarily geared to strengthening and gaining more insight from the causal narratives, so sampling error does not affect this element either. While sampling error could possibly affect Skocpol's use of Millian comparison, she in no way attempts to estimate causal effects or offer independent causal insight based on them. Rather, her ultimate causal claims focus on necessary conditions, proposing that state breakdown and peasant mobilizational capacities are necessary for social revolution. Even more, the ultimate insight from Skocpol's Millian comparisons is not independent and completely depends on the within-case analysis for insight into causal processes.

Although sampling error does not usually cause a problem for comparative-historical analysis, it does affect some works. Specifically, sampling error can affect comparative-historical analysis when researchers employ large-N comparison, which is not surprising because sampling error is an issue that first arose to address problems with statistical analysis. Indeed, the data sets used by comparative-historical researchers are commonly truncated because certain categories of cases—poor, authoritarian, war-torn, etc.—are more likely to lack data. Concerns about sampling error in comparative-historical analysis should, therefore, focus on those works that employ large-N comparisons.

Selection Bias

Sampling error and **selection bias** are very similar concepts and might be considered the same by some. I separate them, however, because only sampling error assumes that researchers apply statistical methods to their comparative-historical analysis. Specifically, sampling error considers how the selection of cases affects estimates of causal effects derived from comparative methods. Alternatively, selection bias is more general and considers the representativeness of cases. It suggests that the selection of non-representative cases promotes inaccurate nomothetic explanations. Such explanations can be based either on estimates of causal effects or insight from within-case analysis.

Although sampling error does not pose a serious threat to comparative-historical analysis because most researchers do not employ comparative-historical methods to estimate causal effects, selection bias is an important issue that many comparative-historical researchers must consider. Specifically, researchers who pursue nomothetic explanations must consider potential problems caused by selection bias, as they might select cases that are not representative and generalize based on non-representative cases. Moreover, **cherry-picking** might bias the results—that is, researchers might select only those cases that conform to their preferred theory.

Selection bias can pose a problem to comparative-historical analysis because most of the methods in the comparative-historical toolkit are not suitable for broad nomothetic explanations. Indeed, within-case methods offer insight into the particulars of only one case and are, therefore, a poor basis for generalization (unless one analyzes many cases through within-case methods), and small-N comparison of only a handful of cases is poorly suited for offering explanations that extend beyond the subset under analysis. Most comparative-historical researchers recognize this and, therefore, do not attempt to make extremely broad claims based on their analyses. Others, however, wish to offer more nomothetic explanations and are, therefore, at greater risk of selection bias. Skocpol's *States and Social Revolutions* (1979), for example, might not have been affected by sampling error, but any attempt to generalize based on her limited set of cases opens her argument up to potential problems caused by selection bias.

For those comparative-historical researchers who pursue broadly nomothetic explanations, there are different ways to minimize the risk of selection bias. The most basic strategy involves using large-N comparison as part of the comparative-historical analysis, as this method is an important means of general insight. One particularly advantaged type of comparative-historical analysis that employs large-N comparison is what Lieberman (2005) calls a **nested analysis**. For this strategy, a researcher runs statistical analyses and chooses cases based on their fit with the statistical findings. A nested analysis therefore allows researchers to select the cases that fit the statistical analysis and that are most likely to be representative of the larger set. At the same time, the statistical findings offer insight into general relationships among the larger set of cases, thereby offering cross-case insight into the research question. When the statistical findings and the within-case analyses support one another, their combination can offer considerable insight on which one can build nomothetic explanations. Nested analysis can therefore be an important means of limiting selection bias.

An alternative strategy simply involves increasing the number of cases under analysis. The analysis of one of many cases is not likely to offer general insight into the larger set of cases, but the ability to offer general insight increases with each additional case. A researcher might, therefore, use within-case methods to analyze a large sample of the set of cases. This is the strategy pursued by Rueschemeyer, Stephens, and Stephens (1991) in their analysis of the relationship between capitalist development and democracy, with case studies of over thirty countries. Although limiting selection bias, this strategy can still be affected by it, as researchers might analyze a number of exceptional cases. Researchers using this strategy must therefore consider the representativeness of their samples. While helping to limit selection bias, there are two main disadvantages of this strategy: each additional case expands the time and resources needed to complete the research project, and additional cases commonly diminish coherence and parsimony while increasing repetitiveness. As described above, the inclusion of multiple abbreviated cases can help limit these costs.

The case selection strategies described above limit selection bias but do not necessarily address potential bias caused by cherry-picking. The one exception is nested analysis, as using statistical fit as a means of case selection helps to limit cherry-picking. When there are multiple on-line cases that the researcher can choose from, however, cherry-picking is still possible. Nested analysis can limit this possibility even further, however, when it also selects outlier cases, thereby purposefully including cases that do not fit the general theory.

Regardless of their strategy of case selection, one way researchers can limit bias caused by cherry-picking is for them to be conscious of it. They should carefully choose cases and refrain from choosing only those cases that conform to their theories. In addition, they must be explicit about case selection so that readers are able to consider whether cherry-picking has occurred.

Fearon and Laitin (2008) are particularly concerned with selection bias that results from cherry-picking; and because the strategies described above do not completely remove case selection from the hands of the researcher, they suggest that selection bias remains a problem. Therefore, they propose a strategy of case selection based on **random selection**. They do not suggest that case selection should be completely random, however. Rather, they claim researchers should use a random sample stratified by both the independent and dependent variables, a technique that ensures considerable variation among the selected cases. While overcoming cherry-picking, this strategy prevents researchers from using case selection strategies that carefully pair cases, attempt to analyze important cases, consider data availability, and consider the general fit of the cases. This strategy thus comes at a heavy price.

Even random selection is not able to avoid potential problems with selection bias altogether, however. Indeed, no matter how one selects cases for comparative-historical analysis, selection bias remains a potential problem for all works that attempt to generalize based on a small sample of cases. To limit this sort of selection bias, random selection must therefore be combined with a research design that addresses the small-N problem—such as the use of large-N comparison, a nested analysis, or the within-case analysis of many cases.

Thus, selection bias is a problem for comparative-historical researchers who wish to pursue highly nomothetic explanations. Some techniques can help limit the problem but cannot eliminate it. However, selection bias is not a problem for most comparative-historical analyses because they do not pursue explanations that apply to the universe of cases; rather they commonly pursue ideographic explanations and explanations that apply to a circumscribed set of cases. Indeed, the middling position between the extremes of ideographic and nomothetic explanations is a common hallmark of comparative-historical analysis and limits the problem of selection bias.

An Example of Case Selection

In order to highlight factors affecting case selection and to give an example of the actual concerns that go into selecting cases, it is helpful to consider case-selection strategies for a real analysis. Although many comparative-historical analyses include sections describing case selection, they are always quite abbreviated and overlook many factors the researcher actually needs to consider for case selection. It is necessary to have personal knowledge of case selection strategies, and I therefore review my own work, *Lineages of Despotism and Development* (Lange 2009) as an example here.

Lineages of Despotism and Development begins by recognizing that former British colonies are presently found at all levels of the global developmental hierarchy and explores the determinants of this variation. Although noting that multiple factors undoubtedly account for such variation, it explores three general hypotheses: variation is determined by precolonial conditions, colonial legacies, or postcolonial policy and transformations. The analysis begins with a cross-national statistical analysis of former British colonies and finds that precolonial factors explain little of postcolonial development, that the form of colonialism (measured as the extent of indirect rule) is strongly related to level of development in 1960, and that the form of colonialism is even more strongly related to the level of development in 2000. The statistical analysis, therefore, offers evidence that colonialism is an influential determinant of long-term development but offers little support for the precolonial and postcolonial hypotheses. More specifically, it suggests that direct rule institutionalized states that were more capable of promoting diverse elements of development than indirect rule.

Although offering important evidence, the statistical analysis could not highlight mechanisms and was in no way conclusive, given potential problems with the statistical analysis. I therefore chose to use within-case methods and narrative comparison to explore whether, and—if so—how, colonialism affected developmental trajectories. With several dozen former British colonies, however, I could not analyze the entire population of former British colonies in any detail. I decided that four was the maximum number of cases I would analyze because of time and monetary constraints and because I believed any additional cases would reduce the depth and detail of the case studies to unacceptable levels. At the same time, my goal was to explore common mechanisms that potentially underlay the statistical findings. Therefore I chose to include a dozen abbreviated case studies of additional former British colonies in order to check whether the findings from the in-depth case studies could be applied to additional cases. In this way, I included a statistical analysis to highlight general relationships, in-depth case studies of four cases to explore potential mechanisms underlying the statistical findings, and several abbreviated case studies to check whether the findings from the four in-depth case studies helped to explain additional cases as well.

Besides the number of cases, I also needed to figure out which cases to analyze. One factor that I considered was case conformity. Given the statistical findings and my goal to explore the impact of direct and indirect rule on state-led development, it was vital that at least one of my in-depth case studies be a directly ruled colony that conformed to the statistical analysis and another be an indirectly ruled colony that conformed to the statistical findings. My statistical analysis used multiple measures of development, however, including per capita GDP, infant mortality, average school attainment, democratization, and state capacity. I therefore had to check the residuals for five different dependent variables, something that complicated the process because few cases conformed to all five. I created a list of all former British colonies with their residuals for all models and created a much smaller pool of cases that conformed to most of the models. Mauritius and Sierra Leone were among this shortlist, and I subsequently selected them as my two on-line cases. Table 7.1 lists the standardized residuals from the statistical analyses of both cases, with 1 representing one standard deviation above the expected value and -1 representing one standard deviation below the expected value. Table 7.1, therefore, shows how both Mauritius and Sierra Leone are generally conforming cases, the main exception being that Sierra Leone had a considerably higher infant mortality rate in 2000 than predicted by the model.

Besides selecting conforming cases, I also chose to select two cases that were statistical outliers. Specifically, I wanted to analyze one indirectly ruled colony that had greater levels of development than expected given its form of colonialism and one directly ruled colony that had lower levels of development than expected given its form of colonialism. I chose to select two outliers to check the generalizability of the findings of the two conforming cases. Specifically, an in-depth analysis of non-conforming

Table 7.1 Standardized residual scores of Botswana, Guyana, Mauritius, and Sierra Leone

	Democracy, 1972–2000	Governance, 1996–2005	GDP, 2000	Infant Mortality, 2000	Education, 1995
Mauritius	0.62	–0.01	0.27	–0.09	–1.30
Sierra Leone	0.09	–0.25	–0.46	3.91	–0.39
Guyana	–0.75	–1.91	–2.23	2.08	–1.01
Botswana	1.59	1.81	1.50	0.70	–0.02

Source: Lange 2009, 64

cases could either offer evidence that the statistical relationship between the form of colonialism and postcolonial development is spurious and that the findings of the conforming cases are unique, highlight contextual conditions on which the form of colonialism depends and which explain the exceptionalism of the outliers, or show exceptions that prove the general rule. Moreover, the selection of non-conforming cases helps limit bias caused by cherry-picking because it explicitly selects cases that do not conform to the statistical findings. Similar to the conforming cases, I used residuals from the models using five different dependent variables to select a pool of cases that were appropriate outliers, including the two that I ultimately selected: Botswana and Guyana. Table 7.1 lists their residuals, showing that Botswana generally had a better developmental record than expected and that Guyana generally had a worse developmental record than expected.

The conformity of a case to the statistical analysis was, therefore, a major criterion I used to select cases for in-depth analysis, having selected a strategy of analyzing one conforming directly ruled colony, one conforming indirectly ruled colony, one non-conforming directly ruled colony, and one non-conforming indirectly ruled colony. Case conformity was not the sole selection criterion, however. Indeed, if it was, I could have found a couple of cases that conformed more closely or were bigger outliers. Three additional factors that I considered were the individual characteristics of cases, how cases paired with one another, and my prior knowledge of the cases.

My main concern about individual characteristics was to select cases that could not be easily explained by other factors in order to isolate the impact of the form of colonialism. For example, I could have chosen Canada or Singapore as typical examples of directly ruled colonies. However, settlement and strategic location were factors that placed both colonies at a developmental advantage regardless of their form of colonial rule, and I wanted to focus on their form of colonial rule. I, therefore, sought a directly ruled colony that—other than its form of colonialism—seemed unlikely to become a developmental success. Ultimately, I decided to analyze one of several directly ruled plantation colonies because all general developmental theories suggest that plantation-based economies with enormous class inequalities are strong deterrents to development. Of the several former British plantation colonies, Mauritius was the most appropriate choice because its developmental record was average among former British plantation colonies (and it conformed most closely to the statistical findings).

Because I planned to use small-N comparison, I also carefully considered how the cases paired with one another. Specifically, I sought to maximize similarities among cases with different outcomes and different forms of colonialism in order to focus on the potential effect of the form of colonialism. Thus, because I chose a plantation colony as the conforming case of a directly ruled colony (Mauritius), I also selected a directly ruled plantation colony as the non–conforming case (Guyana). Moreover, Guyana has a population that—in terms of size and ethnic composition—is similar to that in Mauritius. Given their marked similarities, a comparison of the two therefore helps to highlight factors causing their divergent developmental trajectories.

I also considered pairings of other cases. For example, both Mauritius and Sierra Leone are small tropical countries in the African region with strategic ports, thereby mimimizing differences and helping to highlight the impact of the form of colonialism. Similarly, I selected Botswana and Sierra Leone because both were indirectly ruled African colonies with similar population sizes and rich diamond reserves. They also had similar forms of colonial rule throughout most of the colonial period (although the extent of indirect rule ultimately decreased rapidly during the independence transition in Botswana). The similarities therefore created an opportunity to pinpoint differences that promoted the very different developmental trajectories of the cases.

Finally, the project actually emerged out of an exploratory case study I had completed on the long–term determinants of Mauritian development. My research highlighted the important impact of major political and social reforms during the late colonial period, and the case therefore began my project on the long–term developmental legacies of British colonialism. I was interested in including the Mauritian case because of my previous research. Thankfully, I was able to include it because Mauritius strongly conformed to the statistical findings, had characteristics that allowed me to isolate the impact of colonialism, and paired well with other cases.

These are the main reasons I ultimately selected Mauritius, Sierra Leone, Guyana, and Botswana. Other selection criteria, however, disfavored them, and I ultimately selected them because I believed these cases offered the greatest potential benefits. Here, I briefly go over some of the potential problems with the cases I selected in order to show how researchers must weigh the costs and the benefits and ultimately select imperfect cases.

There was one particular data problem concerning Sierra Leone that nearly prevented me from selecting it. I selected my cases during the Sierra Leonean civil war, and the violence and destruction prevented me from completing fieldwork in Sierra Leone, making data accessibility an important concern. Ultimately, I decided to select the case because quality secondary sources were available and because many important primary sources were available in British archives and libraries. Although a bit uneasy about analyzing a country I had never visited, I therefore decided to select the country given the potential benefits the case could offer.

Concerning Botswana, I was initially hesitant to select it because it had one important difference with Sierra Leone: during the late colonial period, Botswana's level of indirect rule was considerably less than Sierra Leone's. As a result, the pairing matched cases with different degrees of indirect rule, preventing me from holding the form of colonialism constant in an effort to isolate other factors causing their divergent outcomes. Ultimately, I selected Botswana because it paired very well with Sierra Leone in other ways and was a clear outlier that had a much better developmental trajectory than one would have predicted given its relatively high levels of indirect rule.

Another important concern for all of the cases was their marginal positions within the British Empire. Indeed, I ultimately selected four small and peripheral colonies whose population and resources comprised only a tiny segment of the peoples and wealth of the entire empire. Most notably, India stood out as the so-called jewel of the British Empire, and I therefore sought to include it. Moreover, Nigeria, Malaysia, and other former colonies were larger and more central to the empire. In making my ultimate selection, I decided against in-depth analyses of these cases for different reasons. First, a few conformed less nicely to the statistical analysis. Moreover, I felt that the ultimate pairings of cases were important, and the pairings were poorer when including the more significant former British colonies. Moreover, my selection of smaller former colonies allowed me to analyze the cases more thoroughly, as a thorough analysis of a case like India would require a book-length manuscript on its own.

Finally, I really wanted to include an in-depth analysis of a case with a form of colonialism that clearly and evenly mixed both direct and indirect colonial rule. India, Malaysia, Burma, and South Africa are notable examples. Ideally, I would have included either a conforming case with a mixed form of colonial rule (Malaysia or India) or a conforming and a non-conforming case (Malaysia and Burma, given their similarities and that Malaysia is a conforming case and Burma is a non-conforming case). I chose not to do either out of a belief that five or six in-depth cases would be overly burdensome.

My concerns about crucial cases and cases with mixed forms of colonialism did push me to include some in the analysis, however. As mentioned previously, I also selected a dozen former colonies for more abbreviated analysis. Ultimately, these cases were selected based on three main criteria: I selected large and important colonies that might be viewed as crucial, I selected cases with forms of colonialism that mixed direct and indirect rule, and I selected cases that were unique in certain ways. Notably, this design strategy is imperfect because abbreviated case studies cannot go into detail, offer more limited evidence, and are usually very one-sided given their brevity and focus. In the end, I decided abbreviated case studies were an imperfect solution to some of the problems caused by my selection of Mauritius, Sierra Leone, Guyana, and Botswana for in-depth analysis.

Instead of struggling through case selection based on all of these factors, Fearon and Laitin (2008) recommend case selection based on random selection. I decided against such a strategy for different reasons. First, my use of a nested analysis—and, in particular, my strategy of analyzing both on-line and off-line cases—helped limit cherry-picking, which is the main problem that random selection helps eliminate. I did not believe, therefore, that random selection would be very valuable. Moreover, random selection would have prevented me from considering other factors that I believed were important. Most notably, I would not have been able to carefully pair cases or select cases based on their general statistical fit.

This overview of my case selection strategy accurately reviews the factors I considered, but it presents these considerations and the actual case-selection process in an over-simplified manner. Indeed, I did not sit down at one time, consider all of these factors, and then finalize my cases; rather, it was a back-and-forth process that took years to complete. As mentioned previously, the project began as an exploratory case study of the impact of colonialism on long-term development in Mauritius, and this case study inspired a theory that I subsequently tested statistically. After completing an initial statistical analysis, I began to contemplate seriously the selection of additional cases, but even this took considerable time. For example, Sierra Leone seemed like an appropriate case, but I needed to see whether there were sufficient data available in the UK. Moreover, it took me several years and multiple fieldtrips to decide not to include a case study of a former colony with a more mixed form of rule; I wanted to but had limited time and resources and, eventually, I came to the conclusion that the case would add little to the overall analysis. Allied with this decision, I only decided to include a chapter with several abbreviated case studies after I had ruled out the possibility of analyzing a case with a mixed form of rule, deciding at that point that several abbreviated case studies would be more valuable than one long case study. In this way, although it might seem simple and like something one completes at the beginning of a comparative-historical research project, case selection is generally a complicated and messy affair and can extend well into the research project.

Theory and Comparative-Historical Analysis

Comparative-historical researchers are frequently well-versed in theory and commonly teach courses on social theory. Two main factors are likely to underlie the affinity between the two. First, and most importantly, the founding figures of social theory are also the founding figures of comparative-historical analysis, with Marx, Engels, Smith, Weber, and Tocqueville being the most notable examples. Second, these classic social theorists focused on the same issues that most contemporary comparative-historical researchers analyze: large-scale social change, with a special interest in capitalist development, revolutions, democratization, and state building. This common heritage has caused many researchers from the second generation of comparative-historical analysis—especially the early second generation—to draw on classic social theories.

More recently, there has been a move away from the more grandiose classic social theories and a considerable push toward mid-level theory. With this theoretical shift, there has been growing interest in causal mechanisms. Kiser and Hechter (1991) helped usher in this theoretical reorientation through an influential article that questioned the role of theory in comparative-historical analysis and claimed that comparative-historical researchers needed to pay greater attention to mechanisms. Still, their comments reflected changes that were already at work. Most notably, the use of meta-theory within comparative-historical analysis—and the whole social sciences, for that matter—came under increasing scrutiny because social complexity caused problems for social theories that attempted to explain everything. Simultaneously, comparative-historical researchers increasingly recognized that mechanisms allow the analysis of general processes while still highlighting the peculiarities of individual cases. In this way, it is a type of middle ground between nomothetic and ideographic positions, a position that has always been prevalent in comparative-historical analysis—despite temporary swings in one direction or another—and one that caused comparative-historical researchers to embrace mechanisms.

The theoretical shift in comparative-historical analysis is most notable in Rueschemeyer's *Usable Theory* (2010). Rueschemeyer is both a notable social theorist and a comparative-historical researcher. In *Usable Theory*, he lays out how a mid-level theoretical perspective focused on mechanisms is most appropriate for social scientific analysis and describes a number of different mechanisms based on different theoretical perspectives. Although Kiser and Hechter would appear to be pleased with this theoretical reorientation toward mechanisms, Kiser (1996) actually criticizes such an approach in another article. A mechanistic "toolkit" approach, he argues, hinders theory testing by simply allowing a researcher to arbitrarily substitute one mechanism for another when the first does not work. As one potential solution, he proposes limiting the analysis to the mechanism that he believes offers the greatest insight into social processes: the rational-choice mechanism.

The rational-choice mechanism is distinct from others because numerous researchers use it as the sole mechanism for social analysis. In this way, one might view it as a mechanistic meta-theory. That being said, most rational-choice researchers recognize that it is only one of several mechanisms that affect social processes but choose to focus on it out of a belief that it is the most important. Prominent comparative-historical researchers who employ rational-choice theory include Robert H. Bates, Margaret Levi, Michael Hechter, and Edgar Kiser. Although forming a distinct and growing niche, rational-choice-based comparative-historical analysis remains quite rare. However, rational-choice theory has also been the sole theoretical perspective employed by most economists who use comparative-historical methods, and a growing number of political scientists within the methodological tradition take a rational-choice perspective.

Ultimately, Kiser's critique and advocacy for rational-choice theory pushes comparative-historical analysis back to analyses that explain most of the universe of cases based on one theory, something that fell out of favor with the decline of structural functionalism and Marxism. The reason for their long-standing demise is extreme social complexity. In a situation of extreme social complexity, in turn, Rueshemeyer's proposed toolkit of mechanisms appears highly appropriate. Moreover, most analyses that consider multiple mechanisms are still able to test them and do not simply mix and match mechanisms arbitrarily. If a mechanism does not hold, comparative-historical researchers explore the presence of opposing mechanisms and investigate scope conditions that potentially affect the mechanisms, and such an analysis offers powerful tests of mechanisms.

Besides a growing focus on mechanisms, over the past twenty years comparative-historical scholars have increasingly looked beyond the perspectives of early theorists and employed the theories of more recent theorists. Most notably, Pierre Bourdieu, Michel Foucault, and Edward Said have influenced several recent comparative-historical analyses. In so doing, they have brought discourse, culture, and critical views of power more centrally into comparative-historical analysis. For example, Steinmetz (2007) draws on both Said and Bourdieu in *The Devil's Handwriting*, which explores how precolonial discourses affected "native policy" in three former German colonies. Gorski's (2003) *The Disciplinary Revolution* follows the Foucaultian tradition. Specifically,

Gorski uses Foucault's theory of discipline and power to help explain how Calvinism promoted state building in Early Modern Europe. Notably, these theoretical perspectives are not opposed to mechanistic analysis, as both Steinmetz and Gorski clearly focus on causal mechanisms in their analyses.

Theory Development and Theory Testing

Although social theorists might see theory as an end in itself, most social scientists view it as a component of empirical research. Theory, however, can be used for social scientific analyses in different ways. Some attempt to use an empirical analysis to help build theory, whereas others employ an empirical analysis to test preexisting theories. Comparative-historical methods, in turn, are well-suited for both, although particular methods and methodological combinations within the comparative-historical methodological toolkit are more advantaged for one than the other (see Chapter 6). Whether one uses comparative-historical methods to build or to test theories ultimately depends on the research question and the goal of the researcher. Theory building is most likely when existing theories are unable to explain adequately particular phenomena. Theory testing, on the other hand, is most likely when the researcher wants to explore whether existing theories help to explain particular phenomena.

Theory development is largely an inductive process whereby researchers use their in-depth knowledge of a particular phenomenon to postulate theoretical precepts about general phenomena. Comparative-historical methods are ideal for theory development because within-case methods allow researchers to gain great insight into particular cases. This is especially the case for causal narrative and process tracing. Both of these within-case methods also allow researchers to analyze complex causal processes, scope conditions that affect them, and track how causal processes occur over time. In this way, they allow researchers to consider diverse aspects of phenomena that might be theoretically relevant.

In addition to within-case methods, the comparative methods used by comparative-historical researchers can also contribute to theory development. For example, inter-case comparison can be a means of refining theory, as it allows the researcher to consider similarities and differences between cases and such comparisons play a vital role transforming ideographic insight into theory. Mann's *The Sources of Social Power* (1986) offers a notable example. In it, Mann uses comparative methods to highlight commonalities among cases and thereby to formulate a complex theory of social power. Barrington Moore's *Social Origins of Dictatorship and Democracy* (1966) offers another celebrated example. The book follows a standard format for theory building, as it begins with in-depth case studies focusing on internal validity and ends with a comparative review of the cases that explores commonalities and differences. The comparative analysis proves very valuable at theory building and lays out a number of hypotheses about the determinants of democracy and dictatorship, including his famous claim "No bourgeoisie, no democracy" (Moore 1966, 418).

Among the comparative methods, small-N comparisons are particularly well-suited to theory building. Most notably, narrative comparison allows researchers to highlight factors and conditions shaping the process, and such insight plays an important role in building theory. Millian comparison is disadvantaged in this regard, although it can still play an important role in theory building by highlighting similarities and differences between cases.

Instead of building theory, a number of researchers use theory deductively: they test theories by applying them to cases. Comparative-historical researchers commonly use within-case methods to test whether one or more cases conforms to a theory. Most notably, pattern matching is ideally suited for theory testing, as the technique is used to explore whether particular cases support or oppose different theories. To do this, the researcher generates multiple hypotheses based on one or more theories and analyzes whether cases support these hypotheses. In this way, individual cases can offer multiple sources of insight into the validity of a theory. Most commonly, researchers apply pattern matching to multiple cases, as the analysis of more cases increases the strength of the test.

Comparative methods also allow researchers to test theories. Most notably, comparison allows researchers to explore relationships between variables, something that can offer powerful insight into the validity of theory. Similarly, one can employ a type of comparative pattern matching, whereby one develops hypotheses based on a theory and tests the hypotheses through a qualitative comparison of cases.

One work that uses comparative-historical methods to test theory is Paige's *Agrarian Revolution* (1975). It begins by laying out his general theory of agrarian movements. Next, it uses statistics to test whether the hypotheses derived from the theory are supported through cross-case comparison and the analysis supports his theory. Finally, he employs pattern matching as his secondary within-case method and uses detailed case studies to test his hypotheses. Instead of testing their own theories, other researchers test the theories of others and sometimes simultaneously analyze competing theories. Wickham-Crowley's *Guerrillas and Revolution in Latin America* (1993) offers one example. The book lays out the most prominent theories of guerrilla movements and uses both within-case methods and comparative methods to test them, ultimately finding that all theories offer important insight into guerrilla movements in Latin America (see Chapters 5 and 6 for a more detailed methodological review of both books).

Although criticized by some neo–positivists who believe in the necessary distinction between the context of discovery and the context of validation, comparative-historical researchers sometimes combine both theory development and theory testing (see Rueschemeyer and Stephens 1997). Indeed, many works that develop theories attempt to extend the theory to additional cases as an initial test. Similarly, many works that set out to test theories subsequently modify the theory based on their initial findings. For example, Rueschemeyer, Stephens, and Stephens's *Capitalist Development and Democracy* (1991) starts with a theory and tests it on multiple cases. Although the analysis strongly supports their theory, they also discover certain inaccuracies and subsequently refine the theory to make it more nuanced. In this way, the work tests a theory but, in so doing, also refines it.

Most within-case and comparative methods can be used for both theory development and theory testing, but several methods have affinities with one or the other. Most notably, the analytic goal of pattern matching is testing theories, so pattern matching is the ideal within-case method for researchers who wish to use comparative-historical methods to test theory. Alternatively, causal narrative is focused on describing particular causal processes in an effort to highlight the causes of particular social phenomena. In so doing, it is well suited for theory building. Process tracing, in turn, is well suited for either theory testing or theory development, as it can explore new mechanisms or test mechanisms related to preexisting theory.

Among comparative methods, large-N comparative methods are best suited to testing theory. Statistics, for example, is able to include multiple independent variables to simultaneously test competing theories. Small-N comparison, on the other hand, is particularly advantaged at building and refining theory because it allows researchers to explore commonalities and differences among a small number of cases. Most notably, process-oriented narrative comparison allows researchers to compare temporal, contextual, and other factors that can shape the outcome in subtle ways and is, therefore, particularly advantaged in this regard.

Summary

The previous methodological chapters discuss the actual techniques used to analyze data. This chapter changes the focus to analyze three methodological elements that do not deal with the techniques of analysis but are vital for any empirical analysis. First, it discusses the data used by comparative-historical researchers. Comparative-historical researchers use a variety of data sources but are particularly dependent on historical and secondary sources. Different critiques have been raised against the data used by comparative-historical researchers, and different strategies can be used to help reduce data problems. The two main strategies involve being more self-conscious about data quality and increasing the use of primary sources.

Next, the chapter considers case selection. Case selection is an important element of research design for all comparative-historical researchers, and researchers commonly select cases based on their consideration of different factors, including the number of cases, data availability, particular case characteristics, the pairing of multiple cases, and case conformity. Case selection has the potential to introduce bias into the analysis in different ways, including sampling error and selection bias. Although sampling error rarely affects comparative-historical analyses because researchers rarely use comparative-historical method to estimate causal effects, selection bias can affect comparative-historical analysis, so researchers who wish to extend their findings beyond the cases they analyze need to consider ways of limiting it.

Finally, the chapter describes how comparative-historical researchers use theory to guide the methods. Presently, researchers very rarely use comparative-historical methods to build or test meta-theories. Rather, contemporary comparative-historical researchers are usually theoretically eclectic and focus on mid-level theory. Increasingly, comparative-historical researchers pay considerable attention to mechanisms, a mid-level theoretical focus that comparative-historical methods are well suited to analyze. Lastly, comparative-historical researchers actively employ theory both deductively to test theory and inductively to build theory, and different methods within the comparative-historical toolkit are more advantaged at one or the other.

Glossary

Causal-process observation (CPO): An insight or piece of data that provides information about context, process or mechanism, and that contributes distinctive leverage in causal inference. Causal-process observations are distinct from data points, which measure particular variables for particular cases.

Cherry-picking: The act of selecting either data or cases that conform to the researcher's favored theory or explanation and a potential source of error in social scientific analysis.

Crucial case: A case that offers particularly important insight that can be used to either build or test theories. The importance of the case might be caused by its close conformity to a particular category, the fact that a phenomenon originated in the case, or other factors.

Nested analysis: A mixed-methods research design that combines statistical and within-case methods (usually either causal narrative or process tracing). It uses statistical methods to analyze general relationships and to highlight the extent to which individual cases conform to the statistical findings. Next, it uses within-case methods to analyze the causal processes in particular cases. Usually, within-case analysis explores mechanisms that potentially underlie the statistical findings.

Off-line case: A case that does not conform to general statistical findings. That is, it has relatively high residuals, showing that the statistical model produced inaccurate estimates of the case's dependent variable score.

On-line case: A case that conforms to general statistical findings. That is, it has relatively low residuals, showing that the statistical model produced accurate estimates of the case's dependent variable score.

Primary data: Information from original sources, including historical documents, artistic works, experiments, surveys, observations, and interviews.

Random selection: The act of choosing one or more cases at random. Such a procedure removes any source of selection bias, although it prevents the use of selection techniques that offer analytic advantages.

Residual: A statistical term referring to the difference between the observed value of a variable for a particular case and the value predicted by the regression model. It therefore shows the error of the predicted value of a case based on a statistical model, with small residuals showing that the model was a relatively good predictor but larger residuals showing that the model was a poor predictor.

Sampling error: A particular type of selection bias that occurs when a non-representative sample causes researchers to estimate causal effects inaccurately. It affects comparative methods that estimate causal effects, with statistics being the most notable.

Secondary data: Information from non-original sources that has been gathered by researchers and recorded in books, articles, and other publications.

Selection bias: Error that arises when cases are selected according to an unrepresentative sampling rule, which results in inaccurate cross-case insight. That is, general claims of causation are inaccurate because the set of cases analyzed is not representative of the entire set of cases.

Set delimitation: The act of delimiting the cases that share certain characteristics and are sufficiently similar for causal factors to have similar effects on them. Set delimitation therefore attempts to reduce inter-case heterogeneity. It is usually a theory-driven exercise, although empirical analyses can also be used to delimit sets.

Note

1 See Gerring (2007) for several detailed examples of how to select cases based on case conformity.

8

Comparative-Historical Methods: Conclusion and Assessment

Comparative-historical methods are the main methods of comparative-historical analysis, a rich and historic research tradition that was begun by the founding figures of the social sciences and includes a number of the most influential social scientists of all time. Notable researchers whose works use comparative-historical methods include Adam Smith, Alexis de Tocqueville, Karl Marx, Max Weber, Marc Bloch, Karl Polanyi, Barrington Moore Jr., Charles Tilly, Immanuel Wallerstein, and Theda Skocpol among others. It is therefore evident that comparative-historical methods have been used to produce some of the best and most influential social scientific analyses of all time and must be viewed as a major methodological tradition in the social sciences.

Despite a long and prestigious heritage, there has been relatively little work on comparative-historical methods. Indeed, it is quite possibly the only major methodological tradition within the social sciences without a single book outlining its methods. The preceding chapters help fill this methodological lacuna by describing and interpreting the basic methods used for comparative-historical analysis. In this chapter, I conclude the book by giving a final overview of comparative-historical methods and offering an assessment of their analytic benefits.

The Components of Comparative-Historical Methods

Comparative-historical methods are a unique methodological tradition in two important ways. First, as their name implies, comparative-historical methods combine multiple methods. Historically oriented within-case methods are employed to explore what happened in particular cases. In addition, various comparative methods offer more general insight by comparing and contrasting cases. Alternatively, the other major methodological traditions of the social sciences generally employ only one main method: historical and ethnographic methods rely overwhelmingly on within-case analysis, and statistical and experimental methods rely exclusively on comparison.

Second, yet related to the first point, comparative-historical methods generally attempt to offer a combination of ideographic and nomothetic insight, and this middling position is also unique among social scientific methods. Within-case methods offer insight into the particular causal processes of individual cases, whereas the comparative methods offer more generalizable insight. Thus, the particular methodological combination of comparative-historical analysis makes possible both types of insight. As Skocpol puts it, "comparative historical research has successfully developed valid generalizations about many phenomena of great importance without ignoring contextual particularities" (2003, 414). All other major methodological traditions in the social sciences, however, rely overwhelmingly on either within-case or comparative methods, so they are forced to focus on either nomothetic or ideographic insight.

The within-case methods used by comparative-historical researchers include both primary within-case methods and secondary within-case methods. Primary within-case methods offer evidence that can be used to explore the research question. Comparative-historical researchers use diverse primary within-case methods, although historical methods are easily the most common. As the name suggests, historical methods are the main method of historians and offer insight into the characteristics of historical phenomena. Internal comparison, which compares either the same case over time or subcomponents of the case, is also commonly used as a primary within-case method for within-case analysis. Other less common primary within-case methods include— but are not limited to—network analysis, GIS, ethnographic methods, archeological methods, linguistic methods, and game-theoretic methods. Comparative-historical researchers sometimes employ these primary within-case methods themselves. This is most commonly the case for historical methods and internal comparison. Nearly all researchers also depend on evidence from secondary sources that use the primary within-case methods to generate evidence. Because of the latter, comparative-historical researchers frequently do not use the primary within-case methods themselves, and primary within-case methods are commonly hidden from the comparative-historical analysis.

Secondary within-case methods differ from primary within-case methods because they assess and combine the evidence provided by the primary methods. They therefore depend on the primary within-case methods for evidence but guide the overall within-case analysis of the evidence. The three secondary within-case methods commonly used for comparative-historical analysis are causal narrative, process tracing, and pattern matching—each of which pursues different types of insight. A causal narrative is a detective style analysis that explores the causes of a particular outcome in a particular case. It looks at the details of the case, assembles them, and offers a particular narrative account of what contributed to the outcome. Process tracing is similar to causal narrative because it employs narratives to explore causal relationships but differs in important ways. Most notably, process tracing is more focused and explores mechanisms linking either related variables or factors in a causal sequence. Finally, pattern matching is distinct from both causal narrative and process tracing because it does not focus on causal processes—and indeed might not even consider them. Rather, it assesses case-specific data to test one or more theories; that is, it is a technique that allows researchers to test theories through case studies.

In addition to describing the within-case techniques used to analyze data, the book also considers two particular and valuable types of insight that can be gained from within-case methods. All three secondary within-case methods can offer such insight, although causal narrative is particularly advantaged at providing both types of insight. First, within-case methods can analyze temporality, and time can have important effects on the social phenomena under question. Most notably, within-case methods are commonly used to explore causal ordering, covariation over time, threshold effects, asymmetric processes, period effects, and path dependence. Second, cases are commonly shaped by their relationships with other cases, and within-case methods allow researchers to explore the causal impact of inter-case relationships.

Along with within-case methods, comparative-historical researchers also use multiple comparative methods to gain insight into their research questions. Similar to within-case methods, comparative methods include two basic types, each with multiple subtypes.

The first general type of comparison is large-N comparison, which compares multiple cases simultaneously and uses comparison as an independent means of insight. Although very common within the social sciences, it is relatively rare in comparative-historical analysis. The two main subtypes of large-N comparison are statistical and Boolean comparison. Statistical comparison analyzes relationships between variables using a probabilistic logic and estimates causal effects. Boolean comparison, commonly referred to as Boolean algebra, is much rarer than statistical comparison within the social sciences. It differs markedly from statistics because it explicitly explores necessary and sufficient causes—not relationships—through inter-case comparison and does not estimate a causal effect. Moreover, it compares configurations of variables instead of individual variables and sometimes employs a deterministic comparative logic.

The second—and the most common—type of comparison used by comparative-historical researchers is small-N comparison. Unlike large-N comparison, small-N comparison offers very little—if any—independent insight. Instead, it supplements or guides analyses using other methods, offers insight only when combined with other methods, or both. The two main subtypes of small-N comparison are Millian and narrative comparisons, both of which can be further subdivided into additional categories. Like large-N comparison, Millian comparison operationalizes and compares variables. It is usually able to make more detailed comparisons and to compare more complex phenomena than large-N comparison, but its small number of cases severely limits its comparative insight. Narrative comparison, on the other hand, does not compare variables. Instead, it compares complex phenomena that cannot be easily operationalized, including processes, mechanisms, and ideal types. Relative to Millian comparison, it is better suited to analyze actual causal processes and highlight influential causal determinants. Similar to Millian comparison, however, it offers little or no independent comparative insight and has difficulty providing nomothetic insight.

Comparative-historical analysis, therefore, combines both within-case and comparative methods, but comparative-historical researchers do not combine them for the sake of it; one can gain three valuable analytic benefits by combining methods. First, combining methods allows researchers to triangulate or use different methods to offer independent insight into the same phenomenon and see whether the different findings support one another. This is important because social complexity and data problems make the insight provided by any single method suspect, but one can be more confident in social scientific conclusions when they are supported by multiple methods. Second, methods can complement one another, with each having a particular strength that helps make up for a weakness of another. For example, statistical comparison is advantaged at offering general insight but disadvantaged at offering insight into causal processes, causal narrative is advantaged at offering insight into causal processes but disadvantaged at offering general insight, and the combination of both methods therefore helps maximize strengths and minimize weaknesses. Finally, combining methods can promote methodological synergy, whereby combining methods actually strengthens their ability to offer insight. Most notably, small-N comparisons offer little or no independent insight but can offer important insight when combined with different within-case methods.

Because comparative-historical methods actively combine methods in these ways, it is important to consider the total configuration of methods used for comparative-historical analysis instead of considering each method separately. Indeed, one can only gauge the total insight offered by comparative-historical analyses by carefully considering how the methods work together. This is particularly the case because the insight of many methods depends on their combination with other methods, and some methods offer no independent insight. Most notably, within-case methods and small-N comparison—which nearly all comparative-historical analyses include—are usually combined in ways that strengthen each. When only considering methods independently, researchers fail to recognize the total insight offered by comparative-historical methods.

Besides reviewing within-case methods, comparative methods, and the ways that comparative-historical researchers combine them, this book also considers three general methodological issues that researchers must consider in order to complete a comparative-historical analysis. First, all scientific analyses depend on data, and comparative-historical researchers must, therefore, consider their sources and types of data when they are designing and completing their research. Comparative-historical researchers depend on a variety of data but are most likely to use secondary sources and historical primary sources. All data can be erroneous, and comparative-historical researchers must critically assess their data and use different strategies in an effort to limit the use of biased data. This problem can be mitigated—but not eliminated—in different ways, including using techniques to assess contradictory sources, employing primary sources instead of secondary sources, and replicating past analyses. Most basically, however, researchers must be self-conscious and aware of potential problems with the data.

Second, comparative research must also consider case selection, as the cases they select have great bearing on their ultimate findings. There are a number of factors that must be considered when selecting cases, including the number of cases, data availability, case characteristics, pairing cases, and case conformity. Moreover, when researchers pursue nomothetic explanations, they must attempt to limit selection strategies that bias the analysis. Simply being conscious of selection bias and the potential problems it can cause can go a long way in limiting it. In addition, the most important strategies for limiting selection bias are using large-N comparison as a method and increasing the number of cases analyzed through within-case methods. Researchers might also use random selection, a technique that is particularly well-suited to preventing cherry-picking but that also prevents researchers from selecting cases based on other important factors. Because of the latter, random selection comes at a considerable cost, and comparative-historical researchers use it very rarely.

Finally, comparative-historical research is theoretically oriented, and researchers use theory to guide their analyses. Comparative-historical researchers use theory from a variety of theoretical traditions. Although early comparative-historical researchers used meta-theories—and created among the most influential meta-theoretic traditions—most contemporary researchers use mid-level theory focused on mechanisms to guide their analyses. The theoretical focus on mechanisms, in turn, helps to integrate the theory into the analysis and allows researchers to use theory both deductively and inductively. Importantly, comparative-historical methods are well-suited for analyses that either build theory inductively or test theories deductively.

The Value of Comparative-Historical Methods: A Final Assessment

Researchers choose methods—in part—based on their subjective valuation of different methods, and once researchers use a method they have a large stake in it. As a result, researchers often have biases in favor of the methods they use and get into methodological debates about the superiority of their chosen method. In this section, I might be accused of instigating such a debate, as I claim that comparative-historical analysis has one enormous advantage over other methodological traditions. My claims might be more palatable to practitioners of other research traditions, however, because the greatest advantage of comparative-historical analysis is that it actively combines diverse methods. This methodological pluralism not only allows researchers to gain more and different types of insight, but it helps engage researchers in diverse literatures and traditions, thereby preventing them from disregarding the findings and perspectives of different research traditions.

The best way of gaining scientific insight is through controlled laboratory experiments. Unfortunately, many social phenomena cannot be analyzed through controlled experiments because of impracticality or immorality. As a result, most social scientists are left with different methods that offer imperfect insight into social relations, so one can never be certain that the conclusions of social scientific analyses are valid. That said, all methods offer important but limited insight into social relations, so social scientific analysis can increase our understanding of social processes. Combining methods is very beneficial in such an uncertain situation. First, combining insight from different methods is a way to double-check the validity of each method. If the methods offer opposing findings, the researcher will not be able to reach a clear conclusion but, in so doing, is less likely to make invalid conclusions. On the other hand, when the methods point to similar conclusions, researchers can have more confidence in those conclusions. As Hall notes, "natural scientists normally seek many kinds of observations pertinent to the causal processes they are studying. So should social scientists" (2003, 397).

Even more than methodological triangulation, combining methods allows researchers to limit the weaknesses of methods and maximize their advantages. Such a methodological division of labor can thereby allow researchers to limit some of the shortcomings of their methods. Similarly, some methods offer little or no insight on their own, but they are able to offer insight when combined with other methods. In this way, combining methods not only offers multiple types of insight, but it can also improve that insight.

Comparative-historical methods, in turn, include multiple methods in their methodological toolkit. Highlighting this methodological pluralism, the main section for comparative-historical methods in the American Political Science Association is named Qualitative and Multi-Method Research. Because of this methodological pluralism, comparative-historical analysis is not constrained to particular methods but expands its methodological repertoire as researchers discover new methods that offer insight into their research questions. Statistics is a notable past addition; and Boolean comparison, methods of network analysis, and GIS are three more recent additions to the methodological toolkit. Skocpol notes that this methodological pluralism is an important advantage, as "[d]escent into theoretical monism or methodological rigidity is always a risk in academia—and it can easily lead to sterile dead ends" (2003, 419). Comparative-historical methods should, therefore, be an example for all methodological traditions to follow, as breaking down the walls separating research traditions can only improve our understanding and help to curb errors.

Obviously, not everyone agrees with these claims about the value of methodological pluralism. Many—including several comparative-historical researchers—stick by their favored method and suggest its inherent superiority relative to others. Moreover, combining methods is not necessarily straightforward. Ragin (1987) and Mahoney and Goertz (2006), for example, both suggest that different methods make radically different assumptions, are based on different principles, and can therefore be very difficult to integrate successfully. A growing body of comparative-historical research, however, shows that diverse methods can be successfully combined to offer insight into the research question, despite such difficulties.

Methodological pluralism in comparative-historical analysis has also contributed to another analytic benefit that has been emphasized throughout this book: the pursuit of both ideographic and nomothetic explanations. As noted in Chapter 1, this middling position within the ideographic–nomothetic spectrum is the result of the active combination of both comparative and within-case methods, with the former promoting nomethetic explanations and the latter promoting ideographic explanations. In turn, it helps limit the Scylla of overly general explanations in the absence of knowledge about actual causal processes and the Charybdis of getting lost in the details of a single case and overlooking commonalities across cases. In their pursuit of both nomothetic and ideographic explanations, comparative-historical researchers strive to get the cases right and gain knowledge about individual cases while at the same time pushing the envelope to explore whether explanations hold across multiple cases. As a result, comparative-historical methods are well suited simultaneously to analyze both complex and unique social phenomena as well as general processes.

In light of these advantages, it is time to give comparative-historical methods their due recognition, as they offer a superb example of how to combine diverse methods in order to maximize insight. In sociology, both qualitative and quantitative methods courses largely ignore comparative-historical methods, and the methodological tradition has faced rather hostile resistance from researchers using other methods in political science. As a result, comparative-historical methods are not commonly recognized as a major methodological tradition in either discipline. In anthropology, economics, and history, where comparative-historical analysis is rare but still appropriate for the subject matter, the methods are almost completely overlooked. Because of the valuable insight offered by comparative-historical methods, these disciplines could gain enormously from them.

Despite such high praise for comparative-historical methods, the methodological tradition also faces problems. Most notably, comparative-historical analysis is very demanding in a number of ways. For one, researchers must gain expertise in multiple research methods and must possess the mental acumen to adeptly and efficiently sift through and piece together diverse types of evidence. Moreover, broad analyses spanning both large swathes of history and multiple cases require enormous time and effort. Such broad analyses, in turn, hinder the ability of comparative-historical researchers to explore adequately the validity and accuracy of the data they use and to learn the languages of their cases.

Although important, these difficulties hardly prevent quality comparative-historical analysis, as the proliferation of works using comparative-historical methods—including both classics in the social sciences and contemporary award winning books—clearly suggests. Indeed, comparative-historical methods was the method of choice of many of the most influential founding figures of the social sciences and remains the method of choice for many of the most influential social scientists of our time. For the research tradition to continue to prosper, it is vital that the actual methods of comparative-historical analysis be carefully documented so researchers can use them more effectively and improve them, and so readers can better understand the ways comparative-historical methods offer insight. Indeed, the failure of comparative-historical researchers to elaborate their methods must be recognized as an important reason why comparative-historical methods are underappreciated. Many have already begun this task, and the present book has attempted to integrate and expand on these works to offer a general statement on comparative-historical methods.

References

Abbott, Andrew. 1990. "Conceptions of Time and Events in Social Science Methods: Causal and Narrative Approaches." *Historical Methods*, 23 (4): 140–50.

Abbott, Andrew. 1992. "From Causes to Events: Notes on Narrative Positivism." *Sociological Methods Research*, 20 (4): 428–55.

Abbott, Andrew. 1995. "Sequence Analysis: New Methods for Old Ideas." *Annual Review of Sociology*, 21: 93–113.

Abbott, Andrew and John Forrest. 1986. "Optimal Matching Methods for Historical Sequences." *Journal of Interdisciplinary History*, 16 (3): 471–94.

Abbott, Andrew and Alexandra Hrycak. 1990. "Measuring Resemblance in Sequence Data: An Optimal Matching Analysis of Musicians' Careers." *American Journal of Sociology*, 96 (1): 144–85.

Abbott, Andrew and Angela Tsay. 2000. "Sequence Analysis and Optimal Matching Methods in Sociology: Review and Prospect." *Sociological Methods and Research*, 29 (3): 3–33.

Acemoglu, Daron, Simon Johnson, and James Robinson. 2001. "Colonial Origins of Comparative Development: An Empirical Investigation." *American Economic Review*, 91 (5), 1369–401.

Acemoglu, Daron, Simon Johnson, and James Robinson. 2002. "Reversal of Fortune: Geography and Institutions in the Making of the Modern World Income Distribution." *Quarterly Journal of Economics*, 117 (4): 1231–94.

Achen, Christopher and Duncan Snidal. 1989. "Rational Deterrence Theory and Comparative Case Studies." *World Politics*, 41 (2): 143–69.

Adams, Julia, Elisabeth Clemens, and Ann Shola Orloff (eds). 2005. *Making Modernity: Politics, History, and Sociology*. Durham, NC: Duke University Press.

Amenta, Edward. 2003. "What We Know About the Development of Social Policy: Comparative and Historical Research in Comparative and Historical Perspective." *Comparative Historical Analysis in the Social Sciences*, edited by James Mahoney and Dietrich Rueschemeyer. New York: Cambridge University Press, 91–130.

Anderson, Benedict. 1983. *Imagined Communities: Reflections on the Origin and Spread of Nationalism*. London: Verso.

Anderson, Perry. 1974a. *Lineages of the Absolutist State*. London: NLB.

Anderson, Perry. 1974b. *Passages from Antiquity to Feudalism*. London: NLB.

Arrighi, Giovanni. 1994. *The Long Twentieth Century: Money, Power, and the Origins of Our Times*. New York: Verso.

Barkey, Karen. 2008. *Empire of Difference: The Ottomans in Comparative Perspective*. New York: Cambridge University Press.

Bates, Robert H. 1981. *Markets and States in Tropical Africa: The Political Basis of Agricultural Policies*. Berkeley, CA: University of California Press.

Bates, Robert H., Avner Greif, Margaret Levi, Jean-Laurent Rosenthal, and Barry Weingast. 1998. *Analytic Narratives*. Princeton, NJ: Princeton University Press.

Bendix, Reinhard. 1956. *Work and Authority in Industry: Ideologies in the Course of Industrialization*. New York: Harper and Row.

Bendix, Reinhard. 1964. *Nation-Building and Citizenship: Studies of Our Changing Social Order*. New York: Wiley.

Bendix, Reinhard. 1977. *Max Weber: An Intellectual Portrait*. Garden City, NJ: Doubleday.

Bendix, Reinhard. 1978. *Kings or People: Power and the Mandate to Rule*. Berkeley, CA: University of California Press.

Bendix, Reinhard. 1984. *Force, Fate, and Freedom*. Berkeley, CA: University of California Press.

Bloch, Marc. 1924/1990. *The Royal Touch: Sacred Monarchy and Scrofula in England and France*. London: Routledge.

Bloch, Marc. 1931/1970. *French Rural Society: An Essay on Its Basic Characteristics*. Berkeley, CA: University of California Press.

Bloch, Marc. 1939/1965. *Feudal Society*. Chicago: University of Chicago Press.

Bloch, Marc. 1953. *The Historian's Craft*. New York: Vintage Books.

Bloch, Marc. 1967. *Land and Work in Mediaeval Europe: Selected Papers*. London: Routledge & Kegan Paul.

Boone, Catherine. 2003. *Political Topographies of the African State: Territorial Authority and Institutional Choice*. New York: Cambridge University Press.

Brady, Henry and David Collier, eds. 2004. *Rethinking Social Inquiry: Diverse Tools, Shared Standards*. New York: Rowman & Littlefield Publishers.

Breuilly, John. 1982. *Nationalism and the State*. Manchester: Manchester University Press.

Brubaker, Rogers. 1992. *Citizenship and Nationhood in France and Germany*. Cambridge, MA: Harvard University Press.

Burt, Ronald. 1992. *Structural Holes: The Social Structure of Competition*. Cambridge, MA: Harvard University Press.

Bushman, Brad and Roy Baumeister. 1998. "Threatened Egotism, Narcissism, Self-Esteem, and Direct and Displaced Aggression: Does Self-Love or Self-Hate Lead to Violence." *Journal of Personality and Social Psychology*, 75: 219–29.

Campbell, Donald T. 1975. "'Degrees of Freedom' and the Case Study." *Comparative Political Studies*, 8: 178–93.

Castells, Manuel. 1996. *The Rise of Network Society*. Cambridge: Blackwell Publishers.

Centeno, Miguel. 2002. *Blood and Debt: War and the Nation State in Latin America*. University Park, PA: Pennsylvania State University Press.

Charrad, Mounira. 2001. *States and Women's Rights: The Making of Postcolonial Tunisia, Algeria, and Morocco*. Berkeley, CA: University of California Press.

Chibber, Vivek. 2003. *Locked in Place: State-Building and Late Industrialization in India*. Princeton, NJ: Princeton University Press.

Collier, David. 2011. "Understanding Process Tracing." *Political Science and Politics*, 44 (4): 823–30.

Collier, David, Jody LaPorte, and Jason Seawright. 2012. "Putting Typologies to Work: Concept Formation, Measurement, and Analytic Rigor." *Political Research Quarterly*, 65 (1): 217–32.

Collier, Ruth Berins and David Collier. 1991. *Shaping the Political Arena: Critical Junctures, the Labor Movement, and Regime Dynamics in Latin America*. Princeton, NJ: Princeton University Press.

Collins, Randall. 1994. *Four Sociological Traditions*. New York: Oxford University Press.

Diamond, Jared. 1992. *The Third Chimpanzee: The Evolution and Future of the Human Animal*. New York: Harper Perennial.

Diamond, Jared. 1997. *Guns, Germs, and Steel: The Fates of Human Societies*. New York: W.W. Norton.

Diamond, Jared and James Robinson, eds. 2010. *Natural Experiments of History*. Cambridge, MA: Belknap Press.

Eckstein, Harry. 1975. "Case Studies and Theory in Political Science." *Handbook of Political Science, Volume 7. Political Science: Scope and Theory*, edited by Fred Greenstein and Nelson Polsby. Reading, MA: Addison-Wesley, 94–137.

Eisenstadt, Shmuel. 1963. *The Political Systems of Empires*. New York: Free Press.

Engels, Friedrich. 1884/2010. *The Origins of the Family, Private Property, and the State*. New York: Penguin Classics.

Ertman, Thomas. 1997. *Birth of the Leviathan: Building States and Regimes in Medieval and Early Modern Europe*. New York: Cambridge University Press.

Esping-Andersen, Gosta. 1990. *The Three Worlds of Welfare Capitalism*. Princeton, NJ: Princeton University Press.

Evans, Peter. 1995. *Embedded Autonomy: States and Industrial Transformation*. Princeton: Princeton University Press.

Evans, Peter, Dietrich Rueschemeyer, and Theda Skocpol, eds. 1985. *Bringing the State Back In*. New York: Cambridge University Press.

Falleti, Tulia and Julia Lynch. 2009. "Context and Causal Mechanisms in Political Analysis." *Comparative Political Studies*, 42 (9): 1143–66.

Fearon, James and David Laitin. 2008. "Integrating Qualitative and Quantitative Methods." *The Oxford Handbook of Political Methodology*, edited by Janet Box-Steffensmeier, Henry Brady, and David Collier. New York: Oxford University Press, 756–76.

Flora, Peter and Arnold Heidenheimer, eds. 1981. *The Development of Welfare States in Europe and America*. New Brunswick: Transaction Books.

Gal, Susan and Gail Kligman. 2000. *Reproducing Gender: Politics, Publics, and Everyday Life After Socialism*. Princeton, NJ: Princeton University Press.

Geddes, Barbara. 1991. "How the Cases You Choose Affect the Answers You Get: Selection Bias in Comparative Politics." *Political Analysis*, Vol. 2, edited by James A. Stimson. Ann Arbor, MI: University of Michigan Press.

Geertz, Clifford. 1968. *Islam Observed: Religious Development in Morocco and Indonesia*. New Haven, CT: Yale University Press.

Gellner, Ernest. 1983. *Nations and Nationalism*. Ithaca, NY: Cornell University Press.

George, Alexander. 1979. "The Causal Nexus Between Cognitive Beliefs and Decision-Making Behavior." *Psychological Models in International Politics*, edited by Lawrence Falkowski. Boulder, CO: Westview Press. pp.95–124.

George, Alexander and Andrew Bennett. 2005. *Case Studies and Theory Development in the Social Sciences*. Cambridge, MA: MIT Press.

Gerring, John. 2007. *Case Study Research: Principles and Practices*. New York: Cambridge University Press.

Goldstone, Jack. 1991. *Revolution and Rebellion in the Early Modern World*. Berkeley, CA: University of California Press.

Goldstone, Jack. 1997. "Methodological Issues in Comparative Macrosociology." *Comparative Social Research*, 16: 107–20.

Goldthorpe, John H. 1991. "The Uses of History in Sociology: Reflections on Some Recent Tendencies." *British Journal of Sociology*, 42: 211–30.

Goldthorpe, John H. 1997. "Current Issues in Comparative Macrosociology: A Debate on Methodological Issues." *Comparative Social Research*, 16: 1–26.

Goodwin, Jeff. 2001. *No Other Way Out: States and Revolutionary Movements, 1945–1991*. New York: Cambridge University Press.

Gorski, Philip. 2003. *The Disciplinary Revolution: Calvinism and the Rise of the State in Early Modern Europe*. Chicago: University of Chicago Press.

Gould, Roger. 1991. "Multiple Networks and Mobilization in the Paris Commune, 1871." *American Sociological Review*, 56: 716–29.

Gould, Roger. 1996. "Patron-Client Ties, State Centralization, and the Whiskey Rebellion." *American Journal of Sociology*, 102: 400–29.

Gould, Roger. 2003. "Uses of Network Tools in Comparative Historical Research." *Comparative Historical Analysis in the Social Sciences*, edited by James Mahoney and Dietrich Rueschemeyer. New York: Cambridge University Press, 241–69.

Griffin, Larry J. 1993. "Narrative, Event-Structure, and Causal Interpretation in Historical Sociology." *American Journal of Sociology*, 98: 1094–133.

Haggard, Stephan. 1990. *Pathways from the Periphery: The Politics of Growth in the Newly Industrializing Countries*. Ithaca, NY: Cornell University Press.

Haggard, Stephan and Robert Kaufman. 1995. *The Political Economy of Democratic Transition*. Princeton, NJ: Princeton University Press.

Hall, John. 1985. *Powers and Liberties: The Causes and Consequences of the Rise of the West*. Oxford: Blackwell.

Hall, Peter. 2003. "Aligning Ontology and Methodology in Comparative Politics." *Comparative Historical Analysis in the Social Sciences*, edited by James Mahoney and Dietrich Rueschemeyer. New York: Cambridge University Press, 373–404.

Hechter, Michael. 2000. *Containing Nationalism*. New York: Oxford University Press.

Heckman, James. 1976. "The Common Structure of Statistical Models of Truncation, Sample Selection and Limited Dependent Variables and a Simple Estimator for such Models." *Annals of Economic and Social Measurement*, 5 (4): 475–92.

Heckman, James. 1979. "Sample Selection Bias as a Specification Error." *Econometrica*, 47: 153–61.

Heclo, Hugh. 1974. *Modern Social Politics in Britain and Sweden: From Relief to Income Maintenance*. New Haven, CT: Yale University Press.

Hedstrom, Peter. 2008. "Studying Mechanisms to Strengthen Causal Inferences in Quantitative Research." *The Oxford Handbook of Political Methodology*, edited by Janet Box-Steffensmeier, Henry Brady, and David Collier. New York: Oxford University Press, 319–35.

Hedstrom, Peter and Richard Swedberg, eds. 1998. *Social Mechanisms: An Analytical Approach to Social Theory.* New York: Cambridge University Press.

Herbst, Jeffrey. 2000. *States and Power in Africa: Comparative Lessons in Authority and Control.* Princeton, NJ: Princeton University Press.

Htun, Mala. 2003. *Sex and the State: Abortion, Divorce, and the Family under Latin American Dictatorships and Democracies.* New York: Cambridge University Press.

Huber, Evelyne and John Stephens. 2001. *Development and Crisis of the Welfare State: Parties and Policies in Global Markets.* Chicago: University of Chicago Press.

Kalberg, Stephen. 1994. *Max Weber's Comparative-Historical Sociology.* Chicago: University of Chicago Press.

Kalyvas, Stathis. 2006. *The Logic of Violence in Civil War.* New York: Cambridge University Press.

King, Gary, Robert O. Keohane, and Sidney Verba. 1994. *Designing Social Inquiry: Scientific Inference in Qualitative Research.* Princeton, NJ: Princeton University Press.

Kiser, Edgar. 1996. "The Revival of Narrative in Historical Sociology: What Rational Choice Theory Can Contribute." *Politics and Society,* 24 (3): 249–71.

Kiser, Edgar and Justin Baer. 2005. "The Bureaucratization of States: Toward an Analytical Weberianism." *Remaking Modernity: Politics, History, and Sociology,* edited by Julia Adams, Elizabeth Clemens, and Ann Shola Orloff. Durham, NC: Duke University Press, 225–48.

Kiser, Edgar and Michael Hechter. 1991. "The Role of General Theory in Comparative-Historical Sociology." *American Journal of Sociology,* 97 (1): 1–30.

Kocka, Jürgen. 2003. "Comparison and Beyond." *History and Theory,* 42 (1): 39–44.

Kohli, Atul. 2004. *State-Directed Development: Political Power and Industrialization in the Global Periphery.* New York: Cambridge University Press.

Lachmann, Richard. 2000. *Capitalists in Spite of Themselves: Elite Conflict and Economic Transitions in Early Modern Europe.* New York: Oxford University Press.

Lange, Matthew. 2009. *Lineages of Despotism and Development: British Colonialism and State Power.* Chicago: University of Chicago Press.

Lange, Matthew. 2012. *Educations in Ethnic Violence: Identity, Educational Bubbles, and Resource Mobilization.* New York: Cambridge University Press.

Lange, Matthew and Dietrich Rueschemeyer, eds. 2005. *States and Development: Historical Antecedents of Stagnation and Advance.* New York: Palgrave Macmillan.

LaPorta, Rafael, Florencio Lopez-de-Silanes, Andrei Shleifer, and Robert Vishny. 1999. "The Quality of Government." *Journal of Law, Economics, and Organization,* 1 (15): 222–82.

Levi, Margaret. 1988. *Of Rule and Revenue.* Berkeley, CA: University of California Press.

Lieberman, Evan. 2003. *Race and Regionalism in the Politics of Taxation in Brazil and South Africa.* New York: Cambridge University Press.

Lieberman, Evan. 2005. "Nested Analysis as a Mixed-Method Strategy for Comparative Research." *American Political Science Review,* 99 (3): 435–52.

Lieberson, Stanley. 1985. *Making It Count: The Improvement of Social Research and Theory.* Los Angeles, CA: University of California Press.

Lijphart, Arend. 1971. "Comparative Politics and the Comparative Method." *American Political Science Review,* 64: 682–93.

Lijphart, Arend. 1975. "The Comparable-Cases Strategy in Comparative Research." *Comparative Political Science*, 8: 158–77.

Lipset, Seymour Martin, Martin Trow, and James Coleman. 1956. *Union Democracy: The Inside Politics of the International Typographical Union*. New York: Free Press.

Luebbert, Gregory. 1991. *Liberalism, Fascism, or Social Democracy: Social Classes and the Political Origins of Regimes in Interwar Europe*. New York: Oxford University Press.

Lustick, Ian. 1993. *Unsettled States, Disputed Lands: Britain and Ireland, France and Algeria, Israel and West Bank-Gaza*. Ithaca, NY: Cornell University Press.

Mahoney, James. 1999. "Nominal, Ordinal, and Narrative Appraisal in Macrocausal Analysis." *American Journal of Sociology*, 104 (4): 1154–96.

Mahoney, James. 2000a. "Path Dependence in Historical Sociology." *Theory and Society*, 29: 507–48.

Mahoney, James. 2000b. "Strategies of Causal Inference in Small-N Analysis." *Sociological Methods and Research*, 28 (4): 387–424.

Mahoney, James. 2001a. "Beyond Correlational Analysis: Recent Innovations in Theory and Method." *Sociological Forum*, 16: 575–93.

Mahoney, James. 2001b. *The Legacies of Liberalism: Path Dependence and Political Regimes in Central America*. Baltimore, MD: Johns Hopkins University Press.

Mahoney, James. 2006. "On the Second Wave of Historical Sociology, 1970s–Present." *International Journal of Comparative Sociology*, 47: 371–7.

Mahoney, James. 2010. *Colonialism and Postcolonial Development: Spanish America in Comparative Perspective*. New York: Cambridge University Press.

Mahoney, James. 2012. "The Logic of Process Tracing Tests in the Social Sciences." *Sociological Methods and Research*, 20(10): 1–28.

Mahoney, James and Gary Goertz. 2006. "A Tale of Two Cultures: Contrasting Quantitative and Qualitative Research." *Political Analysis*, 14 (3): 227–49.

Mahoney, James and Dietrich Rueschemeyer, eds. 2003. *Comparative Historical Analysis in the Social Sciences*. New York: Cambridge University Press.

Mamdani, Mahmood. 1996. *Citizen and Subject: Contemporary Africa and the Legacy of Late Colonialism*. Princeton, NJ: Princeton University Press.

Mann, Michael. 1981. "Socio-Logic." *Sociology*, 15: 544–50.

Mann, Michael. 1986. *The Sources of Social Power, Volume I: A History of Power from the Beginning to AD 1760*. New York: Cambridge University Press.

Mann, Michael. 1993. *The Sources of Social Power, Volume II: The Rise of Classes and Nation States, 1760–1914*. New York: Cambridge University Press.

Mann, Michael. 2005. *The Dark Side of Democracy: Explaining Ethnic Cleansing*. New York: Cambridge University Press.

Mann, Michael. 2013. *The Sources of Social Power, Volume III: Global Empires and Revolution, 1890–1945, Volume IV: Globalizations, 1945–2011*. New York: Cambridge University Press.

Marx, Anthony. 1998. *Making Race and Nation: A Comparison of South Africa, the United States, and Brazil*. New York: Cambridge University Press.

McNeill, J.R. and William H. McNeill. 2003. *The Human Web: A Bird's-Eye View of World History*. New York: W.W. Norton.

Michels, Robert. 1911/1968. *Political Parties: A Sociological Study of the Oligarchical Tendencies of Modern Democracy*. New York: Free Press.

Mill, John Stuart. 1843/1949. *A System of Logic: Ratiocinative and Inductive*. London: Longmans Green.

Milligan, John D. 1979. "The Treatment of an Historical Source." *History and Theory*, 2: 177–96.

Mills, C. Wright. 1959. *The Sociological Imagination*. New York: Oxford University Press.

Montesquieu, Charles de Secondat. 1748/1952. *The Spirit of Laws*. Chicago: Encyclopedia Britannica.

Moore, Barrington Jr. 1966. *Social Origins of Dictatorship and Democracy: Lord and Peasant in the Making of the Modern World*. Boston: Beacon Press.

Morrill, Richard. 1970. *The Spatial Organization of Society*. Belmont, CA: Duxbury Press.

O'Connor, Julia S., Ann Shola Orloff, and Sheila Shaver. 1999. *States, Markets, Families: Gender, Liberalism and Social Policy in Australia, Canada, Great Britain and the United States*. New York: Cambridge University Press.

O'Donnell, Guillermo. 1979. *Modernization and Bureaucratic-Authoritarianism: Studies in South American Politics*. Berkeley, CA: Institute of International Studies.

Orloff, Ann Shola. 1993. *The Politics of Pension: A Comparative Analysis of Britain, Canada, and the United States, 1880–1940*. Madison, WI: University of Wisconsin Press.

Paige, Jeffrey. 1975. *Agrarian Revolution: Social Movements and Export Agriculture in the Underdeveloped World*. New York: Free Press.

Patterson, Orlando. 1982. *Slavery and Social Death: A Comparative Study*. Cambridge, MA: Harvard University Press.

Petersen, Roger. 2002. *Understanding Ethnic Violence: Fear, Hatred, and Resentment in Twentieth-Century Eastern Europe*. New York: Cambridge University Press.

Pierson, Paul. 1994. *Dismantling the Welfare State? Reagan, Thatcher, and the Politics of Retrenchment*. New York: Cambridge University Press.

Pierson, Paul. 2003. "Big, Slow-Moving, and … Invisible: Macrosocial Processes in the Study of Comparative Politics." *Comparative Historical Analysis in the Social Sciences*, edited by James Mahoney and Dietrich Rueschemeyer. New York: Cambridge University Press, 177–207.

Polanyi, Karl. 1944. *The Great Transformation*. New York: Farrar & Rinehart.

Przeworski, Adam and Henry Teune. 1970. *The Logic of Comparative Social Inquiry*. New York: Wiley.

Ragin, Charles. 1987. *The Comparative Method: Moving Beyond Qualitative and Quantitative Strategies*. Berkeley, CA: University of California Press.

Ragin, Charles. 2000. *Fuzzy-Set Social Science*. Chicago: University of Chicago Press.

Ragin, Charles and David Zaret. 1983. "Theory and Method in Comparative Research: Two Strategies." *Social Forces*, 61 (3): 731–54.

Rueschemeyer, Dietrich. 2003. "Can One or a Few Cases Yield Theoretical Gains?" *Comparative Historical Analysis in the Social Sciences*, edited by James Mahoney and Dietrich Rueschemeyer. New York: Cambridge University Press, 305–36.

Rueschemeyer, Dietrich. 2010. *Usable Theory: Analytic Tools for Social and Political Research*. Princeton, NJ: Princeton Univesity Press.

Rueschemeyer, Dietrich and John Stephens. 1997. "Comparing Social Historical Sequences: A Powerful Tool for Causal Analysis." *Comparative Social Research*, 17: 55–72.

Rueschemeyer, Dietrich, Evelyne Huber Stephens, and John Stephens. 1991. *Capitalist Development and Democracy*. Chicago: University of Chicago Press.

Said, Edward. 1978. *Orientalism*. New York: Pantheon Books.

Sandbrook, Richard, Marc Edelman, Patrick Heller, and Judith Teichman. 2007. *Social Democracy in the Global Periphery: Origins, Challenges, Prospects*. Cambridge: Cambridge University Press.

Saxenian, AnnaLee. 1994. *Regional Advantage: Culture and Competition in Silicon Valley and Route 128*. Cambridge, MA: Harvard University Press.

Schickler, Eric. 2001. *Disjointed Pluralism: Institutional Innovation and the Development of the U.S. Congress*. Princeton, NJ: Princeton University Press.

Scott, James. 1979. *The Moral Economy of the Peasant: Rebellion and Subsistence in Southeast Asia*. New Haven, CT: Yale University Press.

Seavey, C.A., P. A. Katz, and S.R. Zalk. 1975. "Baby X: The Effect of Gender Labels on Adult Responses to Infants." *Sex Roles*, 1: 103–9.

Seawright, Jason and David Collier. 2004. "Glossary." *Rethinking Social Inquiry: Diverse Tools, Shared Standards*, edited by Henry Brady and David Collier. New York: Rowman & Littlefield Publishers, 273–313.

Sewell, William Jr. 1996. "Three Temporalities: Toward an Eventful Sociology." *The Historic Turn in the Human Sciences*, edited by Terrance McDonald. Ann Arbor, MI: University of Michigan Press, 245–80.

Silberman, Bernard. 1993. *Cages of Reason: The Rise of the Rational State in France, Japan, the United States, and Great Britain*. Chicago: University of Chicago Press.

Skocpol, Theda. 1979. *States and Social Revolutions: A Comparative Analysis of France, Russia, and China*. New York: Cambridge University Press.

Skocpol, Theda, ed. 1984. *Vision and Method in Historical Sociology*. New York: Cambridge University Press.

Skocpol, Theda. 2003. "Doubly Engaged Social Science: The Promise of Comparative Historical Analysis." *Comparative Historical Analysis in the Social Sciences*, edited by James Mahoney and Dietrich Rueschemeyer. New York: Cambridge University Press, 407–28.

Skocpol, Theda and Margaret Somers. 1980. "The Uses of Comparative History in Macro-Social Theory." *Comparative Studies in Society and History*, 22 (2): 174–97.

Slater, Dan. 2010. *Ordering Power: Contentious Politics and Authoritarian Leviathans in Southeast Asia*. New York: Cambridge University Press.

Slater, Dan and Erica Simmons. 2010. "Informative Regress: Critical Antecedents in Comparative Politics." *Comparative Political Studies*, 43 (7): 886–917.

Smith, Adam. 1776/1976. *An Inquiry into the Nature and Causes of the Wealth of Nations*. Oxford: Clarendon Press.

Snyder, Richard. 2001. "Scaling Down: The Subnational Comparative Method." *Studies in Comparative International Development*, 36 (1): 93–110.

Soifer, Hillel. Forthcoming. "The Causal Logic of Critical Junctures." *Comparative Political Studies*, 46 (10).

Steinmetz, George. 2004. "Odious Comparisons: Incommensurability, the Case Study, and 'Small N's' in Sociology." *Sociological Theory*, 22 (3): 371–400.

Steinmetz, George. 2007. *The Devil's Handwriting: Precoloniality and the German Colonial State in Quingdao, Samoa, and Southwest Africa*. Chicago: University of Chicago Press.

Stephens, John. 1980. *The Transition from Capitalism to Socialism*. Atlantic Highlands: Humanities Press.

Tilly, Charles. 1975. "Reflections on the History of European State-Making." *The Formation of National States in Western Europe*, edited by Charles Tilly and Gabriel Ardant. Princeton, NJ: Princeton University Press, 3–83.

Tilly, Charles. 1978. *From Mobilization to Revolution*. New York: Random House.

Tilly, Charles. 1984. *Big Structures, Large Processes, Huge Comparisons*. New York: Russell Sage Foundation.

Tilly, Charles. 1986. *The Contentious French*. Cambridge, MA: Belknap Press.

Tilly, Charles. 1990. *Coercion, Capital, and European States, AD 990–1990*. Cambridge: Blackwell Publishers.

Tilly, Charles. 2004. *Contention and Democracy in Europe, 1650–2000*. New York: Cambridge University Press.

Tocqueville, Alexis de. 1835, 1840/2000. *Democracy in America*. New York: Perennial Classics.

Tocqueville, Alexis de. 1856/1998. *The Old Regime and the Revolution*. Chicago: University of Chicago Press.

Wallerstein, Immanuel. 1974. *The Modern World System, Volume I: Capitalist Agriculture and the Origins of the European World-Economy in the Sixteenth Century*. New York: Academic Press.

Wallerstein, Immanuel. 1980. *The Modern World-System, Volume II: Mercantilism and the Consolidation of the European World-Economy, 1600–1750*. New York: Academic Press.

Wallerstein, Immanuel. 1989. *The Modern World-System, Volume III: The Second Great Expansion of the Capitalist World-Economy, 1730–1840s*. San Diego: Academic Press.

Wallerstein, Immanuel. 2011. *The Modern World-System, Volume IV: Centrist Liberalism Triumphant, 1789–1914*. Berkeley, CA: University of California Press.

Wallerstein, Michael. 2000. "Trying to Navigate between Scylla and Charybdis: Misspecified and Unidentified Models in Comparative Politics." *Newsletter of the Organized Section in Comparative Politics of the American Political Science Association*, 11 (2): 1–21.

Weber, Max. 1904/1997. *The Methodology of the Social Sciences*. New York: Free Press.

Weber, Max. 1905/2001. *The Protestant Ethic and the Spirit of Capitalism*. New York: Routledge.

Weber, Max. 1922/1968. *Economy and Society: An Outline of Interpretive Sociology*. New York: Bedminister Press.

Weyland, Kurt. 2009. "The Diffusion of Revolution: '1848' in Europe and Latin America." *International Organization*, 63 (3): 391–423.

Wickham-Crowley, Timothy. 1993. *Guerrillas and Revolution in Latin America: A Comparative Study of Insurgents and Regimes since 1956*. Princeton, NJ: Princeton University Press.

Wimmer, Andreas. 2002. *Nationalist Exclusion and Ethnic Conflict: Shadows of Modernity*. New York: Cambridge University Press.

Wolf, Eric. 1982. *Europe and the People Without History*. Berkeley, CA: University of California Press.

Yashar, Deborah. 1997. *Demanding Democracy: Reform and Reaction in Costa Rica and Guatemala, 1870s–1950s*. Palo Alto, CA: Stanford University Press.

Yashar, Deborah. 2005. *Contesting Citizenship in Latin America: The Rise of Indigenous Movements and the Postliberal Challenge*. New York: Cambridge University Press.

Ziblatt, Daniel. 2006. *Structuring the State: The Formation of Italy and Germany and the Puzzle of Federalism*. Princeton, NJ: Princeton University Press.

Index